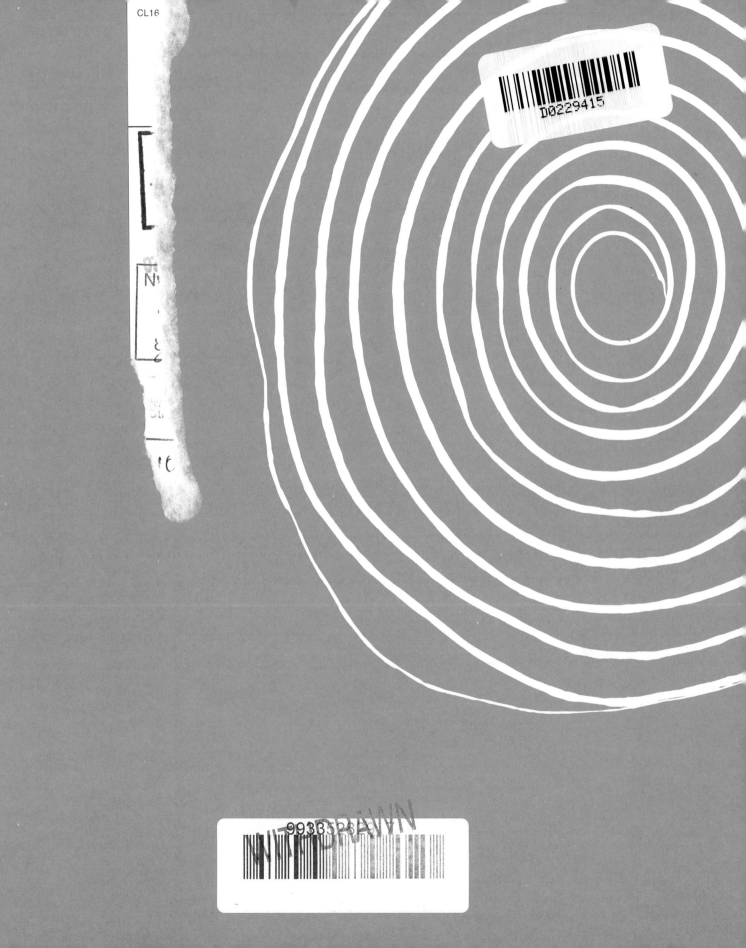

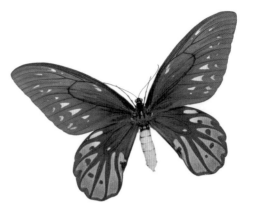

MUSEUM OF LIFE

STEVE PARKER   Foreword by MARK CARWARDINE

PUBLISHED BY THE

NATURAL HISTORY MUSEUM, LONDON

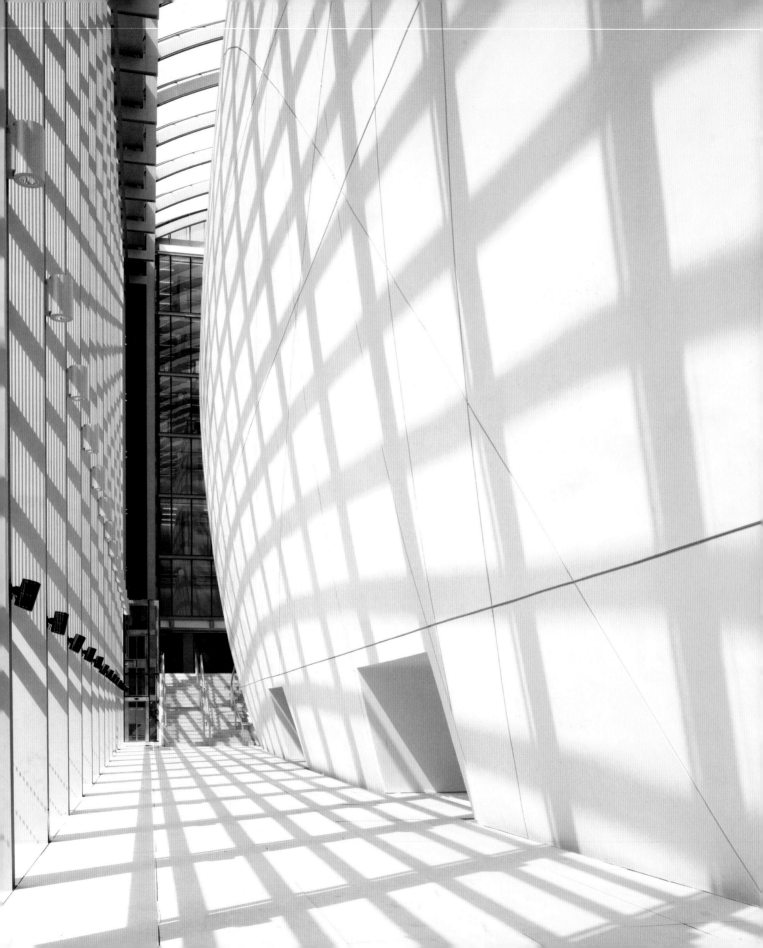

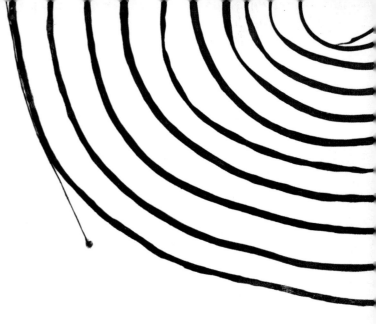

CONTENTS

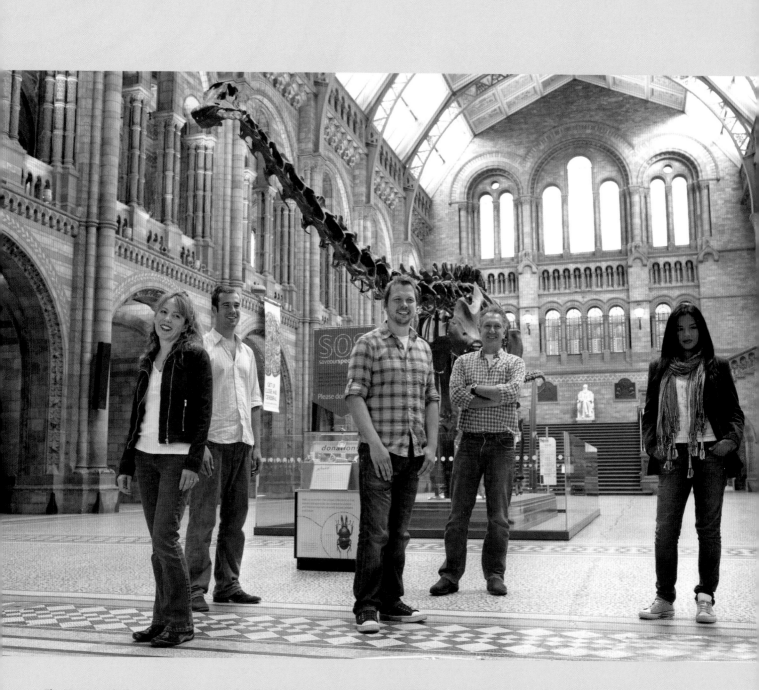

The Museum of Life presenters *(left to right)*: **Kate Bellingham, Chris Van Tulleken, Jimmy Doherty, Mark Carwardine and Liz Bonnin.**

FOREWORD
by Mark Carwardine

I COULDN'T BELIEVE MY LUCK when I was asked to be a presenter on the BBC-TV series *Museum of Life*. Just imagine being paid to rummage around one of the most distinguished and awe-inspiring museums in the world, and to meet some of the 350 botanists, entomologists, mineralogists, palaeontologists, zoologists and other renowned scientists who beaver away behind the scenes doing surprising and often pioneering research work.

The much-loved Natural History Museum houses one of the greatest collections of specimens from the natural world – seventy million of them altogether – in one of the most striking and beautiful buildings on the planet. From 'Dippy' the dinosaur and 'Archie' the giant squid to creatures collected by the great Charles Darwin and historic notebooks handwritten by Alfred Russel Wallace, this cathedral to nature is a never-ending source of wonder and delight.

The collection of objects from every realm of life and every corner of the planet that the general public knows and adores is unimaginably vast. I've been a regular visitor since I was a small boy with a passion for collecting dead beetles and broken eggshells – and I still haven't seen it all.

But the treasure trove behind the scenes is, in many ways, even more astonishing. While we were filming, I spent many happy days and evenings rifling through vast storerooms piled high with yet-to-be-studied and often unique specimens, wandering around a maze of endless corridors, marvelling at tens of kilometres of shelves groaning under the weight of countless preservation jars and specimen boxes, and passing through myriad doors – tantalisingly hidden or secret ones, some marked 'no entry' and others that creaked loudly as if they hadn't been opened for years. There is a whole mesmerizing world back there that few people get to see.

If you're feeling a little bit jealous there's no need to be, because all this – and much more – is in Steve Parker's wonderfully insightful book, written to accompany the television series. He brings these weird and wonderful worlds to life, telling anecdotes about some of the better-known exhibits, explaining where they came from and how they are preserved, revealing what hidden treasures lie behind those secret, creaky doors, and describing some of the remarkable, often ground-breaking work being done by the Museum's scientists.

It's a stimulating and highly readable story of history, adventure, intrigue, discovery, science and passion. If you don't already work at the Museum, you'll soon want to. Enjoy.

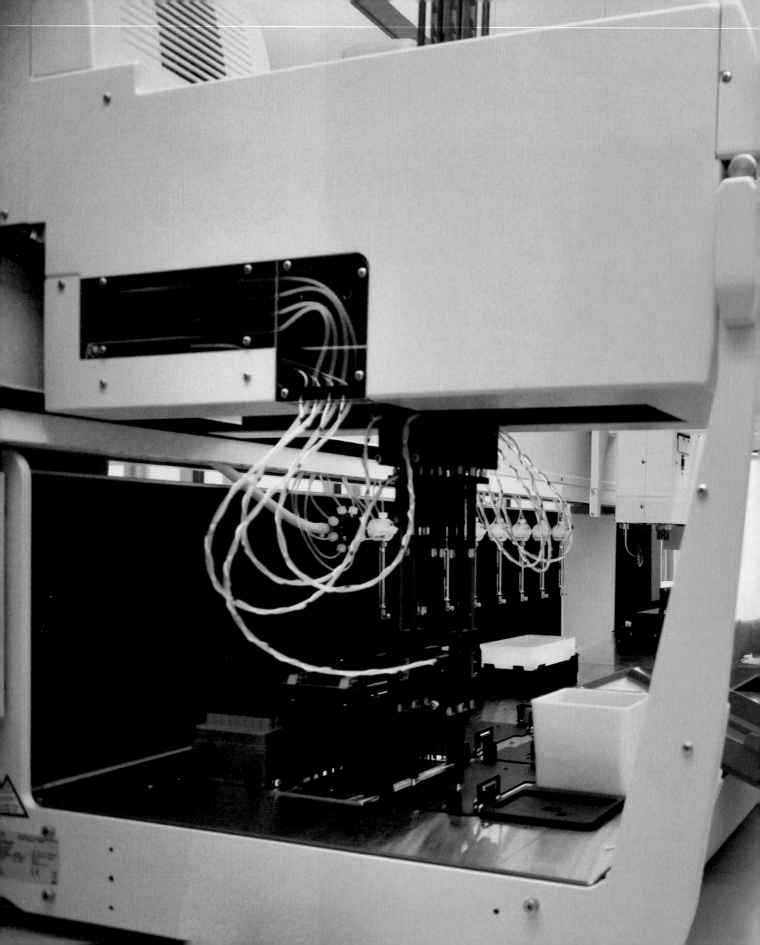

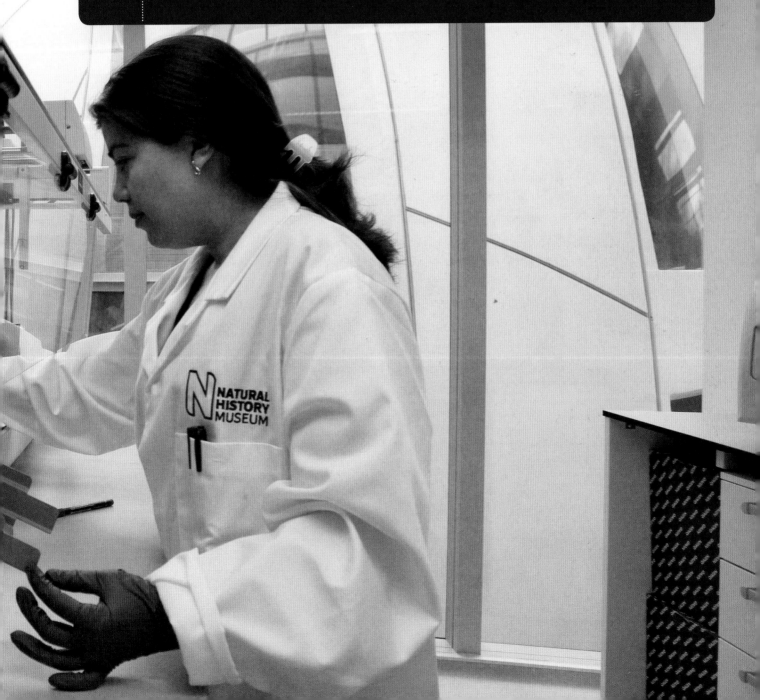

 MUSEUM FOR
A MODERN WORLD

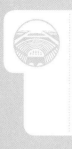

MUSEUM FOR
A MODERN WORLD

Public-access museums as we recognize them today began to appear in the 1700s. They grew from the private curio collections of the rich. For many years they were places where 'ordinary' people came to stare in wonder but not much else. However, times are changing. The Museum is responding to the needs of our modern age in its role as a leading global resource for tackling the challenges of the future.

OPPOSITE: A tray of red-bellied pitta, *Pitta erythrogaster*, preserved skins from the ornithology collection is ready for comparison with recent specimens. This type of work can help detect the effects of changes such as environmental pollution or global warming.

PREVIOUS PAGE: The state-of-the-art Darwin Centre houses high-tech labs for its more than 200 staff.

THE MUSES WERE GODDESSES OF ANCIENT GREECE, believed to be the source of knowledge and the inspiration behind literature, poetry, arts and mythology. Places where earthbound Greeks could think deeply or 'muse', dipping into the well of knowledge as they contemplated the world and created great works, became known as 'muse-eums'. Gradually these sites became populated by wonderful objects and artefacts from nature, the arts and culture – from natural crystals, plants and animals to treasured paintings, sculptures and scripts. And so evolved museums as we know them today.

The Natural History Museum in South Kensington, London, is one of the world's greatest. It houses one of the largest and most important natural history collections: in excess of 70 million individual specimens, more than a million books and half a million works of art. The specimens comprise some 55 million animals, including 28 million insects, as well as around nine million fossils, six million plants, more than half a million rocks and minerals, and well over 3,000 meteorites. With more than 350 scientific staff working within its buildings, around Britain and across the world, it is a leader in many areas of science, from dinosaur fossils and Martian meteorites to the latest research into DNA and sustainable energy.

The scale of the Museum's treasures is staggering, and their potential as sources of information is vast. Each of the millions of specimens has its own story to tell. Individual people collected every one. The majority have been preserved, studied and had scientific reports written on them, but many of them still lie in their cupboards awaiting curation. An object might sit on a shelf or in a cupboard until, one day, a scientist needs or has the time to examine it. From that

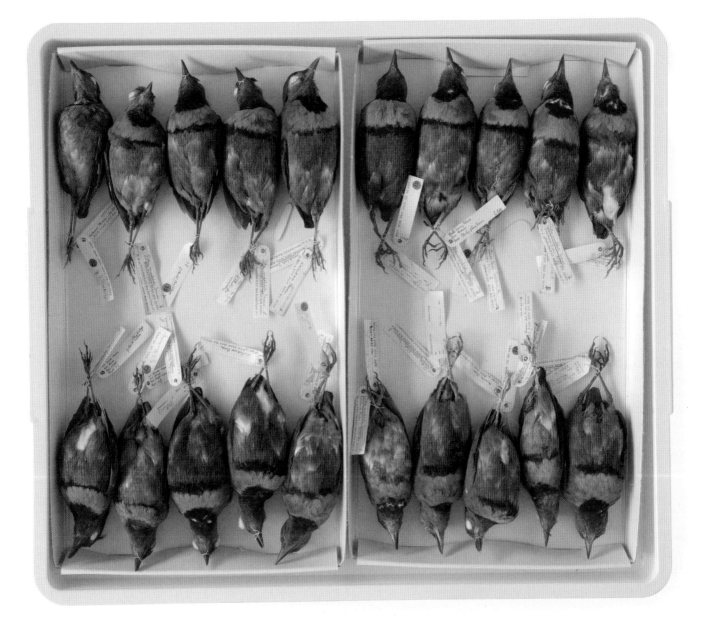

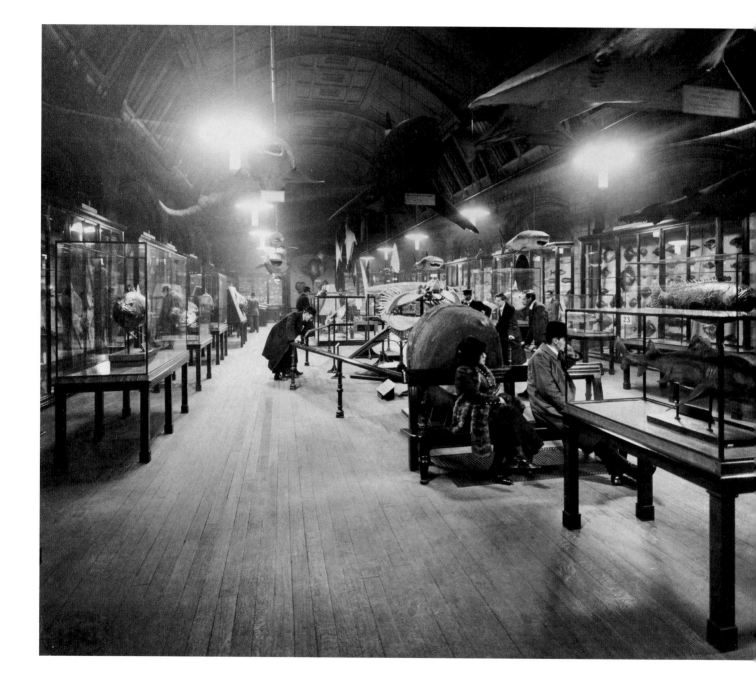

moment, the item could make headline news, solve a puzzle, set up a new theory, and change the way we all think.

Slow beginnings

The Natural History Museum is far from frozen in time. Its vast collections are constantly being maintained, updated, reviewed and improved. New technologies allow specimens to be re-explored and re-interpreted in the light of new theories and observations. But one giant object remains very much as it was when the doors first opened to the public in 1881 – the original building itself.

The objects that form the core of today's Museum collections were originally gathered by Sir Hans Sloane (1660–1753). As explained on later pages, Sloane was not only a physician who attended the fashionable elite. He was also a shrewd businessman, clever investor and inveterate collector – both of his own objects and other people's collections. He bequeathed the bulk of his material to the British Government, which housed it in Bloomsbury, London as the British Museum. The doors opened to the public there in 1759.

Almost a century later, in 1856, the natural history collections had fallen into chaotic disrepair. The British Museum hierarchy, steeped in the arts, cared little for science and nature. Many specimens had decayed, gone missing, been deliberately vandalized or thrown out. Enter Richard Owen (1804–1892), appointed as Superintendent of the British Museum's Natural History Department. An eminent anatomist, biologist and palaeontologist, also coiner of the term 'dinosaur', and general champion of the natural sciences, Owen soon set about to establish his charges in a safe, separate building.

Cathedral to nature

In 1864 architects competed to design the new Natural History Museum in South Kensington. The winner was seen to completion by Alfred Waterhouse, well known in Victorian England for his Renaissance and Gothic revival styles. Work at the five-hectare site started in 1873 and lasted almost eight years. The great building displayed a pioneering use of terracotta, many neo-Romanesque features and hundreds of nature-related adornments – plants and animals, living and extinct, including monkeys, lions, pterosaurs, birds and fish. Owen envisaged the building as a temple or cathedral to the natural objects that were part of God's creation, with its giant, vaulted main hall echoing the church interiors well known to devout Victorians.

Moving the collections was a massive task that demanded military precision. More than 50,000 minerals were transplanted into the new Mineral Gallery. Plants included 25,000 sheets from Joseph Banks, 170,000 specimens from Robert Shuttleworth, Hans Sloane's herbarium of 338 volumes (books of pressed plants), and many others. Only the animal specimens were not in place

11

by opening day. They had to wait until the next year with almost 400 horse-and-cart journeys spread over three months.

On Easter Monday, 1881, the first crowds thronged the galleries to marvel at the newly displayed natural wonders. First day attendance was 17,500. It was a triumphant moment for Owen, whose 25 years of campaigning finally reached fruition. For many years the formal name of British Museum (Natural History), or BMNH, reflected the Museum's unaltered status as a department of the British Museum. Only in 1963 did it attain full independence, and then in 1992 change its official name to the Natural History Museum.

The building we see today has altered very little from that opening success, apart from being flanked by two much newer structures. To the east is the Red Zone including Earth exhibits, the history and treasures of our planet, and natural sources of energy. To the west is the Orange Zone of the recently opened Darwin Centre which houses the animal, insect and some of the plant collections and is described in more detail on later pages.

Inside the original Waterhouse building, the galleries and spaces have been rearranged and reinterpreted many times. From rows of glass cases in Victorian times, the exhibits are now spectacular celebrations of the natural world and how it works, making use of the latest engineering, technology and electronic wizardry.

The tale, and neck, of Dippy

Since 1979, people arriving at the Natural History Museum's main entrance have been welcomed by one of its greatest characters. Small head with a toothy grin and long lugubrious face, an immense neck stretching into the distance, four elephant-like columnar legs, and a tail that seems to taper on and on – it is of course 'Dippy' the dinosaur, officially known as *Diplodocus carnegii*. Along with *Tyrannosaurus rex* and the blue whale, the skeleton of Dippy is an iconic exhibit, familiar not just to dinosaur-mad children, but held in great affection by adults of all ages

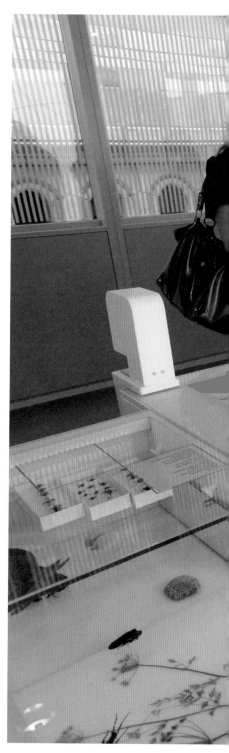

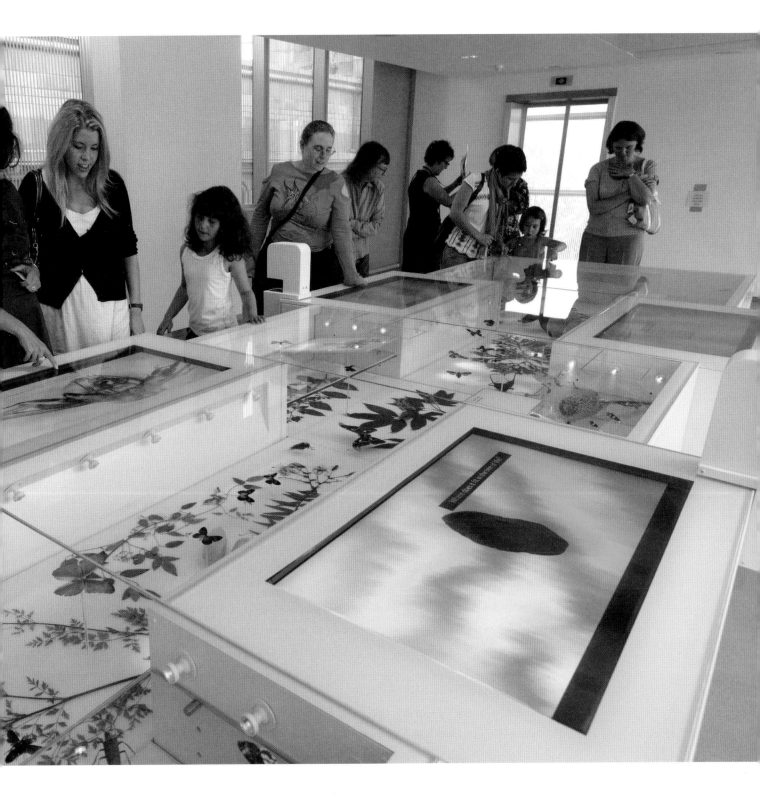

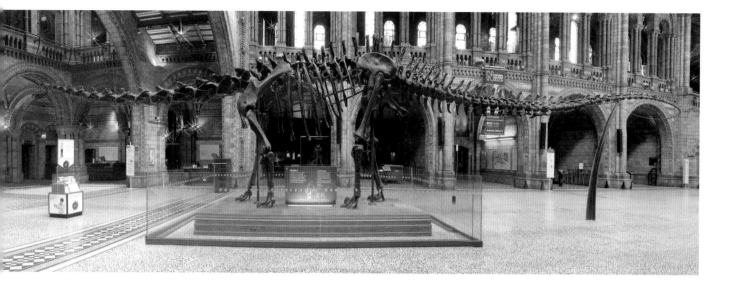

from all corners of the globe. However, what the vast majority of visitors do not realize is that Dippy is not actually a set of fossil bones. It's a replica – a plaster cast copy constructed from sets of real fossils housed in the Carnegie Museum of Natural History, Pittsburgh, USA. The Natural History Museum's copy came about when King Edward VII saw pictures of the Carnegie Museum's *Diplodocus* display in 1902 and mentioned that a big dinosaur like this would look good in London. Andrew Carnegie (1835–1913), the Scottish-born American industrialist whose wealth founded the Carnegie Museum and many other institutions, heard about the King's remarks. At once he set about organizing the gift of a replica plaster skeleton. It took 18 months to cast almost 300 bones from the fossils of five different *Diplodocus* skeletons at the Carnegie Museum, and ship them in 36 crates to England. Carnegie's technicians also arrived to reassemble or mount the bones.

When Dippy was introduced to the public in 1905, it caused a sensation in Edwardian Britain. Newspaper headlines cried 'Welcome, colossal stranger'. At 26 metres in length, it was the longest dinosaur known at the time. In life, a real *Diplodocus* probably weighed around 10–15 tonnes and lived in North America 150–145 million years ago during the Late Jurassic Period. It was the type of herbivorous dinosaur known as a sauropod or long-neck, along with other, even more gigantic kinds such as *Brachiosaurus* and the more recently discovered and even more gargantuan *Argentinosaurus*. Dippy soon became a firm favourite with the museum-going public, who continue to regard it with great affection.

The name *Diplodocus* means 'double beam' and refers to the twin ski-like chevron structures on the undersides of some of the caudal vertebrae, or tail bones. When Dippy was first constructed its head was close to the floor and its tail trailed along the ground, supported by the chevrons. This was in line with the view that *Diplodocus* was a swamp-dweller, wading through wetland habitats, where the water helped to buoy up its massive bulk, and munching on soft aquatic herbage.

More fossil discoveries and increasing knowledge of *Diplodocus* and its fellow sauropods led scientists to propose that it was not semi-aquatic at all. It lived on solid ground and craned its neck like a giant reptilian giraffe to browse in the treetops. The neck and tail were mobile and often held horizontal, to balance each other cantilever-fashion over the main body. So the posture of Dippy was altered to reflect this more active stance, with a slightly raised head and the tail stretching out behind in mid air.

Dippy to Dizzy

Of course, scientific opinions about Dippy and other sauropods continued to change. From the 1980s some experts contended that the neck could not have been held upright because the dinosaur's heart would have found it impossible to pump blood to its brain high above. If the heart did generate enough force to do this, then when the dinosaur lowered its head, the enormous blood pressure would not quite blow its head off, but it could damage the brain. So the view grew that Dippy probably fed close to the ground, swinging its neck and head from side to side in giant arcs as it grazed while plodding forwards.

Fossils cannot tell us the details of a dinosaur's heart and circulatory system, although we can get some ideas from comparative anatomy by studying related living creatures such as crocodiles and birds. Maybe sauropods had a valve system in their vessels to control blood pressure, as we see today in the giraffe. In 2009 an X-ray survey of various vertebrate groups (animals with backbones) added to evidence that sauropods like Dippy could raise their heads high after all. And so the arguments, perhaps like the dinosaur's neck, swing to and fro. However, there was no need to alter the current posture of Dippy because this reptilian giraffe view did not exclude the neck and tail sometimes being held horizontal, for example, as the beast prepared to take a drink. It is perhaps just as well that the pose of Dippy is not altered to reflect each new theory, otherwise it might have to be renamed Dizzy.

Although major remountings of Dippy are few, the exhibit receives the occasional 'refurb' and also an annual spruce-up. Specialist cleaners, usually each spring, spend one to two days (and perhaps nights) removing the accumulated dust and debris of the previous year and touching up here and there.

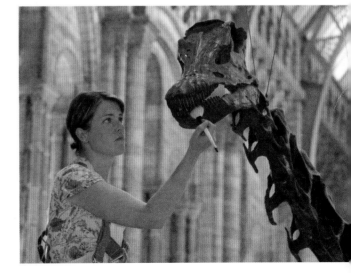

In 2004, in preparation for Dippy's 100th birthday, staff from the Museum's Palaeontology Conservation Unit and Design and Installation Team repaired some of the parts that had been damaged or turned brittle with age. Moulds were taken using the jelly-like setting compound dentists use to make impressions of teeth. From these replacement plaster pieces were cast, which were then carefully painted and colour-matched to blend in with the neighbouring original parts.

Today, Dippy is the first awesome exhibit that most visitors cannot fail to notice as they enter the Museum, and it is also the last item they see on the way out. It has created a lasting impression on millions of people over the years.

The early bird

A much smaller specimen than Dippy, but an actual fossil of immeasurable value, is *Archaeopteryx lithographica*, the earliest known bird. There are only about ten fossils of this creature in the world, plus a fossil feather that may have belonged to it. They all date to the Late Jurassic Period (the same time as Dippy) about 150–145 million years ago and come from the world-famous fossil sites in the Solnhofen area of Bavaria, Southern Germany. Exceedingly fine-grained rock known as lithographic limestone was once quarried here for use in printing. Because of the tiny grains, fossils are preserved in this rock in breathtaking detail – not just *Archaeopteryx* but many other creatures, including one of the smallest dinosaurs, *Compsognathus*, as well as pterosaurs and other reptiles, fish, insects and plants.

The Natural History Museum's so-precious fossil of *Archaeopteryx* (BMNH 37001) – often termed 'the most valuable specimen in the Museum's whole collection' – is known, not unsurprisingly, as the London specimen. It was perhaps the second to be found, in 1861, and certainly the first with most of the body, following a single feather fossil excavated the previous year that may come from the same species. In the London specimen parts of the head and neck are missing, but otherwise it is stunningly preserved with most of the skeleton, and also delicate impressions of the feathers spreading out fan-like from the wings and along the tail. The discovery of the specimen stunned the world and it was sold to the museum for £700. This is more than £60,000 in today's money, but even that is a fraction of the fossil's value if it were ever sold on the open market.

Archaeopteryx revived

Archaeopteryx reconstructions show an obviously bird-like animal, with feathers and wings, about the size of a crow – some 50 centimetres in total length. Its feathers, which strongly resemble those of today's birds, and forelimb structure suggest that this animal could have been a flier rather than a simple glider. Recent medical-style CT (computed tomography) scans of *Archaeopteryx* specimens

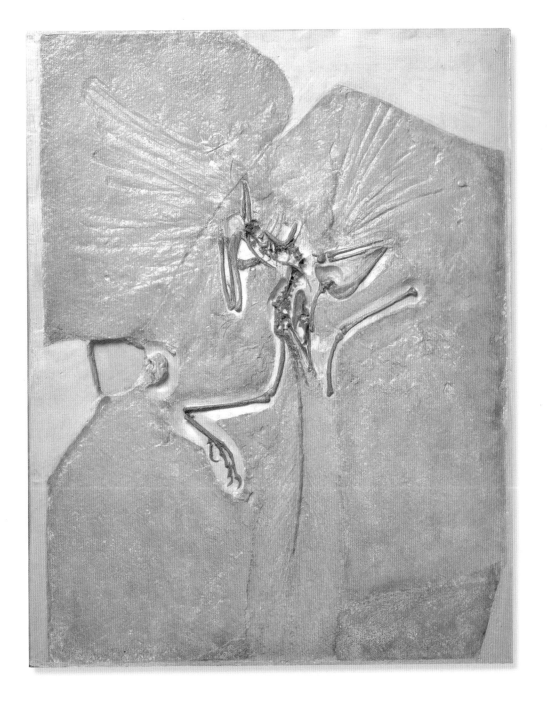

LEFT: The Natural History Museum's fabulous London specimen of *Archaeopteryx lithographica* shows its wing feathers fanned out to the upper left and right, and the long chain of caudal vertebrae (tail bones) with their feathers pointing downwards.

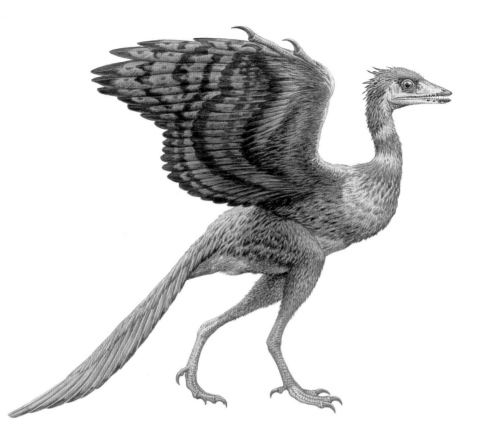

RIGHT: The wings of *Archaeopteryx* had the same number and arrangement of flight feathers as modern birds, with large primaries at the wing tip and secondaries towards the body. The feather colours, as with all reconstructions from fossils, are intelligent guesswork.

with skulls reveal the shape of the braincase, and so the brain within. The brain parts concerned with sight, hearing, balance and muscle coordination were developed enough to enable flight, but the aerobatic powers of *Archaeopteryx* were probably limited.

Although bird-like, *Archaeopteryx* has some definitely unusual features compared to today's avian species. The jaws were not covered by a horny beak and possessed small, sharp teeth along their length. Each wing had three small finger claws part-way along its leading edge. And the tail was not simply long feathers, as in modern birds; it had a long row of backbones, or caudal vertebrae, along the centre. These features are found in typical reptiles, and especially dinosaurs.

The world of *Archaeopteryx*

When it was discovered *Archaeopteryx* was hailed as a 'missing link' between reptiles such as dinosaurs, and birds. In recent years many more fossil finds, including dinosaurs with feathers, have strengthened the view that birds evolved from some kind of smallish, bipedal (walking on two legs), meat-eating dinosaur – probably a dromaeosaur, well known to dinosaur fans as a raptor. Because of details in its skeleton, and the time when it lived, it's doubtful that *Archaeopteryx* itself was the ancestor of all birds. But it may well have been a relative of the ancestor.

The plethora of wondrous fossils from Solnhofen allow experts to describe the whole habitat or environment of *Archaeopteryx* – a branch of science known as palaeoecology. In the Late Jurassic, the area was a mosaic of islands and shallow salt-water lagoons, with a fairly arid subtropical climate. Whether this early bird stayed mainly on the ground, or clambered among the

ARCHAEOPTERYX RENOVATED

LIKE DIPPY, *Archaeopteryx* has been subjected to many changing views over the years. But unlike the replica Dippy, the Museum's London specimen is the real thing – an incredibly rare and valuable fossil. It is kept under lock and key in an exceptionally safe place within the Museum, and only a limited number of people know of its location. The specimen on display in the public galleries is a replica cast – one of more than 200 that have been carefully prepared from a mould of the original fossil and distributed to museums and exhibitions around the world.

Despite its significance, the London specimen is not immune from ongoing studies and even renovations. As techniques and equipment improve for exposing fossils, it has been periodically re-cleaned with greater care and detail, to try and remove more minute particles of rock and get ever closer to the extraordinary detail of the naked fossil. This means that *Archaeopteryx* casts made from the specimen, even just 10 years ago, and which have been distributed worldwide, are now out of date. So in 2009 a new mould was produced of the recently re-cleaned London specimen, from which new casts can be produced with the added depth of detail now seen in the original fossil. It was a nerve-wracking procedure handling such a world-famous fossil, but the expert staff ensured that the process went well. And now the new updated casts are becoming available.

MUSEUM OF LIFE

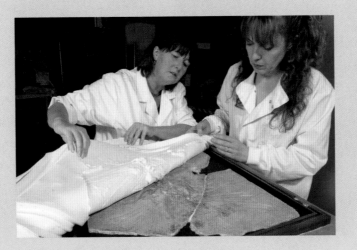

BELOW: This carved
hippo tooth is an
example of the exotic
natural artefacts that
people have tried to
smuggle into the UK
and that have been
seized by Customs and
then donated to the
Museum.

shrubs and small trees, or did both, is not clear. But its skull and teeth show a diet of small prey such as bugs, worms and other creepy-crawlies.

Quite how the first birds came to have wings and feathers and the power of flight are questions waiting for definitive answers. Did the earliest 'proto-feathers', seen in some dinosaurs as a covering of thready filaments, perhaps evolve as insulation, like the mammal's fur? In which case, this would imply that those dinosaurs were warm-blooded. Did the first birds evolve flying wings by running along the ground and flapping their feathered arms to become airborne? Or did they leap from trees using the arms to glide to safety? One day, perhaps in the Museum, specimens will be examined that answer such questions.

Expert witnesses

The 1980s saw a campaign to cast doubt on the authenticity of the London specimen and other fossils of *Archaeopteryx* by claiming that the feather impressions were forged using some kind of man-made cement layer. The fraud, it was alleged, could even date back to the Museum's founder, Richard Owen himself. Perhaps Owen intended the fossil to be lauded as a missing link in support of Charles Darwin's theory of evolution, an idea that Owen definitely did not support in terms of how evolution happened. Then, when Darwin's supporters triumphantly pointed to *Archaeopteryx* as a dinosaur gradually becoming a bird, Owen could shoot them down in flames by exposing the fossil as a hoax. However, Owen wrote a report himself on the specimen, without mentioning any forgery. So that scenario was not at all likely.

The Natural History Museum repudiated the accusations thoroughly by a series of scientific reports and press releases. In this case, Museum specialists were not actually summoned to court and called into the witness box. But it does happen regularly to some Museum staff members in a wide range of legal situations. They are asked to become expert witnesses and give their studied, professional opinions in all kinds of legal wrangles.

For example, suspicious imported trinkets are seized by the Customs authorities. It's difficult for the layperson to identify what they are made of: plastic, bone, horn, teeth, ivory? If their origins are organic (from living tissue), is the material from a common source that is legal? Or does it derive from a rare and perhaps protected species such as a rhinoceros, sea turtle, tiger or Arabian oryx? Sadly, cases of poaching and smuggling are on the rise, with big money paid for sought-after consignments. The trinkets could be a clear breach of wildlife regulations such as the CITES agreement, the Convention on International Trade in Endangered Species.

Open and shut case

The Customs authorities call the obvious place – the Natural History Museum. Could an expert please take a look and tell us what the items are made of? Depending on the case, this may vary from a fairly rapid once-over to a battery of technical analyses such as microscopic examination of cell patterns, and testing the substances for reactions with acids and other chemicals. These take place in the dozens of science and research laboratories scattered all around the Museum, away from public view – apart from the new facilities in the Darwin Centre, where people can watch this type of science in action.

The results are communicated to Customs. It is a rare and protected species. There is enough evidence for a prosecution. In court, the Museum specialist is called as expert witness to explain how the material was identified. Well, your honour, it was the result of several technical procedures, including histological examination using a particular stain, bioassay, and DNA extraction or gel electrophoresis. The accused's defence team caves in and accepts the authoritative evidence. The prosecution seals a guilty verdict. The Museum's staff have played a vital part in disrupting another smuggling operation.

Diagnosis murder

By no means all cases go so smoothly. A shocking murder hits the news when a decaying human corpse is found in a derelict building. It's time for CSI-style forensic examination. The body has lain around for some time, and flies have laid eggs on it, from which maggots have hatched and eaten their way through the flesh. Identifying the species of fly will give some clue as to how long ago the murder was committed.

Enter an expert witness from the Museum to help the investigation team with the forensic entomology (use of insects to solve crimes). Identify the type of fly, or dipteran, its laying habits and preferences, and to which stage the larvae (maggots) have developed. Dipteran larval growth is affected by environmental conditions, especially temperature, so take these into account. Work backwards to find an approximate time 'window' for when the eggs or, in some species, the larvae were originally laid.

However, under cross-examination in the witness stand, the defence has some knowledgeable questions about forensic entomology. Is the expert really sure about the speed of larval development? How can the ambient conditions be known accurately? Can the 'window'

21

BELOW: Darwin's closely-related Galapagos finches have different beak sizes and shapes but are otherwise very similar. This shows how they have adapted to different types of foods. Big, strong beaks crack hard seeds while smaller, more pointed beaks snap up insects.

really be defined so precisely? Isn't it a fairly inexact science? Could the estimated time of death be a few days out? If so, the accused has secure alibis and could not have committed the crime, and so must be innocent, rather than go to jail for murder. The future, nay, the whole life of a surely innocent person is in the balance.

It can be very difficult for the expert witness to hold steady and remain unflustered under intense questioning while offering an opinion that is based on solid science. Barristers and other legal specialists are themselves experts in picking holes in every small detail as they strive to defend their clients. It's perhaps not what Museum staff foresee when they first join as juniors, pinning specimens into cases or studying insect genitalia under a microscope (often the sex organs are one of the best ways to distinguish closely similar species).

Darwin's finches

Very different kinds of expert witness are witnesses to evolution. These are plants or animals with similar features that show they are closely related, having evolved from a common ancestor. Many clear examples in the modern life sciences are known, but perhaps the most famous of all are Darwin's finches. This group of some 13 finch species (14 including the Cocos Island finch), making

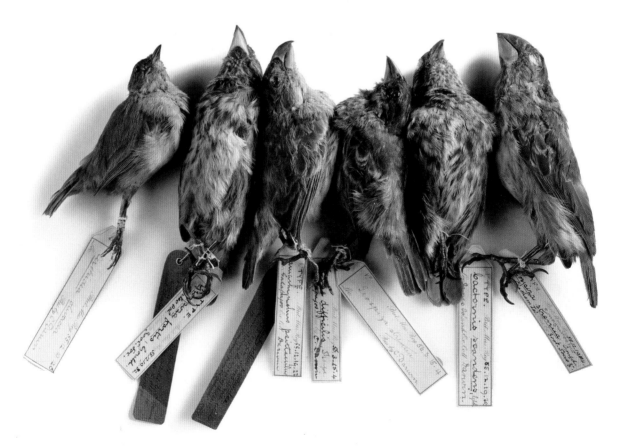

MOCKINGBIRDS AND PIGEONS

IT WAS TWO OTHER KINDS OF BIRDS, and some massive reptiles, that were instrumental in Darwin's **On the Origin of Species**. On the Galapagos Islands he had been struck by the giant tortoises – not only their massive size, lumbering habits and slow lifestyles, but by the observation that they were the same yet different. Tortoises from different islands had slightly different shapes of shells. Apparently a local expert could tell which type of tortoise belonged to which island. This was one clue. Other hints that guided Darwin's thoughts were the Galapagos mockingbirds (*see* below). As he collected these from different islands, and studied them on the next phase of the trip, he noticed that he had at least three species – again, similar yet different, from various islands. He also realized that a mockingbird he had seen on the South America mainland was another and similar species. So it was the mockingbirds, rather than the finches, that probably helped to seed Darwin's theory of evolution.

The third bird associated with Darwin's groundbreaking ideas was the humble domestic pigeon. For several years he kept pigeons at his home and workplace of Down House, Kent. He discussed their breeding and varieties with many pigeon-fanciers from far and wide, even as far as India. He also set out to select individual pigeons and breed them to continue or exaggerate certain features or traits such as a particular shape of tail. This was artificial selection, a major piece of supporting evidence for his theory of evolution by natural selection.

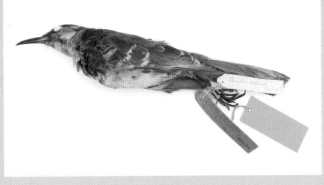

OPPOSITE LEFT: From 2008, Charles Darwin once again resides in the Museum's Central Hall. Looking at visitors surging through the Museum's main entrance, this mild-mannered man might be somewhat surprised at how his ideas on evolution have shaped modern life sciences.

OPPOSITE RIGHT: Apart from coining the name dinosaur, Richard Owen was central in establishing the Natural History Museum as we know it. He was appointed first Superintendent of the Natural History Departments of the British Museum in 1856, a post he kept until 1883, two years after the new building opened in South Kensington.

up the subfamily Geospizinae, live on the Galapagos Islands in the East Pacific. They are relatively small, drab birds, ranging from 10 to 20 centimetres in total length, mottled mainly in shades of brown and black. Most people would not give them a second glance.

Many specimens of these finches were observed and collected by Charles Darwin (1809–1882) when he visited the islands in 1835, on his five-year round-the-world voyage on HMS *Beagle*. Darwin's finches have become symbolic of the theory of evolution. After all, they were the initial inspiration for the great naturalist as he began to crystallize the notion of evolution. As Darwin gazed in wonder at the amazing and unique Galapagos wildlife, explored the islands, and collected specimens for preservation and later study, the finches were foremost in his thoughts.

Not quite. Darwin's curiosity was first spiked, not by the finches, but by other birds. In fact, during the voyage and for some months afterwards he did not examine the finches closely, or understand their significance, or even identify them. He thought that they were a mix of finches, grosbeaks, warblers, wrens and perhaps blackbirds. On his return to England, Darwin passed them and many other bird specimens he had collected to the Zoological Society of London. Within a week the famed ornithologist John Gould (1804–1881) had studied and identified them as a group of closely related finches, all new to science, and very worthy of further work. Darwin asked around for more specimens and gathered them from the captain and crew of the *Beagle*, and he was sufficiently intrigued by Gould's observations to open his first notebook on 'Transmutations' shortly afterwards. Later, once he had been working on his theory of evolution by natural selection for some time, he realized that the finches could be excellent examples. He saw how each finch's features, and especially its beak shape, were adapted to the particular habitat and food sources of its island. Yet to the trained eye there was also an unmistakeable family resemblance. The finches now reside at the Natural History Museum, as probably its most famous modern bird inhabitants.

Darwin and Owen

In 1867 Darwin donated his collection of more than 100 pigeon skins and skeletons, along with specimens of other domestic birds, to the Natural History Museum. They still bear his handwritten labels and identification codes, and his personal notes accompany them. They are the most tangible and awe-inspiring reminders of Darwin's momentous contribution to the natural sciences.

In common with several other great men of science at this time, Richard Owen was not at all a fan of Charles Darwin. Owen was the leading figure in establishing the Natural History Museum as a separate entity from the British Museum, relocating it to South Kensington, and organizing and displaying its collections. He also aimed to increase public awareness of the wonders of nature and encourage access to the exhibits. But he became a dedicated opponent of Darwin's theory of evolution by natural selection and the implication that humans were included.

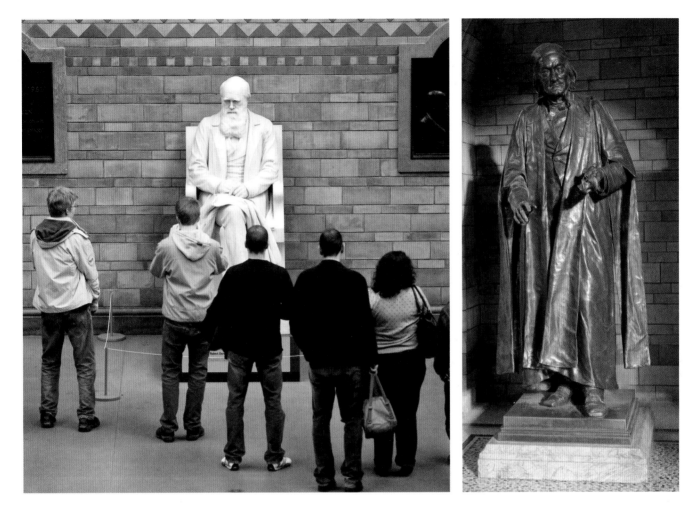

Friends to enemies

Before the publication of *On the Origin of Species*, Owen and Darwin had collaborated on several projects. Owen studied fossils collected by Darwin on his *Beagle* trip and reconstructed some of the great beasts they represented, such as the giant ground sloth *Megatherium* (*see* pages 90–93) and the giant 'armadillo' *Glyptodon*. When Darwin fell ill, as he often did following his epic voyage, Owen visited him at Down House. During the 1840s Owen came to think that some sort of change or evolution among species could be possible, and he considered several mechanisms or processes that might bring it about.

After the publication of *On the Origin of Species*, Owen and Darwin had several discussions about evolutionary theory and its applications. But their views diverged, and were sharpened by various attacks by both supporters and opponents of the *Origin* against each other – including

25

many colleagues and even good friends of Darwin and Owen. The latter said that Darwin's book was 'an abuse of science' while Darwin thought it 'painful to be hated in the intense degree with which Owen hates me.'

Changing places

The Natural History Museum honours both Richard Owen and Charles Darwin with beautiful statues. The gowned Owen, unveiled in 1897, stands in his lecturing pose. The long-bearded Darwin, who arrived three years after his death in 1885, sits benignly, hands on lap. He was originally installed in the prime location at the top of the main staircase, looking south over the Central Hall. But in the 100-plus years since, these statues, along with others of luminaries such as Thomas Henry Huxley and Alfred Russel Wallace, have been moved several times around the Museum's Central Hall, Central Hall Café and landings.

In 2008, in anticipation of the bicentenary of Darwin's birth the following year, it seemed fitting that the great man should resume his original location facing the throngs of incoming visitors from his lofty perch. However, Owen was there. So an eight-person team took about 26 hours to lift and transport the one-tonne bronze Owen to its new position up on the balcony. Then the 2.2-tonne marble Darwin was shifted from the Central Hall Café to the landing at the top of the main staircase in the Central Hall. Once again he has pride of place – the best seat in the house.

The face of conservation

Not far from Charles Darwin, near the Café, is another of the Museum's most popular objects – but a very different one, furry not rock-hard. This is Chi-Chi, the giant panda, *Ailuropoda melanoleuca*, from London Zoo. She sits quietly in a glass case, unaware that she inspired the globally recognized panda logo of the WorldWide Fund for Nature (World Wildlife Fund).

Chi-Chi, roughly translated as 'naughty little girl', was caught while still a baby in China's Sichuan Province in late 1957 and spent her first months in Beijing Zoo. At the time, pandas were known to be rare. But they were mysterious animals, little known scientifically and shrouded in myths from their restricted and remote homelands, the mountain bamboo forests of southwest China. One Tibetan legend describes how young shepherdesses were attacked by a leopard as they played with a giant panda cub. They sacrificed themselves and were killed, but the cub was saved. To remember these human heroines, other pandas followed the local people's tradition when mourning of smearing black ashes on their arms. As they mourned, they rubbed the tears from their eyes, covered their ears to block out the wails of grief, and hugged each other around the shoulders – thereby transferring the black colour to these other body parts. This is how, it is said, giant pandas gained their striking black-and-white markings.

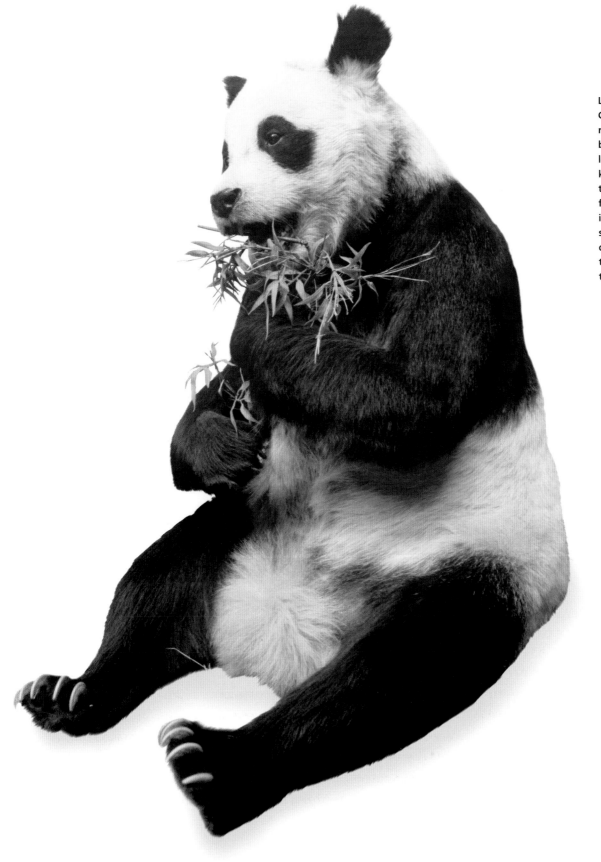

LEFT: At the Museum, Chi-Chi's lifelike posture reflects her love of bamboo shoots and leaves. Not clearly known in her time was that pandas eat other foods occasionally, including eggs, fish, small creatures and carrion – reflecting their membership of the bear family.

RIGHT: Chi-Chi
underwent her first
London Zoo medical
in October 1958 and
passed with flying
colours. Here the
superstar panda is
occupied with a bowl
of food while zoo
veterinary officer Oliver
Graham-Jones checks
her heart.

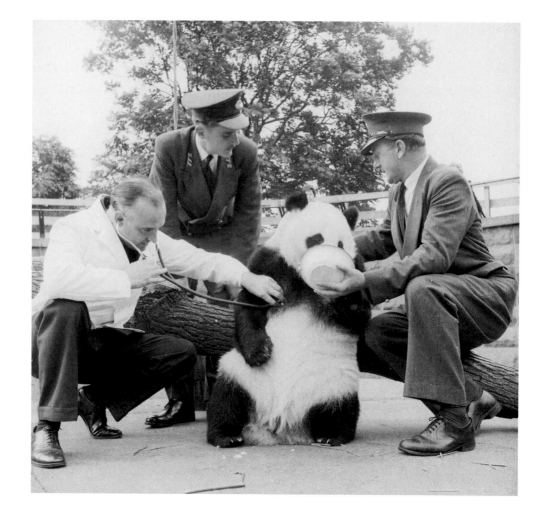

The giant panda's definite monochrome coloration was not lost on foremost naturalist, artist and conservationist Sir Peter Scott (1909–1989), one of the WWF's founders. He worked on the WWF logo, advising that a giant panda was cute and seemed cuddly and attractive to the public. It would represent the plight of rare species. Also, more practically, it was hardly changed if the logo had to printed or copied in black-and-white rather than colour, which was ideal for cheaper reproduction.

Chi-Chi's story

Due to a series of political manoeuvrings typical of the Cold War era, the infant Chi-Chi went through several transfers from Beijing to Moscow to Berlin, then Frankfurt and Copenhagen, before arriving at Regent Park's London Zoo in September 1958. She was due to stay for three weeks, and was only accepted by the Zoological Society of London because she was already in captivity, since the Society had announced that it could not encourage collection of rare creatures such as wild pandas. Commercialism came into play when Chi-Chi was such an instant hit and huge box-office draw, and she enjoyed 14 years as one of Britain's best-known and much loved zoo inmates.

During her stay, Chi-Chi vied for the limelight with the Zoo's other big hairy star, Guy the gorilla. Guy was a Regent's Park resident from 1947 to 1978, outlasting Chi-Chi, who passed away in 1972. The giant panda's skin was given to the Museum and she was carefully mounted in a lifelike posture, sitting upright on her behind, thoughtfully using her forepaws to manipulate her staple food of bamboo. Guy followed her to the Museum when he passed away.

Precarious pandas

For many years there were strenuous efforts worldwide to bring together captive giant pandas for breeding. Chi-Chi twice entertained An-An, a male at Moscow Zoo, but there was no baby. There were also great efforts among scientists to work out exactly which kind of animal the giant panda was. Due to its unusual anatomy, it has been variously classified as a bear, a member of the raccoon group, or something somewhere between. Studies of its morphology, along with DNA evidence, finally showed it to be an unusual member of the bear family, Ursidae.

The giant panda's situation in the wild has changed somewhat since Chi-Chi's time. Vigorous and focused efforts by the Chinese authorities, who are all too conscious of the panda's worldwide image, have led to protected areas where these bears are (in theory) safe from poaching and other interference. Several recent surveys indicate that their numbers are on the rise, with perhaps more than 2,000 in the wild. But the giant pandas' predicament is still terribly precarious, with fragmented ranges connected by 'bamboo corridors' under huge pressure from the surrounding and growing human population. They are designated as Endangered on the 'Red Lists' of threatened species compiled by the IUCN, the International Union for the Conservation of Nature and Natural Resources.

A puzzling spiral

Far more is known about Chi-Chi's life than for the vast majority of the Natural History Museum's specimens. One of the most puzzling, sometimes known as the 'mystery spiral', is a lump of rock more than two metres long and 40 centimetres in diameter. It resembles an elongated, solidified helix or corkscrew, or perhaps an unfortunate giant snail with about 24 turns to its shell that has been stretched on the torture rack. From this latter resemblance it has been named *Dinocochlea*, meaning 'giant snail'. But it is no kind of snail. Its smooth surface has no traces of a shell. None of the typical growth lines that mark a snail's development, as the shell gets longer and wider, have left any marks on the fossil. This would happen if the object had formed from rock particles filling in a giant shell, which then fragmented and disappeared as the infill hardened.

The mystery spiral came from rocks dated to the Early Cretaceous Period, about 135 million years ago, in East Sussex, southern England. Several were recovered during road-building excavations, with spirals that were in some clockwise, and in others anti-clockwise. Another suggested identity for them is a coprolite – in essence, fossilized dung or droppings. Preserved bones of the five-tonne, plant-eating dinosaur *Iguanodon* and other large beasts have been uncovered from the same rocks. The shape is not that unusual, since spiral or corkscrew droppings are known from ancient and modern creatures such as sharks. But no coprolites from anywhere else, that formed as the preserved poo of dinosaurs or any other creatures, resemble the mystery spiral in its almost mechanically regular shape and sheer size.

Recent study of *Dinocochlea* has led to another, very plausible explanation. The specimen shows signs of concentric rings, rather like a tree's growth rings, starting from a central point. Such patterns are known from mineral growths termed concretions. These are inorganic, that is, formed by non-living processes, in the way that crystals grow. Concretions are well known in geology, enlarging as minerals 'condense' or precipitate within hardening rock around an original small item or nucleus, such as a fragment of fossil. They form rocks that are slightly different in hardness or colour from the surrounding sediments. Concretions can be shaped like spheres, rugby balls, eggs, tubes, discs and bunches of grapes. Some are enormous, almost ten metres across.

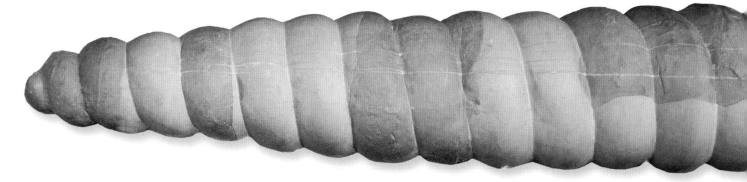

No spiral or helical concretions are known from inorganic origins. But several kinds of worms, shrimps and similar small creatures make helical or spiral burrows in the mud and sand on the bottom of lakes and seas. Did such a burrow become infilled to form an object that acted as a nucleus for concretion, with mineralization growing layer by layer around it over thousands and millions of years? Research using computer programs has revealed that spiral or helical shapes can be expanded according to certain mathematical simulations to create shapes that are very similar to *Dinocochlea*.

Museum workers propose this process as the answer to the mystery spiral. It does not identify the creature that made the burrow, which for now can be given the name *Helicondromites* while remaining anonymous. *Helicondromites* is an ichnospecies – a creature (or plant) based on the traces or the work it leaves behind for fossilization, such as burrow remains, footprints, tail drags, claw marks and the like, rather than remains of the organism itself. Perhaps, after more than a century of wondering, the object dubbed 'one of nature's biggest riddles' may have given up its secret at last.

A new kind of collection

Looking back into the past helps to solve puzzles today, such as the mystery spiral. Work at the Natural History Museum today aims to help combat incalculably greater challenges in the future. Global warming is predicted to change our planet's climate, habitats and wildlife, and affect almost every aspect of our lives. One looming example is the spread of tropical diseases into warmer temperate lands, such as one of the most terrible infections, malaria. It is caused by a parasite of the genus *Plasmodium* and is spread by the bites of female *Anopheles* mosquitoes.

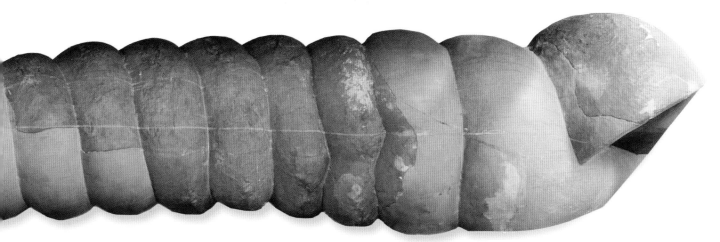

RIGHT: Mosquito nets may seem low-tech, but they are very effective at keeping away all kinds of disease-spreading bugs. Globally, malaria kills around 3 million people a year, many of them children.

OPPOSITE: So small, yet so deadly – the bloodsucking *Anopheles* mosquito is the chief spreading agent, or vector, of malaria. It pierces the skin with needle-like mouthparts and pumps in its saliva, carrying the microscopic parasites, to prevent blood clotting.

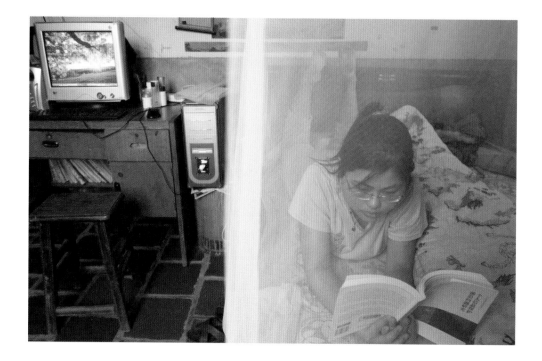

Globally, malaria infects up to 450 million new people each year and kills around three million, mainly children in Africa. The infection was eradicated from some areas in the 1950s using the pesticide DDT. But the harmful effects of this chemical gradually became apparent on nature's food chains – work in which the Museum was involved (*see* pages 85-87). So the use of DDT was severely limited and is now tightly controlled. Today the malaria is being fought on many fronts. These include work to develop a vaccine, research into better anti-malarial drugs for prevention and treatment, distributing mosquito nets to prevent people being bitten, creating improved pesticides that target only mosquitoes (with minimal side-effects on other wildlife) and even genetically altering the mosquitoes themselves, either so that they cannot carry the parasite or so that they are unable to breed.

Museum staff play a leading role in fighting this scourge and its possible reintroduction or range spread due to climate change, to regions such as Britain. Mosquitoes collected by Museum staff and others are examined not just anatomically but also genetically. They are ground up and their DNA is extracted and sequenced to determine which species live where and whether they are involved in the spread of malaria or other diseases. This work results in the creation of an entirely new kind of Museum collection, the DNA specimen bank, which will eventually encompass thousands of species. This collection will be used as a vital resource for scientists working on a wide range of projects in the future.

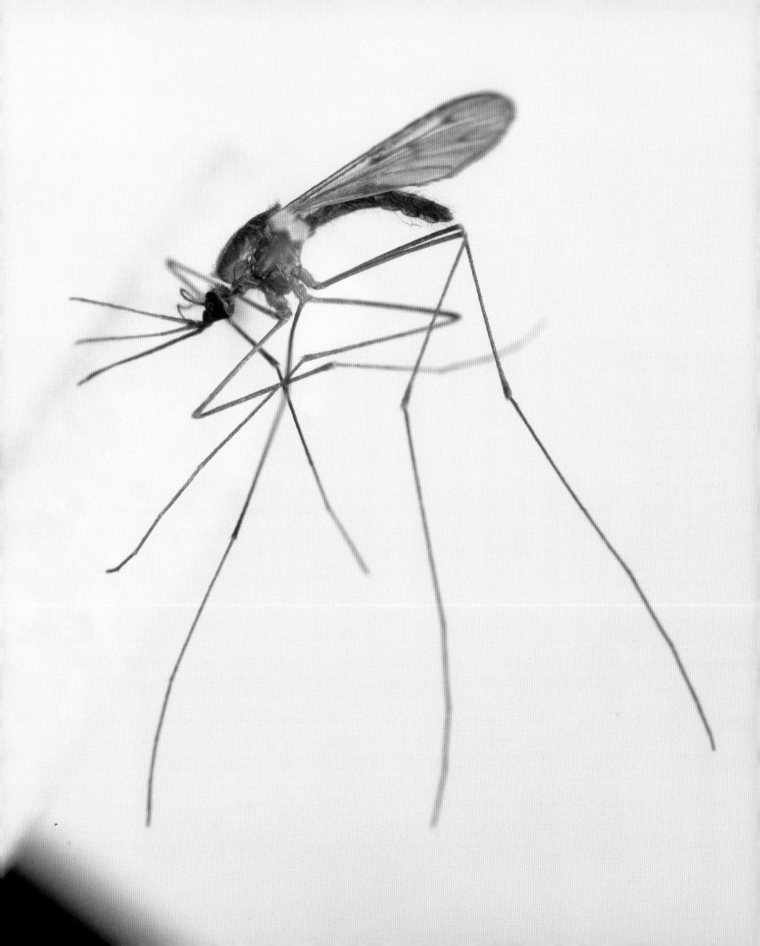

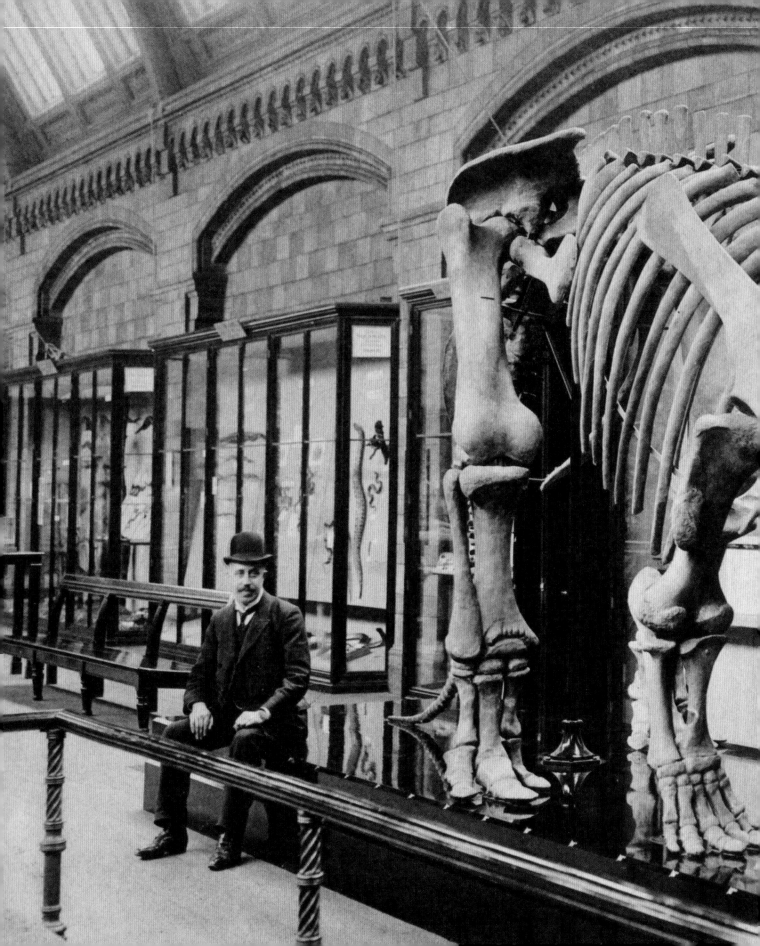

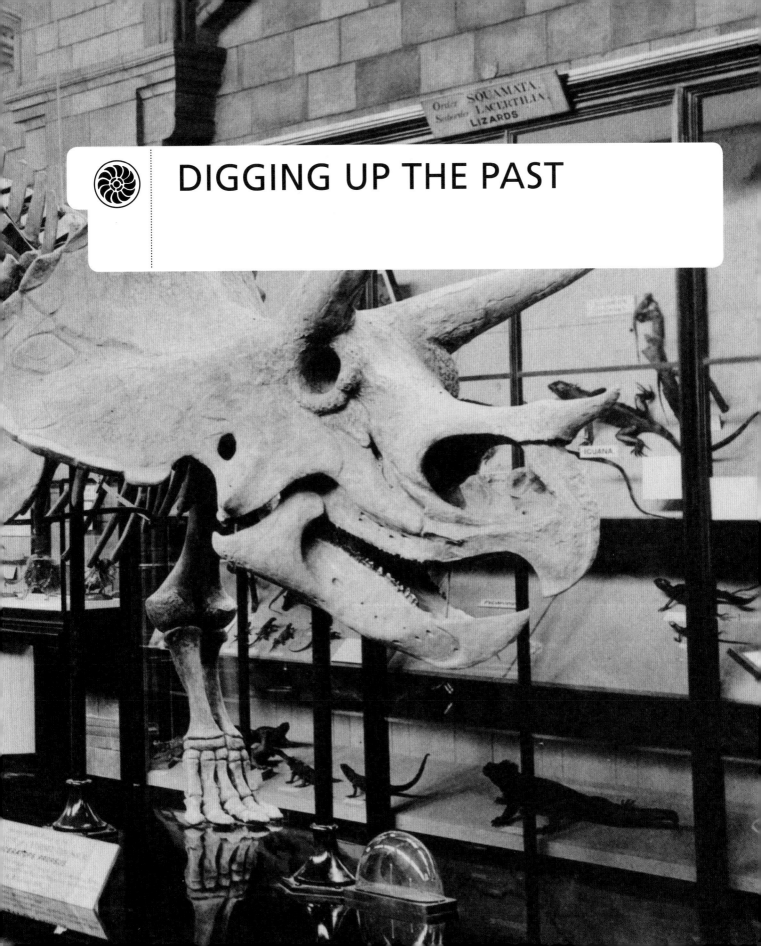

DIGGING UP THE PAST

DIGGING UP THE PAST

With more than nine million specimens, and up to hundreds added weekly, the
Natural History Museum's fossil collection is a global celebration of life's incredibly
long and diverse history. Every fossil tells many tales – the living thing that left it, the
person who found it, the scientists who studied it, and much more. Using the latest
technology to read these clues from the past is vital for predicting our future.

OPPOSITE: Not quite
a woolly mammoth,
but from the closely
related and even larger
steppe mammoth, this
Museum specimen
gives an impression
of how huge these
beasts were. Excavated
at Ilford, Essex in the
1860s, its tusks are two
metres long.

PREVIOUS PAGE: This
photograph shows
the Museum's fossil
galleries in 1907.

In medieval times, a fossil was almost anything dug out of the ground. Weird-shaped flints,
glistening crystal gemstones and shiny gold nuggets all qualified as fossils. Gradually, however,
the term became limited to the remains of living things or imprints that were somehow buried
or trapped in sediments and slowly turned to stone. The scientific study of fossils, the living things
they came from and how they interacted and survived, is known as palaeontology.

There's an ongoing misconception that only dinosaurs left fossils. But all living things, or
organisms, are eligible. Usually fossils derive from the hardest, toughest parts that persist longest
after death – animal teeth, bones, horns, claws and shells, and the bark, roots, seeds and even
tiny pollen grains of plants. Rarely, exceptional conditions – especially rapid burial in a low-oxygen
environment where rotting hardly happens – preserve impressions of softer or more delicate
organisms, floppy jellyfish, squidgy worms, lacy leaves and delicate flower petals.

Little of this crossed the minds of visitors as the Natural History Museum opened its doors
to the public in 1881. The buzz was all about the most famous of fossil-related topics, which still
fascinate and terrify us today – dinosaurs!

The first dino-stars

The word dinosaur, meaning 'terrible lizard', was coined in 1841–1842 by the man who became
the Museum's founding superintendent, Richard Owen. He recognized features in the fossils of
certain large reptiles that marked them out from other reptilian groups. Stories of the 'terribles' as
huge, fierce monsters from long ago began to sneak from scientific reports into the public domain.

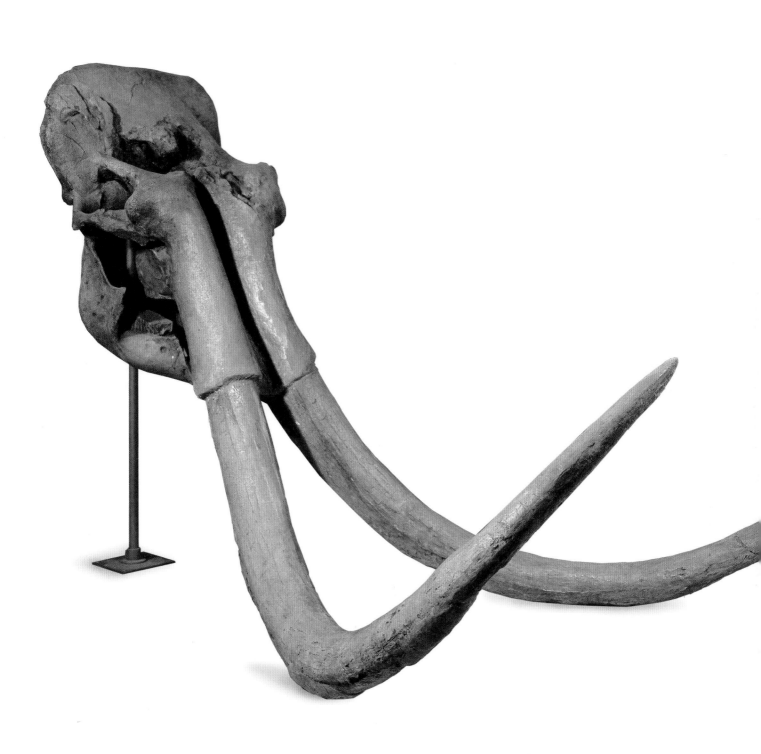

RIGHT: The Crystal Palace's Dinosaur Court sculptures were the world's first dinosaur models. From 1973 they were given the official status of Grade II listed buildings, and after extensive restoration they were promoted to Grade I listed in 2007.

OPPOSITE: *Iguanodon* peers across the Museum's Dinosaur Gallery. This creature is one of the best known of all dinosaurs, mainly as a result of the painstaking excavation of more than 40 individuals from 300 metres below ground in a coal mine near Bernissart, Belgium during the 1870s and 1880s.

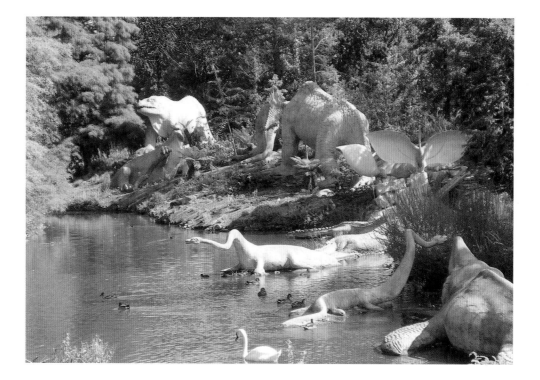

Fossils of dinosaurs and other great extinct beasts had long caused wonder at their origins, with many people believing them to be remains of huge dragons, ogres and other mythical monsters.

The first science-based dinosaur models to go on display were included in the Great Exhibition of 1851 in Hyde Park, London. By 1854 the giant glass building that housed the exhibition, known as the Crystal Palace, had been transplanted to Sydenham in South London. To celebrate its re-opening, what better than 33 life-sized models of dinosaurs, designed and constructed over the previous two years by Owen and the acclaimed natural history artist and sculptor Benjamin Waterhouse Hawkins. Built mainly from concrete to Owen's estimated sizes and shapes, the great monsters were an instant hit. People flocked to gaze in wonder. Dino-mania had truly arrived!

Sadly, over the following decades these particular dinosaur models not only fell into disrepair, some actually fell to bits. But in the early 2000s the remainder were recognized as items of great historic and scientific interest. They were renovated and put proudly back on display in 2007 at the Crystal Palace Park.

Dinosaurs get real

Hawkins did not stop there, and neither did dino-mania. In 1868 he began a lecture tour of North America. Working with the eminent American palaeontologist (and parasitologist) Joseph Leidy, he took casts of the first almost complete dinosaur skeleton to be excavated, from a marlstone pit in Haddonfield, New Jersey. Leidy named this 'duck-bill' plant-eater *Hadrosaurus foulkii*, and Hawkins masterminded the casting and mounting of its fossils into the world's first full-sized dinosaur skeleton to be re-assembled into a lifelike pose. It was put on display at the Philadelphia Academy of Natural Sciences, and dinomania was given another boost as crowds thronged around the great reptile's towering bones.

In a move reminiscent of Crystal Palace, in 2008 a revised version of the *Hadrosaurus* skeleton was again put on show at the Academy – the original had long gone, apart from its plaster skull. The new exhibit included information about the Leidy and Hawkins skeleton and the way its remains were interpreted by the palaeontologists of Leidy's time – including its upright, bipedal (two-footed) 'kangaroo' posture, which differs from the views of today's palaeontologists.

In 1868 *Hadrosaurus* set new trends. No longer were dinosaurian and other fossils left in drawers or displayed as rows of separate items in glass cabinets. Any museum worth its salt needed reconstructions of the skeletons and lifelike models of these long-gone beasts. Apart from their scientific value, they were marvellous crowd-pullers. Back in London, the Natural History Museum soon jumped onto the bandwagon, which has been rolling ever since. Today the drawing power of

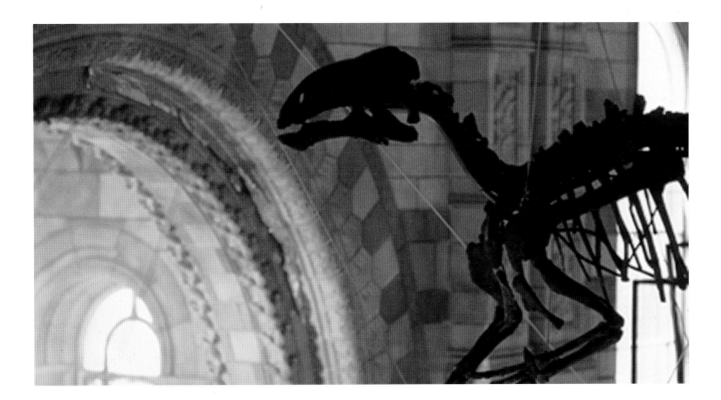

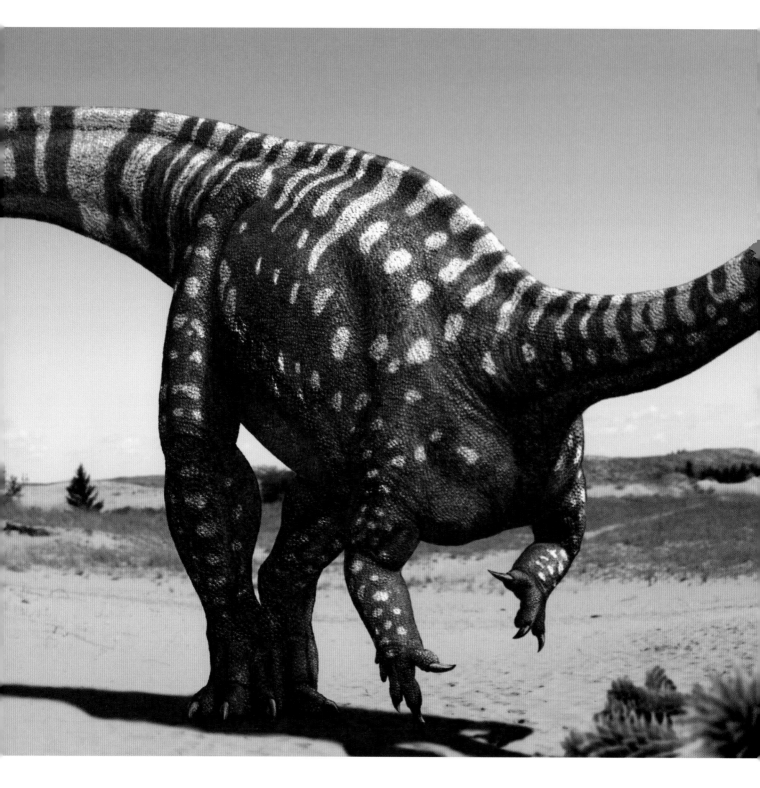

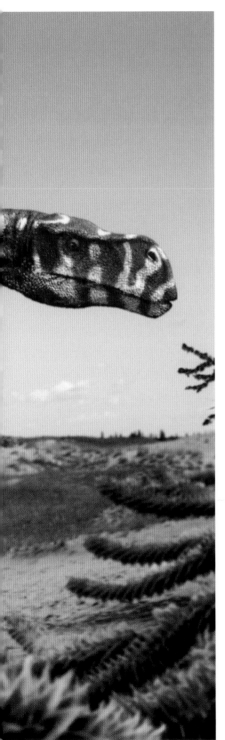

dinosaurs continues to rise, and three million people pass through the Museum's main fossil galleries every year.

New discoveries

Many hundreds of different dinosaurs are known from the fossil record. But the search for new kinds continues unabated. Natural History Museum scientists travel the world to search for the latest exciting finds, often working with colleagues from other museums, universities and research institutes.

One of the most illuminating recent discoveries is the seven-metre-long, half-tonne, ten-year-old at death plant-eater *Aardonyx celestae*, 'earth claw', from the Senekal district of South Africa. It was excavated by Adam Yates at the University of Witwatersrand and his team, which included Natural History Museum scientists. It is generally accepted that the earliest dinosaurs were bipedal, that is, walked and ran habitually on their two back legs, which were longer and stronger than the forelegs. However, the later group called sauropods – real giants such as *Brachiosaurus* and *Diplodocus* – had tiny heads, lengthy necks and tails, barrel-shaped bodies and four column-like legs. This showed that they were quadrupedal and that they moved normally on all fours.

The 2009 report on *Aardonyx* describes an intermediate bi/quad form. The limb structure suggests that *Aardonyx* moved most often bipedally, but that it could also drop down relatively comfortably to walk or trot on all fours. Among its key features are foreleg bones that could rotate or twist to place the front foot fairly flat on the ground, in order to take body weight. To fit with this transition, *Aardonyx* fossils are from the expected time of almost 200 million years ago, in the Early Jurassic Period, which places them after the early bipedal dinosaurs but before the colossal quadrupedal sauropods.

Significant and satisfying finds such as *Aardonyx* are often dubbed 'missing links', although they are of course 'found links'. They are yet more pieces of the immense jigsaw that

LEFT: *Aardonyx celestae* from South Africa is considered a fine example of a transitional form – what some people might call a 'missing link'. As a bipedal prosauropod, it shows the dinosaurian change or transition from habitual two-legged walking towards moving on all fours.

41

BELOW: Life restorations of Ida show a lemur-like creature well adapted to living in the branches, with grasping hands and feet, large forward-facing eyes and a long balancing tail.

OPPOSITE: The little primate 'Ida', *Darwinius masillae*, was probably only nine or ten months old when she died. Very few fossils are found in such a complete and detailed state of preservation.

increases our understanding of not just dinosaurs but all living things, and how evolution has worked in the past and may continue from the present.

The story of 'Ida'

Another 2009 announcement involved 'Ida', or *Darwinius masillae*. This creature was a primate – the mammal group comprising lemurs, bushbabies, monkeys and apes (including ourselves). Several reports in the popular and semi-scientific media hailed 'Ida' as the discovery of the century, and the 'missing link' that shed light on the evolution of humans and our close cousins from more primitive primate forms. Confusion reigned for a time as both the scientific community and the public tried to make sense of the discovery. So what exactly was 'Ida', and was it the fossil of a century that still had 91 years to run?

Darwinius masillae was named in honour of Charles Darwin (b. 1809) to recognize his bicentenary and the Messel Pit shale quarry near Frankfurt, Germany, which has long been famed for its exquisite fossils. These date to about 47 million years ago during the Eocene Epoch – about 18 million years after the mass extinction that saw the demise of the non-avian dinosaurs. Even for Messel, *Darwinius masillae* is in an amazing state of preservation. About the size of a smallish pet cat, and resembling a modern lemur in overall shape, some 95 per cent of this little tree-dweller's skeleton is present in incredible detail. Not only bones and teeth have been preserved. There are also impressions of the furry coat, and of leaves and fruits inside the body area, where the stomach and

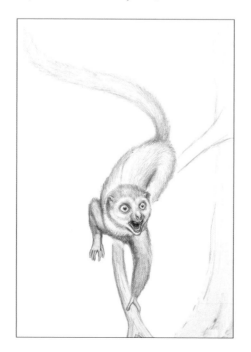

intestines would have been. The lack of a penis bone found in males of these primate groups indicates that 'Ida' was indeed a she, named after the daughter of team leader Dr Jom Hurum who conducted much of the research.

The two main *Darwinius masillae* fossils were unearthed in 1983 but then separated, and since that time they have passed through several sets of hands. Only when they were reunited in 2007 was full scientific scrutiny possible, albeit with some secrecy. Even so, stories began to circulate about the momentous discovery of 'the vital missing link in human evolution' followed by a highly orchestrated public unveiling of 'Ida' during the spring of 2009. In fact, the position of *Darwinius masillae* on the primate family tree

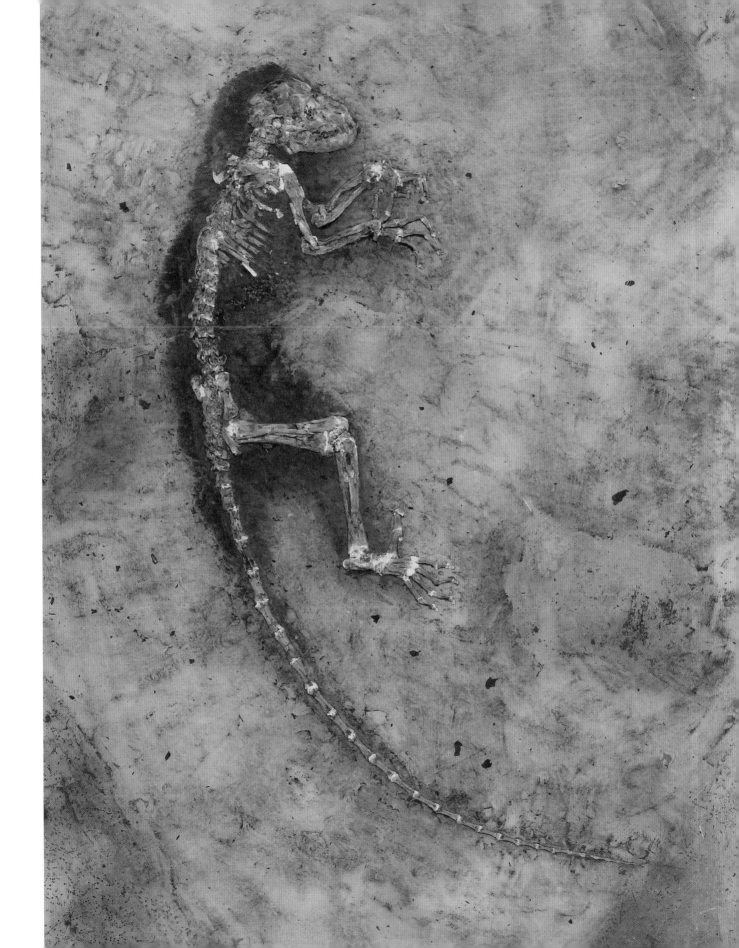

is much debated, and it may well not be on the direct line of human evolution. Even though it lacks some of the features common to modern lemurs it does not appear to possess any features unique to our own lineage of anthropoid primates. Until there is a full description of the Ida fossil with detailed comparisons to the morphological features present in early primates, the controversy cannot be resolved. Even if the species Ida represents is on the direct line of human evolution, it lived a very long time ago – some 40 million years before the traits that we think of as human began to appear.

Ida may well be the victim of a degree of hype and exaggeration. Yet she is enormously significant in other ways. Her extraordinary detail of preservation makes her the best, most complete fossil primate from any prehistoric age. This fossil sheds light on early primate diversity during the Eocene Epoch, and how the primate group may have split into its major subgroups of the strepsirrhines (formerly prosimians) including lemurs, lorises and bushbabies, and the haplorrhines (formerly simians) of tarsiers, monkeys and apes. Ida also helps to further complete our picture of the warm forest environment demonstrated by Messel's thousands of other scientifically significant and beautiful fossils.

The king dethroned

Apart from the occasional Ida, great scaly reptiles that had vanished by 65 million years ago still reign today's natural history museums. So what's your favourite dinosaur? Almost any straw poll of Natural History Museum visitors, of any age, yields the same answer: *Tyrannosaurus rex*. 'It's so big.' 'It's really fast.' 'It kills other dinosaurs.' 'It eats you up.' *T. rex* has ruled today's dinosaur world for more than a century. But with a name that translates as 'king of the tyrant lizards', does it still deserve its superstar status? Has modern science kicked holes in its immense and fearsome reputation? And who are pretenders to its throne?

Tyrannosaurus rex's basic statistics are awesome enough. It was more than 12 metres from nose to tail-tip, four metres tall at the hips, and is estimated to have tipped the scales at six tonnes. These measurements are based on the famous 'Sue' skeleton, the biggest and one of the most complete and best-known of more than 30 sets of *T. rex* fossils found to date. Named after the discoverer Sue Hendrickson, 'Sue' was dug up in 1990 near the town of Faith, South Dakota. Today she (or he, the sex of the individual is not clear) resides at the Field Museum of Natural History in Chicago, Illinois, USA. The largest land meat-eater of its Late Cretaceous age, 68–65 million years ago, *T. rex* would dwarf the same record-holders today, such as the Siberian tiger and grizzly bear.

Tyrannosaurus rex had a skull the size of a small car, teeth 15 centimetres long, a bite estimated at three times more powerful than an African lion's, and enormous eyes suggesting exceptionally sharp eyesight. But these features can be interpreted in several ways. They may indicate one of the most terrifying predators ever on Earth – or they could belong to a lumbering, skulking scavenger.

Changing views on *T. rex*

One of the Natural History Museum's prize fossils is the left lower jawbone of the very first *Tyrannosaurus rex* discovered. It was unearthed in 1900 in Wyoming, USA. Close inspection of its teeth reveal that they are not so much slim, sharp-edged, blade-like steak knives, as in some other big carnivorous dinosaurs, but more like tall cones resembling railway spikes. The full complement of 60-plus teeth seems more designed for crunching through bone than for slicing into flesh. Another clue comes from inside the skull, where the shape of the brain can be deduced from the bony chamber that housed it. The brain's olfactory lobe – the part that analyzed smells – is relatively huge. This could imply that *T. rex* sniffed out the scent of rotting carcasses, rather than chasing down living victims.

More evidence for a hyaena-like super-scavenger role comes from the heavily muscled neck, perhaps used for yanking at old meat, sinew and bone, and the deep jawbone, which could withstand tremendous twisting and pulling forces. A top predator might be expected to have strong front limbs, as in several of *T. rex*'s counterparts, able to grapple and subdue quarry. But the pathetic front arms of *T. rex* were hardly larger than our own and unable to reach its mouth for feeding purposes. An alternative explanation for these mini-arms is some type of holding role when mating. Or they were vestigial – body parts that had lost their original use and were in the process of shrinking away over evolutionary time.

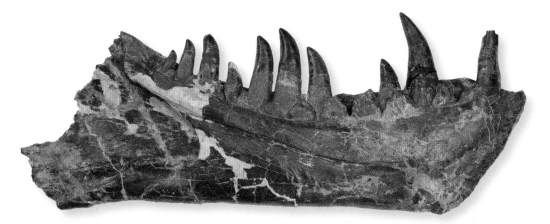

The image of a fleet-footed *T. rex* racing after terrified dinosaurs has also been called into question. True, its hind legs are huge and powerful. But they do not have the thigh, shin and foot proportions of a fast runner, and the bone thickness and muscle bulk are too chunky. They seem more suited to carrying the great body at a pounding trot rather than a flying sprint.

Bigger – but better?

To add insult to injury, *T. rex* no longer holds the crown as the biggest land predator of all time. In 1993 in Argentina, fossils came to light of an even greater meat-eating dinosaur, *Giganotosaurus carolinii*. Dated to 30 million years before *T. rex*, reconstructions show it was a metre or more longer and a couple of tonnes heavier. Since then we have also had *Spinosaurus aegyptiacus*, a massive sail-backed predatory dinosaur from some 100 million years ago in North Africa. In 2005 new fossil specimens of *Spinosaurus aegyptiacus* yielded an estimated length of 16–17 metres and a weight of perhaps nine tonnes. Not forgetting, of course, another pretender, *Carcharodontosaurus saharicus*. This similar but sail-less giant killer from North Africa was perhaps slightly smaller than *S. aegyptiacus* but still outsized *T. rex*.

Despite these usurpers, *T. rex* continues to rule the public imagination. The Natural History Museum's £250,000 animatronic moving model of *T. rex* is by far the most popular exhibit, pulling in more than 40,000 visitors weekly. With its gaping jaws, huge teeth and terrifying roars, it has been fitted with its own camera to sense movements around it and zero in on a likely human victim. Other great predators may come, and perhaps go, and the debate will rumble on about *T. rex* as either a noble, fast-moving hunter or a slouching, cowardly scavenger – or perhaps a combination of both. But what does the dinosaur itself care? For another human generation at least, *T. rex* will hold the title of most-feared and best-loved dinosaur, fulfilling everything that our imaginations want a monster to be.

The most perfect fossils

Known in legend as 'solid sunshine', the substance amber has been treasured for thousands of years. It is fossilized resin – the thick, sticky liquid produced by various trees, especially certain conifers. Quite why these plants manufacture resins is not clear. The various chemical ingredients may be wastes that the tree needs to exude and remove, or repellents for creatures such as bugs that cause damage, or for physical protection. The resins ooze in gloopy gobs from broken twigs, cracked bark, buds and shoots, covering any nearby items with their glacial flow. After a time they go harder as they lose volatile components and begin to set. After an even longer time, they fossilize. The clear varieties of amber, rather than cloudy, are greatly valued for jewellery and all kinds of ornamentation.

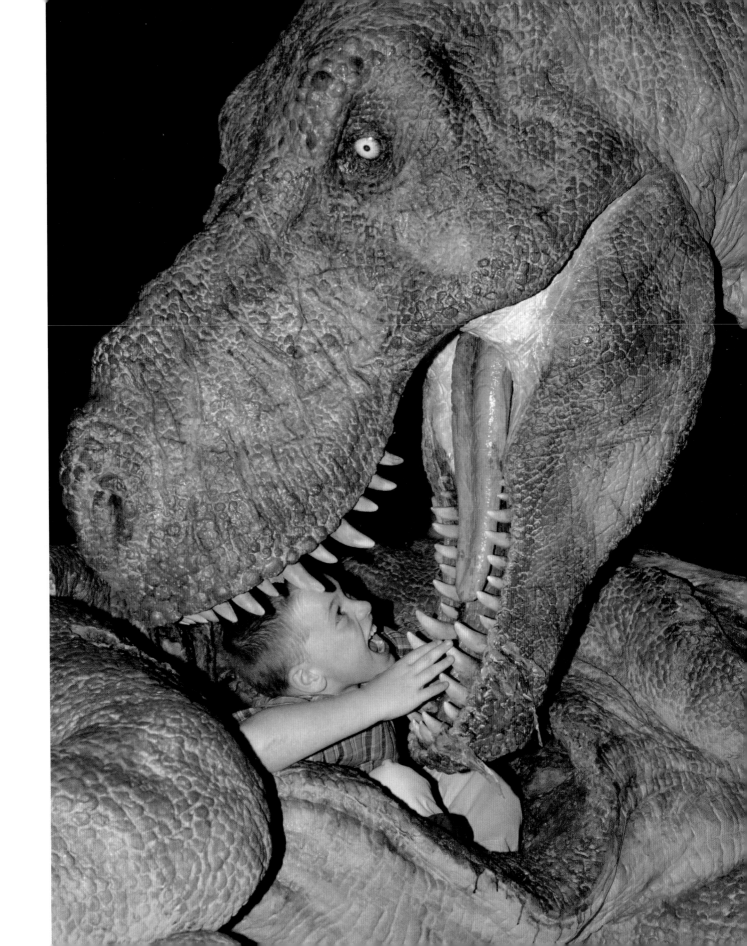

RIGHT: Dating from about 35 million years ago, this wonderfully preserved cockroach looks as if it might shake itself and scuttle out of its Baltic amber tomb.

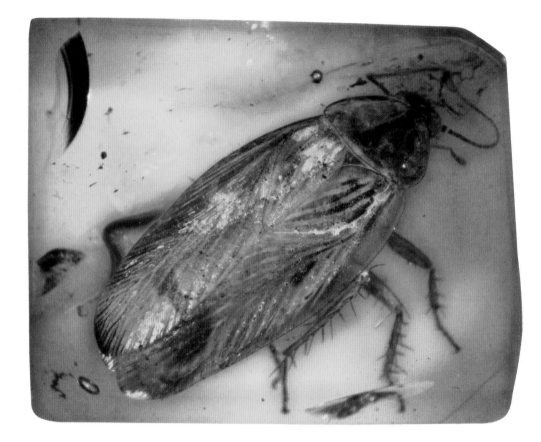

Back to life?

The *Jurassic Park* books and films (1993–2001) infamously portrayed scientists bringing dinosaurs, pterosaurs and other Mesozoic monsters back to life. The source was DNA (de-oxyribonucleic acid), the substance that carries the genes or 'instructions for life' in chemical form, extracted from dinosaur blood within blood-sucking mosquitoes and similar flies trapped and fossilized inside amber. Will this ever be feasible? Most scientists exercise caution in never saying 'never', and current technology has a long way to go for such goals. But if any substance is suitable for this aim, it's amber. Its degree of preservation, acting as a natural antibiotic wrapping and oxygen-excluding barrier, goes way beyond naked-eye features into the microscopic cells and molecules of once-living tissues. Freezing is another contender for preserving at least some DNA intact, as are certain structures known as crystal aggregates found in some types of fossilized bones and teeth.

There are many major hurdles to recreating long-extinct species such as dinosaurs, or even mammoths that died out just a few thousand years ago. For example, there are two main kinds of DNA in living cells. Nuclear DNA in a cell's control centre, or nucleus, carries most of

THE NATURAL TIME CAPSULE

THE NATURAL HISTORY MUSEUM HAS THOUSANDS of amber specimens dating from more than 100 million years ago, prized both for their glowing beauty and for their palaeontological significance. In many cases, as the resin flowed from the living tree it engulfed not only microscopic organisms such as amoebas and bacteria, but also leaves, seeds and other plant fragments, and tiny flies, beetles, termites, bees, ants and other insects, and perhaps worms, snails, spiders or centipedes. More plentiful amounts trapped larger creatures such as frogs, lizards and even mice. Entombed in their now-solid prisons, these inclusions are often preserved to an astonishing degree of precision, for example, with every separate hair visible on the body of a fly as small as this 'o'. Hundreds of long-gone species have been identified from amber, especially Dominican amber dating mainly from 40 to 10 million years ago. It was produced by the now-extinct evergreen hardwood tree *Hymenaea protera*, a cousin of today's locust and stinktoe trees such as jatoba. This specimen of a bee trapped in Dominican amber has been used to attempt DNA extraction. This work is very much ongoing, with problems such as contamination from workplace DNA gradually being solved.

MUSEUM OF LIFE

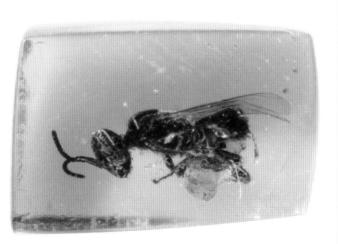

49

OPPOSITE: Mary
Anning is pictured in
her outdoor clothing
with her faithful dog,
geological hammer and
fossil-collecting basket,
in this 1847 painting
by B J Donne that
commemorated her life.

the thousands of genes needed by each organism for its development, growth and general life processes. Mitochondrial DNA is in much shorter lengths and contained within mitochondria – sausage-shaped 'power stations' that provide the cell with its energy for life. This mitochondrial DNA is also passed from one generation to the next, but only via the female line, the egg, with no male contribution. Added to these two may be a third type – DNA from people handling or working with the specimens, or simply from the general environment. This problem of contamination is very real and extremely demanding.

Obtaining unbroken and appreciable lengths or sequences of DNA is very tricky. Usually it falls to bits with time, many fragments disintegrate, and piecing together the few remainders is a gigantic challenge, true. But impossible? Bits of DNA are being recovered from fossil insects more than 100 million years old, and from bacterial microbes that thrived in salt-rich environments an incredible 420 million years ago. Huge strides in gene technology occur every year. If we can get even a few bits of DNA from an extinct species, we could use DNA from its close living cousins to help fill some of the gaps. In another century or two, who knows how close we may get?

As a comparison, imagine what the first lady of fossil collecting would have thought of today's hi-tech museums with their animatronic dinosaurs, DNA sequencers, virtual displays, lasers and holograms. She lived about 200 years ago and her name was Mary Anning.

First lady of fossils

Mary Anning (1799–1847) was one of the first known commercial fossil hunters. She was born, lived and worked all her life in the coastal town of Lyme Regis, Dorset. Apparently, when she was just over one year old, a lightning bolt killed three people who were with her, including the woman holding her, but Mary survived. A local legend grew that this event shaped her curious nature and lively intelligence.

Mary was from a poor family that did not follow the orthodox Anglican religious views of the time. These views included literal belief in the Bible's Old Testament. The Earth and all the creatures, plants and other living things on it were created in six days some 6,000 years ago. But fossils were something of a problem with respect to this notion. Some people recognized them as being the remains of long-disappeared creatures and plants that – to fit them into the Biblical view – had perished in the Great Flood as described therein. Others held out against this explanation and stated that fossils were lumps of stone specially shaped and wrought by God's hand to test the faith of his believers.

Mary did not delve into all of this too deeply. She discovered that she had a talent for spotting fossils eroding from the rocks – and there were few better places for her to practise this skill. Lyme Regis is sited on the 'Jurassic Coast', a line of rugged cliffs, collapses and rough, tumbling

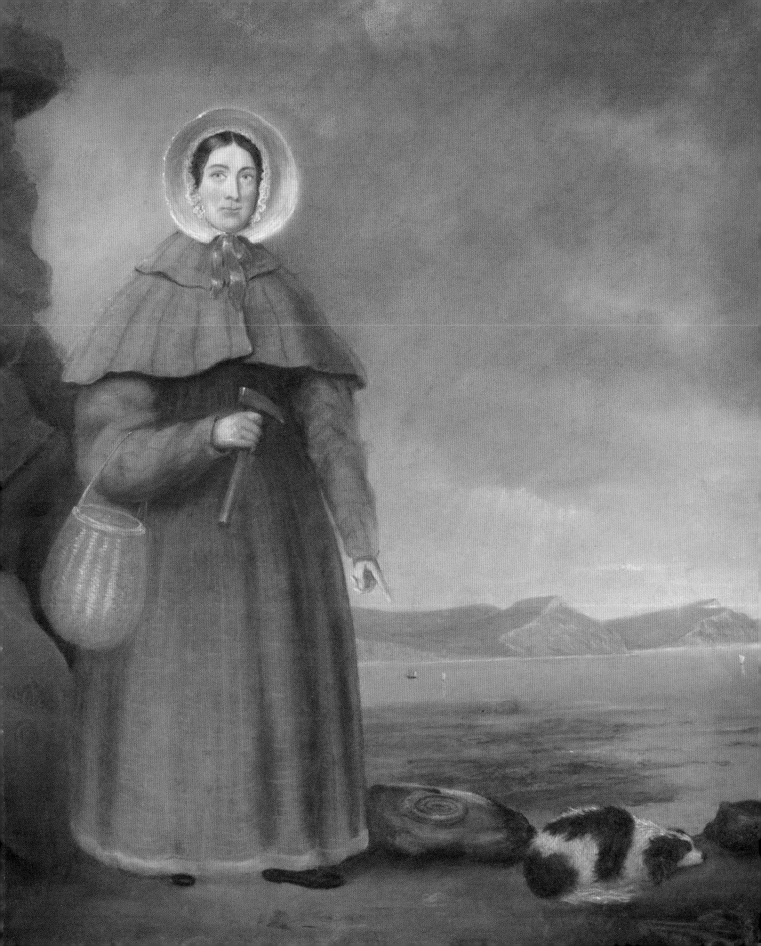

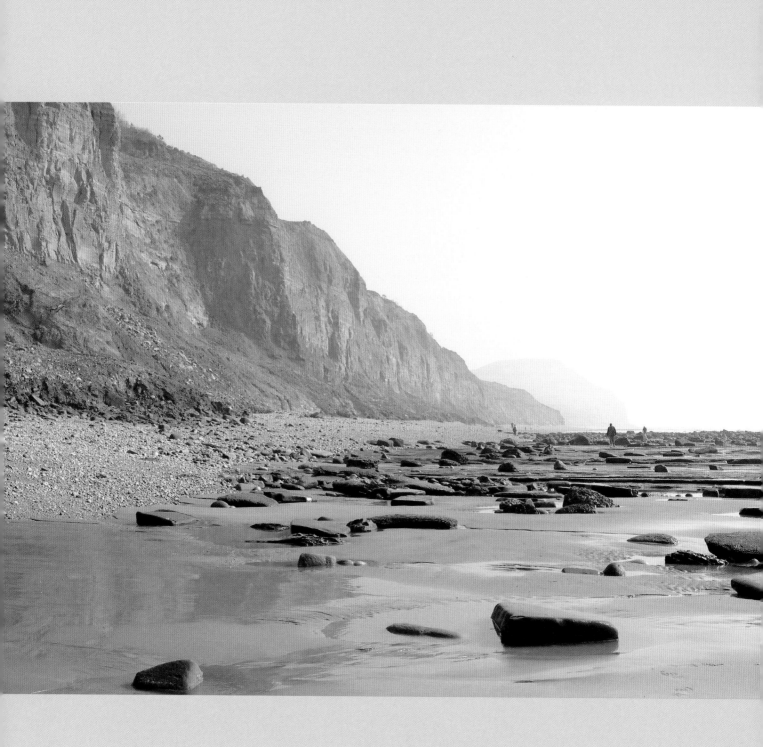

stones stretching some 153 kilometres from near Exmouth in Dorset west to the Swanage area of Devon. The limestones and other sedimentary rocks along this coast were mostly once ancient sea beds, laid down during an immense time span of more than 170 million years from the Triassic to the Cretaceous Periods. The global importance of the Jurassic Coast was recognized in 2001 when it became a World Heritage Site.

Beachcombing for a profit

Back in the early nineteenth century, Mary was little concerned with such matters. Her family was poor and to earn a living she took to roaming Lyme's shore with her dog Tray, especially after storms when the crashing waves loosened and collapsed large chunks of rocks. Each fresh fall brought to light amazing new fossils, which we now know date from the Early Jurassic Period, 180–190 million years ago. Natural history enthusiasts and collectors were prepared to pay for such 'treasures' to display in many places, from humble mantelpieces to stately home libraries to fully-fledged museums. The fossils included many ammonites, which are curly-shelled relatives of today's squid and octopus, along with the even more squid-like belemnites, as well as sharks' teeth, bits of fish and other marine life.

Mary's skills lay in noticing and recovering fossils that were unusual and worthwhile, that is, would fetch a higher price. In 1811 she and her brother saw part of a fossil skull sticking out of the cliff. Over the following months she carefully uncovered an almost complete skeleton. This was a creature less familiar than the ammonites – the first known specimen of an ichthyosaur. This fierce, fast marine predator was similar in size and overall shape to a dolphin, and probably led a similar lifestyle. However, its tail flukes (fins) were vertical, like a fish, and not horizontal, as in the dolphin. The ichthyosaur was a reptile, and ruled the sea at the same time as dinosaurs reigned on land. Mary eventually sold the skeleton for £23. She was becoming well known to palaeontologists and the scientific community in general.

It was hard and dangerous work on the shore. One of the frequent landslides killed Mary's dog Tray. In the wider world, more troubles were brewing. Some free-thinking people began to

OPPOSITE: The coast in the Lyme Regis area is continually eroded by wave action, currents and tides to reveal marvellous new finds. This stretch is at Cain's Folly, Charmouth and shows the vertical cliffs and landslips.

BELOW: This is the ichthyosaur, *Temnodontosaurus platyodon*, whose skull was discovered in 1811 by Mary Anning's elder brother, Joseph. The neck region was found the next year by Mary when she was only thirteen years old. The ichthyosaur lived between 199 and 195 million years ago and now resides at the Museum.

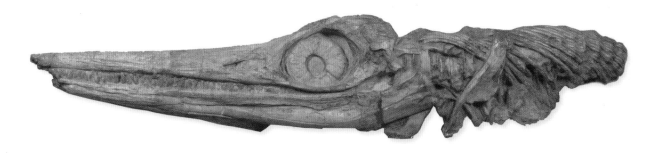

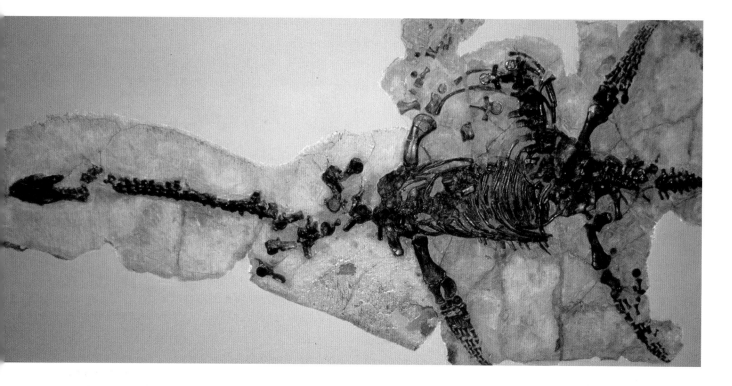

consider the amazing numbers and richness of fossils. Did they suggest that the Earth had a much longer history than 6,000 years? A scientific revolution was brewing, and Mary's work – even though she was a woman, not from nobility, and a non-Anglican – was an important part of it.

With the help of local benefactor Thomas Birch, Mary's reputation grew. In 1826 she set up her *Anning's Fossil Depot* store in the town. The rich and famous visited, including renowned geologists, palaeontologists and general scientists such as William Buckland from Oxford, Louis Agassiz from Switzerland, and the Natural History Museum's founder, Richard Owen. Her further achievements included excavating several excellent skeletons of plesiosaurs, the first to be found for science. Plesiosaurs were marine reptiles with a small head, long neck, tubby body, four flipper-like limbs and a shortish tail, often said to be the original model for the fabled Loch Ness Monster. In addition Mary excavated the first fossils in Britain of pterosaurs – winged creatures related to the dinosaurs that were sometimes referred to informally as 'pterodactyls'. And she contributed to the view that 'bezoar stones' were actually the fossilized droppings or dung of prehistoric animals, now known as coprolites.

Each late spring, since 2004, people gather in Lyme Regis to celebrate Mary's life and works as part of the Fossil Festival. This carnival-style event visits Mary's grave in the churchyard and acknowledges how her achievements helped influence people's literal interpretations of The Bible.

They contributed enormously to a growing feeling among scientists that the Earth was very, very old, and that fossils were remains of creatures and plants that went extinct a very, very long time ago. Great names such as Baron Georges Cuvier and then Charles Darwin would continue the trend. Mary herself is honoured by a portrait in the Natural History Museum.

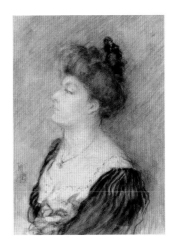

Off to the Med

About a century after Mary, another eminent female fossil-gatherer helped to chip away at the view of palaeontology as the preserve of well-bred, well-connected men. Dorothea Bate (1878–1951) from Carmarthenshire said that her education 'was only briefly interrupted by school'. She took to palaeontology at the age of 19 when she took a job working with bird feathers and skins, and then cleaning and preparing fossils, at the Natural History Museum. By 1901 she was publishing scientific reports on the fossil bones of small mammals from the recent ice ages, less than 2.5 million years ago.

Dorothea soaked up knowledge at an amazing rate and decided to spread her wings by taking off, at her own expense and with no formal scientific organization, to explore the fossil-rich caves of the Mediterranean, especially Cyprus, Crete, Malta, Corsica and Sicily. She travelled without security escorts, which was terribly risky for the time, braving local ne'er-do-wells, bandits and squalid living conditions as she dug into caves and cliffs for fossil treasures. Her hard work in tough conditions was rewarded with a string of breakthrough discoveries including several 'dwarf' species of large mammals such as elephants and hippopotamus.

In particular, one of Dorothea's prizes was the Cyprus dwarf elephant, *Elephas cypriotes*. As she came upon its molar (cheek) teeth, which were less than half the size of closely-related species on the continental mainland, she knew they were something special. Fully reconstructed, this mini-elephant was the size of a very small pony and probably weighed around 200 kilograms.

OPPOSITE: One of Mary Anning's greatest discoveries was the 2.9-metre *Plesiosaurus dolichodeirus* skeleton. It was the first articulated plesiosaur ever found – one with its parts preserved in position, as in life, rather than jumbled and broken.

LEFT & BELOW: Dorothea Minola Alice Bate was strong-minded and exceptionally determined. She employed almost any means to obtain specimens, from charming influential men to blowing up rocks with dynamite. The model skull below on the left of the tiny Cyprus hippo was made by Dorothea in 1906, as part of a full skeletal reconstruction. On the right is one of the actual fossils she used as a basis for her reconstruction.

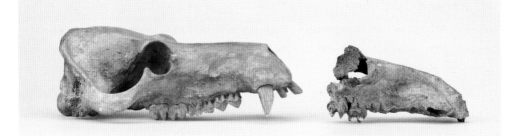

BELOW: This tooth
from a dwarf elephant
sits next to one
from a full-sized but
extinct counterpart,
the straight-tusked
elephant. The mini-
tooth was collected
in about 1901 by
Dorothea Bate. Note
how similar their shape
is despite their disparity
in size.

It survived until perhaps 10,000 years ago, and became extinct perhaps through a combination of climate change and human hunting, as described below for its giant cousins, the mammoths. About the same size was another of Dorothea's discoveries, the even smaller Cyprus pygmy hippo, *Hippopotamus (Phanourios) minor*, just 80 centimetres tall. She also collected new species of birds, mammals and other creatures, often shooting, skinning and preparing the specimens herself.

Island dwarfism

Dorothea was amassing evidence for the now well-known phenomenon of island or insular dwarfism. On a small patch of land with limited space, food and other resources, it may well be the smaller members of a species that survive in times of hardship. Their bodies need less sustenance and they can better cope with environmental stresses. As this trend continues, a once-mighty creature can evolve to a fraction of its former size. Also, most islands lack big predators since there is not the prey to sustain them. So large size as a form of self defence against ending up prey becomes less important, thereby helping the trend to dwarfism.

Many cases of dwarfed animals and plants have been documented from islands around the world, going as far back as dinosaurs, but mainly from fairly recent times during the last batch of ice ages. They include fossil elephants, mammoths, deer and ground sloths. Two of the most intriguing are the Wrangel Island woolly mammoth and the 'hobbit human'. The mini-mammoth from Wrangel, an island north of the eastern tip of Siberia, Asia, may have survived until less than 4,000 years ago, compared with the 'normal' woollies that died out around 10,000–9,000 years ago. The

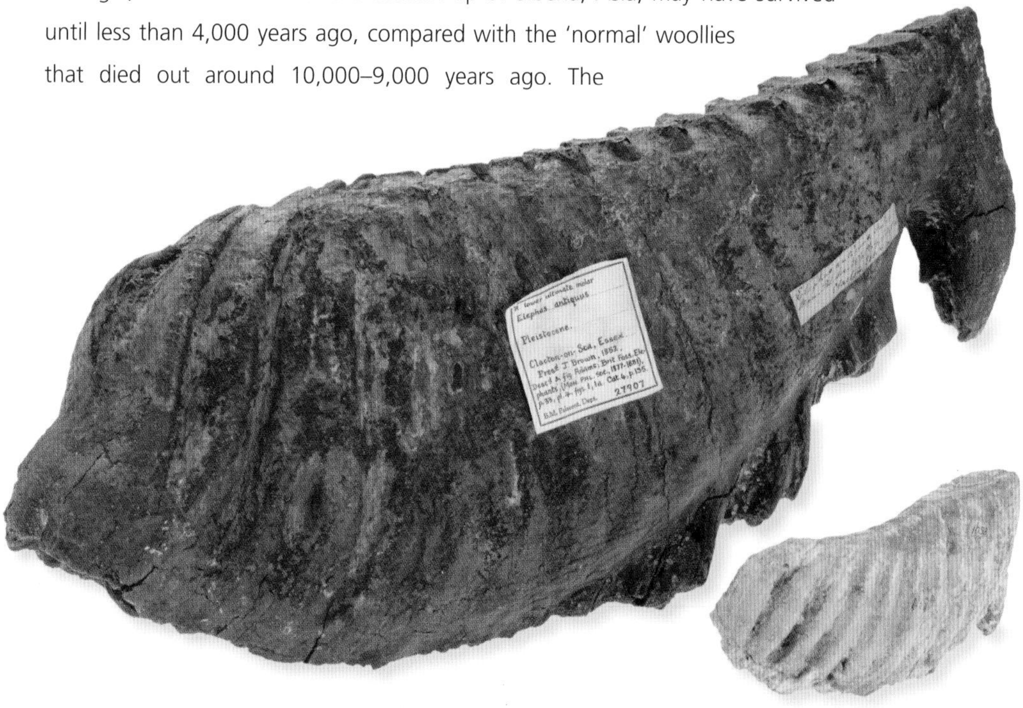

THE HOBBIT HUMAN

THE 'HOBBIT HUMAN', *Homo floresiensis*, (shown below next to a normal human) is a controversial find from caves on the island of Flores, in Southeast Asia. First excavated in 2003, this very small human – more diminutive than the earliest representatives of our genus *Homo*, such as *Homo habilis* – could have lived until just 12,000 years ago. The status of the hobbit's fossil bones and stone tools are much debated. Some experts say that the miniature skull and stature are due to some kind of pathology, such as an inherited condition, while others cite it as another example of island dwarfism. More recent studies show that these 'hobbits' are a strange mix of very primitive or old-fashioned human traits, with other features that are much more modern. Cropping up as it did during the epic *Lord of the Rings* movie trilogy, the fossil hobbit controversy may well have some distance to run.

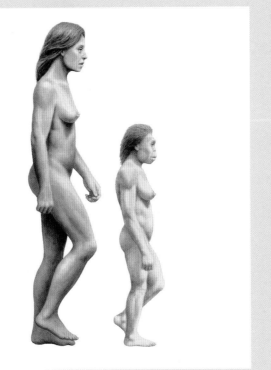

Wrangel mammoth probably weighed a little over two tonnes and stood two metres tall.

Dorothea stayed as a Natural History Museum worker for 50 years and she would doubtless have been amazed at where, a century after her pioneering efforts, her work has led.

Fossil hospital

Mary Anning, Dorothea Bate and others excavated and cleaned their fossil finds with hand tools such as chisels, picks, scrapers, gouges and similar tools. Without the aid of powerful microscopes, it was often not clear where the fossil ended and the surrounding rock, or matrix, began. Once again, times have changed. The Natural History Museum's Palaeontological Conservation Unit is the 'fossil hospital' where specimens go to be mended, cleaned up, renovated and generally made healthy again.

Modern fossil preparators and conservators use a wide array of high-tech devices and gadgets that might seem more suited to the dentist's chair and microsurgery operating theatre. Under a two-eyed or stereo binocular microscope – similar to a high-powered pair of binoculars – the view has depth as well as width and height. Extraction and cleaning proceed slowly with painstaking care, using high-speed pneumatic or air drills with a variety of diamond and hard alloy tips, as well as delicate cutters, grinders, probes, sandblasters and similar tools. It's vital to make sure that the fossil itself is not altered by tool marks that could later be interpreted by other workers as channels for blood vessels, holes for nerves, roughened areas for muscle attachment, or the tooth and claw marks of a predator or scavenger on the original object. On a special fossil it may take a whole week to clean up an area as small as a postage stamp.

A newish gadget is the laser gun. The intensity and wavelength of its beam can be adjusted so that it cracks or vapourizes the surrounding rock, leaving the fossil itself unscathed. Other methods involve painting or immersing fossils in particular combinations of acids and other chemicals, specially

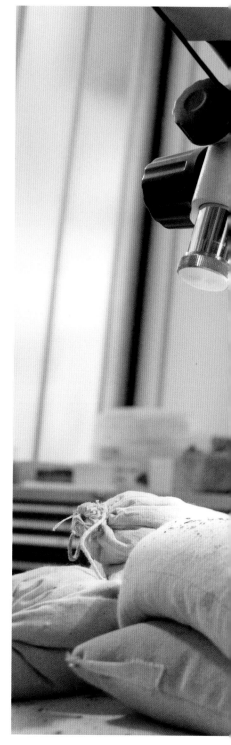

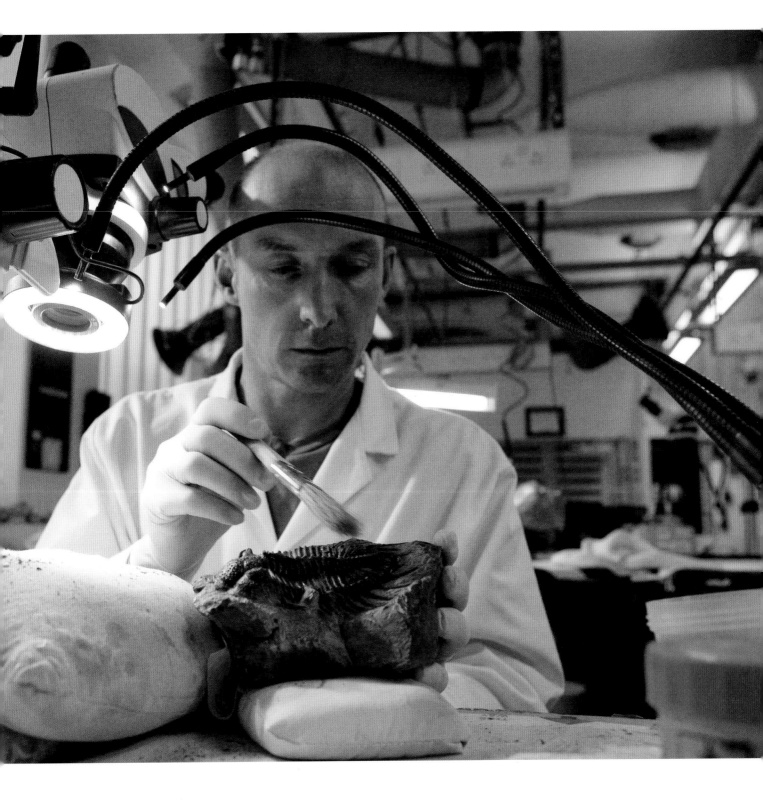

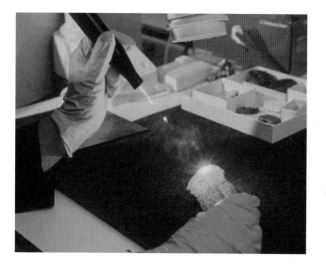

mixed to attack the matrix around the specimen but leave the fossil itself uneroded. There are many cocktails of these chemicals, each suited to a certain type of rock or mineral, and each has to be tested first on a small, unimportant patch of the specimen. It can be a slow process. Several coats or dips to remove the unwanted rock may take weeks, even months.

Battle against decay

With so many million specimens to bring up to scratch, the Museum's Palaeontological Conservation Unit has an estimated 5,000 years of work. Routine specimen preparation is occasionally enlivened by an unlucky palaeontologist who has accidentally chipped, cracked or even dropped and shattered a specimen.

Most fossils are made of rock or stone and might seem everlasting. But a condition called pyrite decay can inflict great damage on certain kinds of minerals that make up particular fossils. Like an infection it spreads through collections and afflicts more than 50,000 of the Museum's specimens. Its signs include yellowish and yellow-green powder coatings where the pyrite minerals have oxidized and deteriorated. Left unchecked, pyrite decay could turn a precious fossil specimen into dust. Museum workers are pioneering new methods of stopping the rot and rescuing fossils from pyrite decay. One involves putting the specimen into an ammonia gas environment, safe in a fume cupboard, to halt the deterioration, then storing it in oxygen-free conditions so that the chemical degradation cannot occur.

A colossal challenge

One of the Natural History Museum's biggest-ever fossil specimens arrived in 2009 – in more than 100 parts. It was a tree from the Late Jurassic Period, 145 million years ago. To be more accurate, it was about 130 pieces of the trunk and/or main branches from a cypress-like conifer, dug out of clay up to one and a half metres deep in Wiltshire, in the West of England. After 180 hours of excavation spread over months by its discoverer, stonemason and part-time fossil sleuth John Needham, and his daughter Izzy, the specimens were transported to Museum premises in several batches – after all, the biggest sections weighed more than half a tonne.

The tree's pieces resemble a gigantic 3D jigsaw. Picking up normal 2D jigsaw pieces between your thumb and forefinger bears no relation to trying to reassemble a fossil tree, when even a strong person has no chance of lifting or even turning many of the bits. Physical manipulation, by trying to fit the different parts to each other using guesswork, was pretty much out of the question.

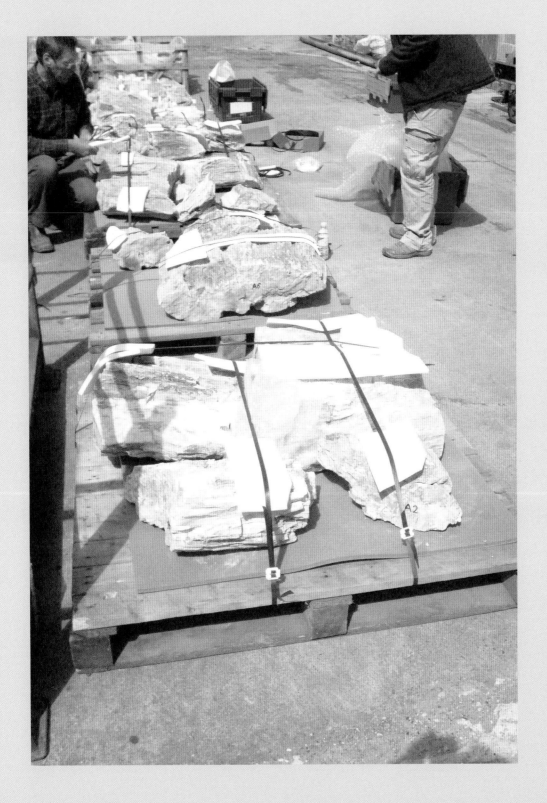

OPPOSITE: Laser guns are just one of the high-tech tools used to extract and clean fossils – here a reptile specimen. This work demands enormous skill, dexterity and concentration for long periods.

LEFT: Chunks of the Wiltshire fossil tree trunk were packed onto pallets, secured and loaded into vans, ready for their journey to the Museum's store in Wandsworth, southwest London.

RIGHT: The Wiltshire fossil tree is reassembled on a computer screen into a section of trunk that was, in real life, about 12 metres long. It was found lying horizontal, its lower end close to a very large upright stump.

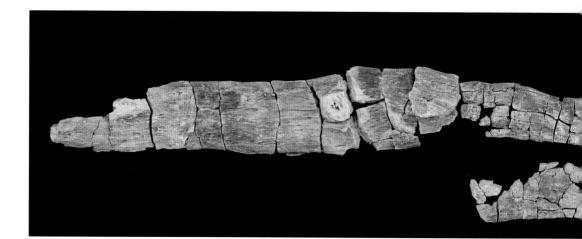

New technology in the form of 3D laser scanners came to the rescue. The fossil tree fragments were scanned into a computer using a 3D laser system, similar to those used for designing sleek cars, crane girders or tiny gearboxes in miniature medical equipment. Once the digitized 3D shape of each tree part was in the computer, its virtual representation on screen could be moved and turned and spun around at the touch of a key or mouse. It was then much easier to fit the bits by trial and error against other likely pieces, and so rebuild the complete object.

Dinosaur forests

The results for the Jurassic fossil tree were surprising. What had seemed to be its main trunk instead could have been a major branch that grew from the trunk, with the latter not preserved. So the whole tree was larger than at first envisaged. The shapes of the fossil parts were rather flattened from one side to another, being almost elliptical in cross section, rather than rounded as the tree would have grown in life. The cross sections showed tree growth rings in some detail, and their patterns indicated a climate of hot, dry summers and fairly wet, cool winters. Looking even closer, details of preserved microscopic cells arranged in rows and patterns suggested that the tree was some kind of cypress.

Sifting this mass of evidence, which included fossils of other plants and creatures from the same area, allowed Museum scientists to work out the likely story of the tree's life and death. It was probably 15–20 metres tall, cypress-like with a broad expanding crown of branches towards the top. It grew in an open woodland with scattered trees and bushes – but no grasses, which had probably not evolved at this time – in a generally warm, relatively arid climate. This was the Late Jurassic Period, heyday of some of the greatest dinosaurs. Both meat-eaters and herbivores would have wandered beneath its branches.

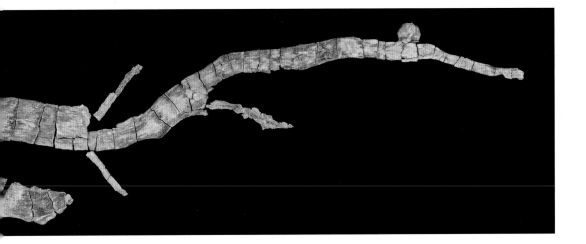

The environmental and fossil clues show that the tree grew near a saltwater lagoon. Some local event, perhaps a landslip, caused the water to flood the woodland and kill the tree. But it stayed upright for another 10, 20 or even 30 years, slowly rotting where it stood. Tiny holes are evidence of insects, perhaps similar to termites and ants, boring into the wood. After years of this active animal decay, the tree finally toppled into the salty water, and its long fossilization began. In this way what is probably the Museum's largest fossil provides a wonderfully fresh glimpse into the climate and vegetation in Western England slap bang in the middle of the Age of Dinosaurs.

A mammoth problem

Much more recent prehistoric giants – animals this time – are the famed woolly mammoths, *Mammuthus primigenius,* of Ice Age northern lands. They were superbly adapted to the bitter cold and polar tundra conditions, with thick shaggy coats, an insulating fatty layer more than six centimetres thick under the skin, and great curving tusks up to five metres long for sweeping snow from vegetation. The mammoth's great body, up to four metres tall and weighing eight tonnes in a full-grown bull, lost heat very slowly because of its low surface to volume ratio. This follows the biological or ecogeographic trend known as Bergmann's rule, suggested in 1847 by German life scientist Christian Bergmann (1814–1865). It states that animals from cold climates, in higher latitudes or higher altitudes, tend towards greater heat-retaining body bulk and smaller heat-losing extremities than their warmth-dwelling relatives.

Accepted wisdom had it that woolly mammoths lived in Britain and most of North West Europe until roughly 20,000 years ago, when there was an intense freezing period known as the Last Glacial Maximum, LGM – the last great Ice Age. (These 'standard' woolly mammoths may have persisted until 10,000 years ago in other locations, while the variety known as the Wrangel Island

RIGHT: Fossils of many animals and plants allow us to reconstruct the woolly mammoths' habitat. In this spring scene mammoths, horses and a wolverine leave the shelter of the larch and pine forests and trek out onto the treeless tundra of sedges and cottongrass.

OPPOSITE: More than 100,000 hand axes have been recovered from Swanscombe, in Kent. They date to between 500,000 and 300,000 years ago. Exactly who made them has been much debated – possibly Neanderthals, probably *Homo erectus*.

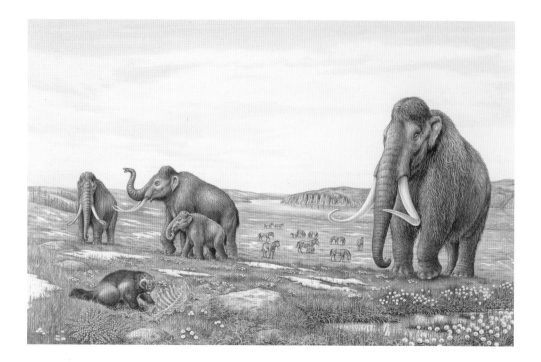

dwarf mammoth, mentioned previously (*see* page 56), persisted on its cold outpost until less than 4,000 years ago.)

The disappearance of the woolly mammoth coincided with the last Ice Age and also the spread of mammoth-hunting humans across their lands. It was thought that these two factors, combined, probably caused their demise. Not just the hairy mammoths but many other huge creatures – known collectively as the 'Pleistocene megafauna' from the name of the geological time span, the Pleistocene Epoch – died out at about the same time. They included woolly rhinos, giant deer, bison, dire wolves, cave lions, cave bears and more.

Climate changes, past and future

Museum scientists have been studying new evidence that has helped overturn these views. New carbon-dating of mammoth bones from Condover, Shropshire put them at around 14,000 years old, which is some 6,000 years later than previously thought. The specimens had been radioisotopically dated before, but newer technology involving a process called ultra-filtration has allowed much purer samples, freer from contamination, to be prepared. Results from other bone and teeth samples had suggested that some previous dates, using older purification methods, could be out by a significant amount. So the mammoth remains were re-tested, and sure enough, a more accurate and much younger date emerged.

At the Natural History Museum, evidence from other fossils has been added to the new woolly mammoth dates to try and glean a more accurate picture of how and why the beasts met their end. The picture now painted is that climate change probably played a major role by affecting vegetation across vast areas. Woods and forests began to encroach on the mammoths' preferred habitat of steppe grassland, where they were adapted to grazing on tough grassy vegetation. Their range became squeezed more and more into small remnant areas or refuges, as their populations shrank from millions to thousands. Local extinctions were perhaps followed by recovery as small groups migrated from refuges elsewhere, as could have happened in southern England. But there was no resisting the changing climate – in effect, it was a relatively rapid episode of natural global warming.

Stone-age humans with their spears, axes, pit traps and control of fire may have hastened the mammoths' end. But the species was likely already heading for extinction. The mammoths' fate is teaching us valuable lessons about the future of our world, and perhaps our own species, as a superfast episode of climate change and global warming gets under way.

Human extinctions

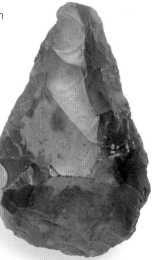

Fossils and other remains show that woolly mammoths were hunted by Neanderthal humans, *Homo neanderthalensis* – a species closely related to ourselves that also went extinct, probably by 30,000 years ago. Again, what was the cause? Climate change is a prominent suggestion. Neanderthals were a cold-adapted species, able to live through the harsh conditions of major Ice Ages or glacials. As the world warmed during interglacial episodes, perhaps they found the going tougher. Then along came another possible threat, that could have finished them off – ourselves, modern humans, *Homo sapiens sapiens*.

Researchers at the Natural History Museum are world leaders in finding the answers to one of the most fascinating and evocative of all questions: the origins of our own kind. The leading notion is known as the 'Out of Africa' theory, or the 'Recent single-origin' hypothesis. In simple terms – its bare bones – it proposes that in Africa some time between 200,000 and 100,000 years ago, a relatively small population of our direct ancestors, known as archaic *Homo sapiens*, went through a fairly rapid speciation event and evolved into what we call fully modern humans – basically, ourselves. These people multiplied and spread within Africa. Some time before 60,000 years ago pioneering groups made their way from that continent into the Middle East and Europe, and also eastwards into Asia, Southeast Asia, and Australia by 40,000 years ago. Yet more populations headed across the Bering Land Bridge from Asia into North America and down into South America.

RIGHT: The map shows how modern humans were thought to spread from about 200,000 years ago, first around Africa, then radiating to other continents. The Middle East may have seen two waves, the first only temporary and followed by Neanderthals.

OPPOSITE: The Cro-Magnon people were anatomically modern humans, derived from populations that left Africa many millennia previously. They were first described from remains about 30,000 years old, discovered in 1868 in the Dordogne region of France.

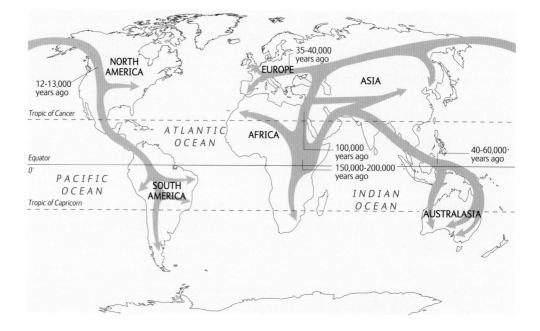

Out of Africa

On the way out of Africa and around the globe, these modern humans may have displaced other human species such as Neanderthals in Europe and *Homo erectus* in Africa and Asia. Quite what 'displaced' means is debated. The modern humans may have used violence, killing off who they deemed to be their rivals. The newcomers could have had superior intelligence, communications, planning, weapons and tools to out-compete the existing locals for resources, especially food. There may have been interbreeding – occasional fossil specimens are said by some experts to show combined features.

Whatever the mechanisms, and these could have varied in different places and times, almost all of the previous human types disappeared, leaving just our own kind. Following these epic spreading migrations, groups of modern humans around the world became adapted to their own local environment, with changes in skin and hair colour, facial features and so on. In this way, the extensive diversity of human ethnic groups arose that we see today.

Fossils and genes

There is plenty of evidence for the Out of Africa idea. Many fossils and archaeological remains track the spread of the modern humans. Anthropologists point to the physical and biological features of various ethnic groups that fit the scheme. There is also genetic evidence, for example, in the form of mitochondrial DNA (which is described earlier). Analyzing this DNA in people from a wide range of ethnic groups shows how changes in its make-up trace the migrations of human populations. Going back and back, the mitochondrial genes – which are passed through the female lines, not male – point to a semi-hypothetical woman known as 'Mitochondrial Eve'. She probably lived in East Africa approaching 200,000 years ago and was, in effect, symbolic as the first fully modern human female. Scientists use terms for her such as the matrilineal most recent common ancestor, MRCA. A more basic title might be 'mother of us all'.

Looking at the male lines, there is also evidence for a PRCA, patrilineal most recent common ancestor, 'Y chromosome Adam'. He is arrived at by tracing back changes or mutations to the genes carried on the Y chromosome. This is one of 46 chromosomes – packages of genetic material – found in most of the microscopic cells that make up the human body. Y is a male sex chromosome and its female counterpart is X. Having the combination XX means a person is female, while XY decrees a male. Of course, 'Mitochondrial Eve' was almost certainly not the partner of 'Y chromosome Adam'. Indeed the two probably lived thousands of years apart, and for neither of them do we have any idea of exactly where they spent their lives. But they represent momentous turning points in prehistory as our own kind, the subspecies *Homo sapiens sapiens*, came into being.

The leading contender to the Out of Africa theory is known as the multiregional hypothesis. It describes how a previous species to our own, *Homo erectus*, itself spread around the world from about two million years ago. Then various geographical populations evolved in their particular regions into the ethnic groups that make up modern humans.

Filling in the details

The above account is a broad, simplified outline of the Out of Africa theory. With support from palaeontology, genetics, archaeology and anthropology, researchers at the Museum and elsewhere are firming up the details. How many dispersals were there, when and to where? What happened to other types of humans as the various continents were populated – for example, the 'hobbit humans' of Flores, mentioned earlier? As work continues, recent evidence suggests that the first spread from Africa may have happened 20,000 years earlier than was thought. As usual, there will be further refinements and some surprises along the way.

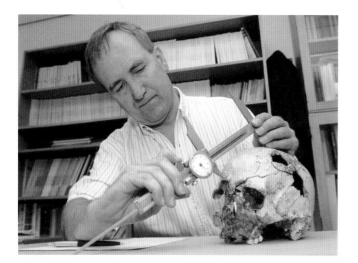

It is difficult to keep Charles Darwin out of most areas of natural history. In 1871 his book *The Descent of Man* proposed that humans came originally from Africa, because our closest living cousins, chimps and gorillas, are found there. He would be very satisfied at the way his idea has progressed.

The Piltdown fiasco

Looking through more jaundiced eyes at the origins of our species brings us to perhaps the most cautionary tale of all regarding fossils and museums. The village of Piltdown, near Uckfield in East Sussex, shot to fame in 1912 with the announcement that fossils found there represented a 'missing link' between apes and humans. Piltdown Man or *Eoanthropus dawsoni* ('Dawn Man of Dawson'), as the fossils became known, consisted of some pieces of upper skull, likened to 'a smashed coconut', and a partial lower jaw plus teeth. These were recovered from a gravel pit by a small team led by amateur archaeologist Charles Dawson (1864–1916). Eminent palaeontologist Arthur Smith Woodward, Keeper of Geology at the Natural History Museum, was involved in their study and reconstruction.

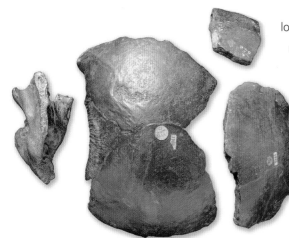

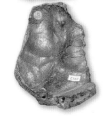

Piltdown Man fitted the bill at the time as to what a 'missing link' should look like. He had a fairly large and human-like skull and brain, which had evolved much of the way towards our present skull condition. But he also had an ape-like jaw, as a remnant of his ape ancestry, although its teeth seemed curiously human. His age was estimated from the fossils' appearance and details from the site at about half a million years. This was far earlier than another famous 'ape-man' fossil find, the Neanderthal remains from Germany. Given the political rivalries in Europe at the time, Piltdown Man was celebrated as the earliest ape–human 'missing link' yet found – and he was British! The Museum was proud of its involvement and took advantage of the ensuing publicity.

In 1953 came the admission. Various experts including Kenneth Oakley, who had fluorine-dated the Piltdown remains at the Museum, and Sir Wilfrid Le Gros Clark, anatomist and surgeon, exposed the hoax. The upper skull was from a human being of the medieval period, about 500 years old. The lower jaw was definitely ape-like, in fact it was from an orang-utan that had died relatively recently. The teeth were a chimpanzee's, filed to make them look more human. The whole package, deliberately assembled as a hoax, was stained with chemicals to give an aged appearance. 'The earliest Englishman' became a laughing stock. The popular press had a field day. Questions were asked in Parliament. How had so many experts been fooled for 40 years? Admittedly, doubts had been raised during this time, not least by German anatomist Franz Weidenrich in 1923. He saw at once that the skull was relatively recent and the jaw came from an orang-utan, although some of the diagnostic features that marked it out as such had been broken away – deliberately? But these dissenting voices were put to one side. The 'missing link' was British, he had what was expected – big brain, ape jaw – and national pride ruled.

Who was the Piltdown perpetrator? Almost everyone involved has fallen under suspicion at some time. It could have been Dawson, one of his team, a mystery visitor who planted the fossils at the site, someone at the Museum involved in their study – or a combination of these. Most fingers now point to Dawson. A 2003 report showed that as well as Piltdown, he carried out more than 30 other fakes and frauds, including supposed Roman artefacts, a prehistoric boat and alleged Stone Age axes.

More frauds

In 1999 a 'dino-bird' fossil from Liaoning, northeast China, made splashy headlines with its detailed preservation and yet another 'missing link' label. Dated at 125 million years ago, it was named *Archaeoraptor liaoningensis* and palaeontologists queued to explain its tremendous significance in showing that certain dinosaurs had indeed developed feathers, then wing-like arms, then the power of flight as they became birds. But a medical-style X-ray CT (computed tomography) scanner undid the forgery by showing it was a composite of several fossil specimens and other bits and pieces skilfully fixed together. The general premise that certain dinosaurs evolved into birds has since gained strength. But such frauds are an occupational hazard for palaeontologists studying celebrated fossil sites such as those in Liaoning, because notable specimens from these areas fetch considerable sums on the open market – and the black market.

The original Piltdown affair, like those described above, provides an ongoing lesson for all fossil experts and other scientists. Looking back, Piltdown Man was constructed in a relatively crude and clumsy way. Perhaps Dawson, if it was he, expected to be found out quite quickly, but he died a few years later without leaving any explanation. At the time, too many eminent people wanted this find to be real and genuine. So they dropped their scientific guard, and it became so. Note to us all: Proceed with extreme caution.

OPPOSITE: Museum human origins expert Chris Stringer measures the skull of Cheddar Man, which dates to about 9,000 years ago. This is one of hundreds of measurements and the minute study of every surface, line, ridge and gap.

OPPOSITE BELOW & BELOW: These are the five pieces of the Piltdown skull (opposite). They come from an individual who lived a few hundred years ago, of our own species *Homo sapiens*. This left side view of the Piltdown jaw or mandible shows its two molar teeth artificially abraded to appear human. The Piltdown material had all been stained to give an aged appearance.

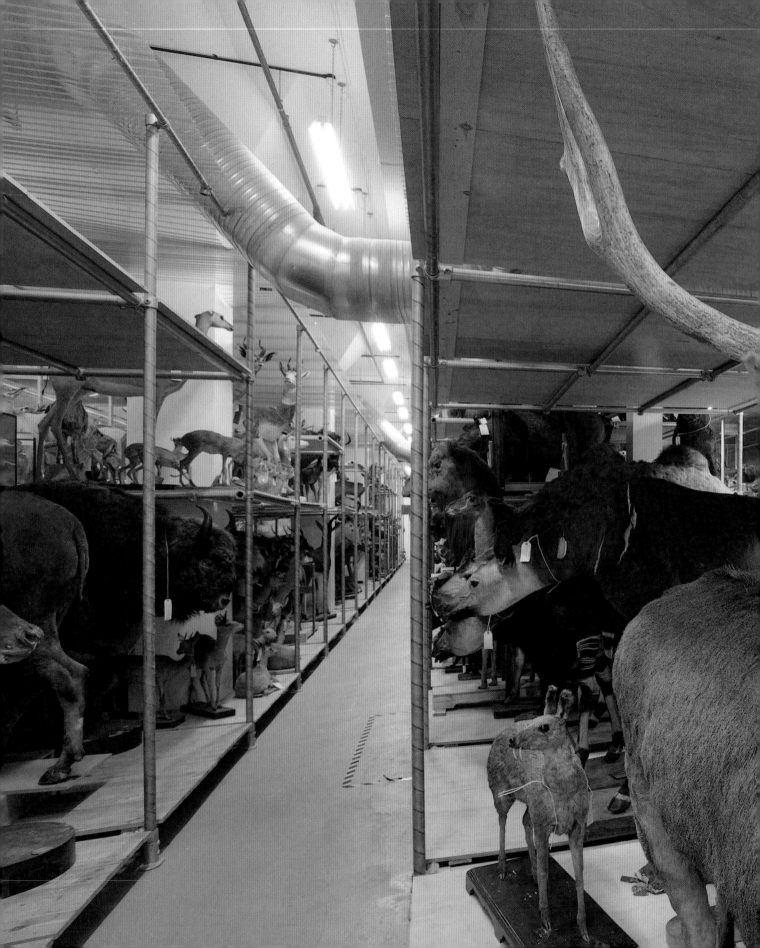

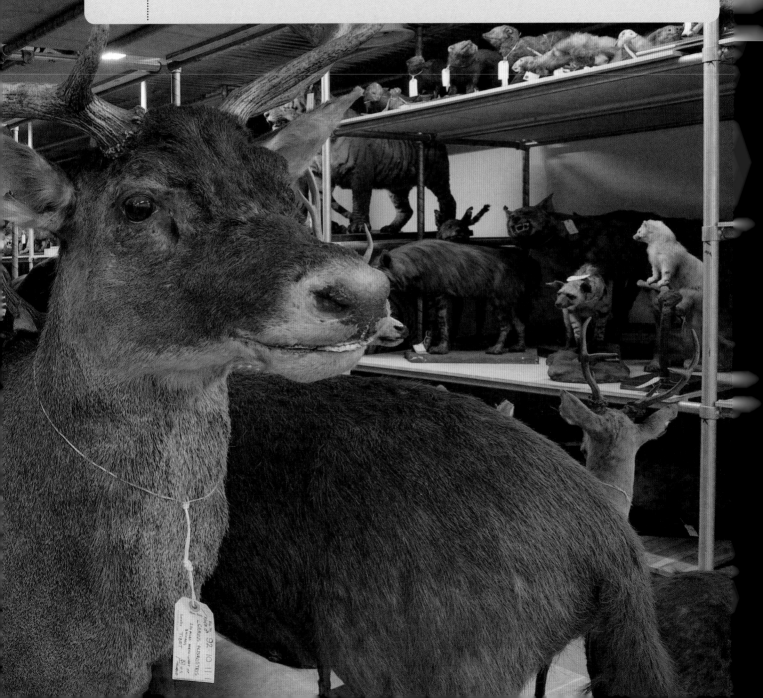

ALL CREATURES GREAT AND SMALL

ALL CREATURES GREAT AND SMALL

From the giant blue whale to the tiniest mosquito or worm, visitors and scientists agree on the magnificence of the Museum's public displays and research collections. What most people never see, however, is the immense behind-the-scenes effort needed to maintain its leading role as a science organization. And this work has its fair share of ups and down, oddities and idiosyncracies, and even hoaxes and frauds.

The Natural History Museum's largest-ever single donation was not a fossil tree, or a whale skeleton. It was another entire, self-contained museum, itself full of millions of specimens collected by explorers and adventurers from all parts of the world, over a period of more than 50 years. This is the Natural History Museum at Tring, formerly known as the Walter Rothschild Zoological Museum. It is situated in Tring, a small market town in Hertfordshire, about 50 kilometres northwest of London.

The Natural History Museum has many outposts and buildings away from the main South Kensington site. Known simply as 'Tring' among staff, the story of this site is perhaps the most fascinating. This amazing donation occurred in 1937, following the death of Lionel Walter, Second Baron Rothschild, at his request and with approval of his family. The Tring Museum is still open daily to the public, as it has been since 1892, when it was described by *The Times* of London as 'a nearly complete collection of the birds and animals of the British Isles and, as regards the rest of the world, examples of the most interesting and sometimes of the rarest species, whether actually existing or recent or long since extinct.'

The beginning of Tring

Walter Rothschild (1868–1937) was born into the immensely wealthy Rothschild banking family. As a child he collected all kinds of animals, including butterflies and other insects, declaring his interest in having his own zoological museum. He even started one at the age of ten, in a garden shed. From his late teens, he kept exotic pets such as kangaroos and cassowaries for study. When Walter

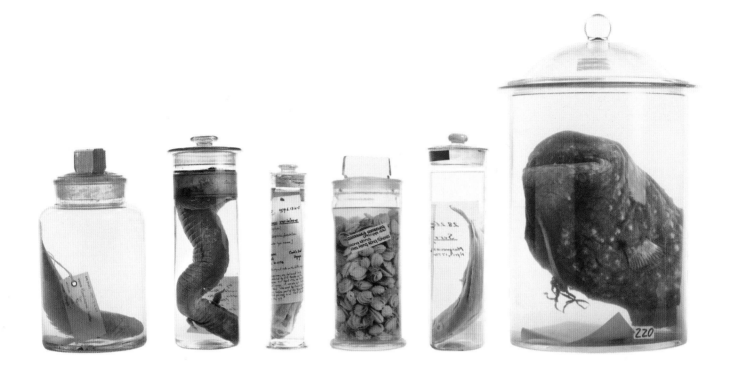

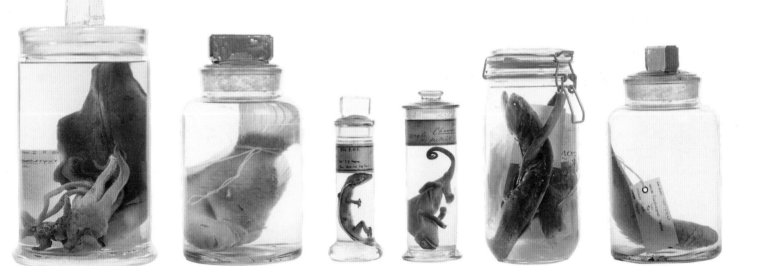

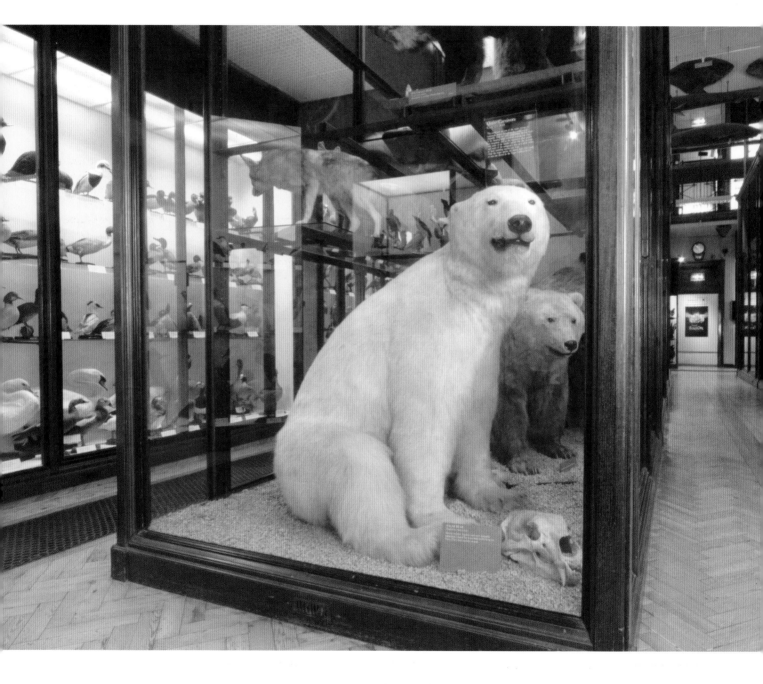

approached working age the family decided to bring him into their business, high finance. But after years of trying, the family recognized that his heart wasn't in it and he was allowed to leave.

In the meantime his father Nathaniel, the Lord Rothschild, and the family had indulged Walter in his passion for nature by building him a museum in 1889 to fulfil his childhood ambition. His special interests were insects and birds, but almost no items were refused. Walter also organized and paid for expeditions to all kinds of remote and exotic places to gather specimens. He himself travelled around Europe and North Africa, gathering specimens as he went. He hired professional animal and plant collectors, and employed staff and consultants for his museum, including librarians, taxidermists and scientific experts. His professional curators, zoologist Ernst Hartert and entomologist Karl Jordan, were leaders in their field – they had to be because Rothschild had very high standards.

Shy and somewhat eccentric, Rothschild struggled with a speech difficulty. However, he had a flamboyant side, being photographed riding one of his pet giant tortoises (he kept a total of 144 of them for study) and also training zebras to pull a horse carriage, which on one occasion he drove along Piccadilly to the forecourt of Buckingham Palace. He became well known at the Natural History Museum, on account of both his vast and growing collections and his scientific knowledge. In 1899 he was elected to the Museum's Board of Trustees as his Tring Museum collaborated with South Kensington in many areas.

Tring's treasures

By the 1920s the Tring Museum represented the greatest ever collection of animals amassed by one individual. In Walter's research collections there were more than two million butterflies, half a million bird skins and eggs, tens of thousands of beetles and other insects, and in the public museum were several thousand display specimens, including crabs and shellfish, fish, lizards and crocodiles and turtles and other reptiles, insects and birds and all kinds of mammals from tiny rodents to rhinos. His wealth and influence are evident from more than 230 animals of all kinds whose official scientific names include his own, from the Rothschild's birdwing butterfly, *Ornithoptera rothschildi*, to the subspecies known as Rothschild's giraffe, *Giraffa camelopardis rothschildi*.

In 1931 mounting debts forced Rothschild to sell most of his bird skin research collection to the American Museum of Natural History. By now he had also decided to bequeath the remainder of his collections, manuscripts, books, buildings and land at Tring to the Natural History Museum.

Since that time, Tring's public displays have changed little. Of course they are by no means neglected. There is an ongoing programme of essential cleaning, maintenance and upkeep. In 2008 Gallery 6 underwent a major renovation, which involved cleaning 837 specimens, including the popular array of domestic dog breeds, and improving the lighting and displays in the original

OPPOSITE: Tring's polar bear in Gallery 1 has a curiously resigned, wry smile, perhaps the result of its Victorian taxidermist's imagination. It was the model for illustrator-author Raymond Briggs in his book *The Bear* (1994), and has since become a potent symbol of climate change, with Arctic habitats threatened by global warming.

RIGHT: Gallery 6 at
the Natural History
Museum at Tring was
recently renovated
with new lighting
and climate control.
Among its residents are
amphibians, reptiles,
flightless birds, bats,
domestic dogs and
many small mammals
such as hares.

floor-to-ceiling glass cases. Gallery 2 hosts temporary and travelling exhibitions that change three times annually. The atmospheric Rothschild Room displays original furniture once used by Walter and his team, and specimens and images that illustrate the history of his museum.

Towards today's Tring

Behind the scenes, Tring's workrooms and research collections have been altered and reorganized through the decades. During the Second World War the outpost was a store for some of the specimens evacuated from London. After the war, many of the non-bird collections, apart from the public displays, were gradually relocated to South Kensington. Over the years, thousands of bird specimens also went the other way, from London to Tring.

From the 1970s, Tring has been home to the Museum's bird research collections and staff, known now as the Bird Group, and so is referred to light-heartedly as its 'Bird Wing'. Today, in these behind-the-scenes study collections, is a wonderworld of ornithology that includes more than 700,000 skins, 400,000 clutches of eggs, 4,000 nests, 16,000 skeletons and 17,000 specimens preserved in spirit. Researchers the world over visit to study, compare, contrast and catalogue.

Tring is a national treasure, an amazing memorial to the achievements of one man with a consuming passion for nature and wildlife and with a vast amount of money to spend on it. Walter Rothschild himself had a quirky sense of humour and he might have smiled at some of the more recent events involving his Tring Museum. For example, one of the biggest and most popular exhibits is an elephant seal, placed in position in 1927 and never moved since. It was so large that it had to be positioned high on top of the display cases, peering up into the roof. During the seal's most recent clean, a card unseen for more than 80 years fell out from between the animal itself and the rock on which it resides. Its information detailed where the seal was caught and when. New knowledge from an old resident.

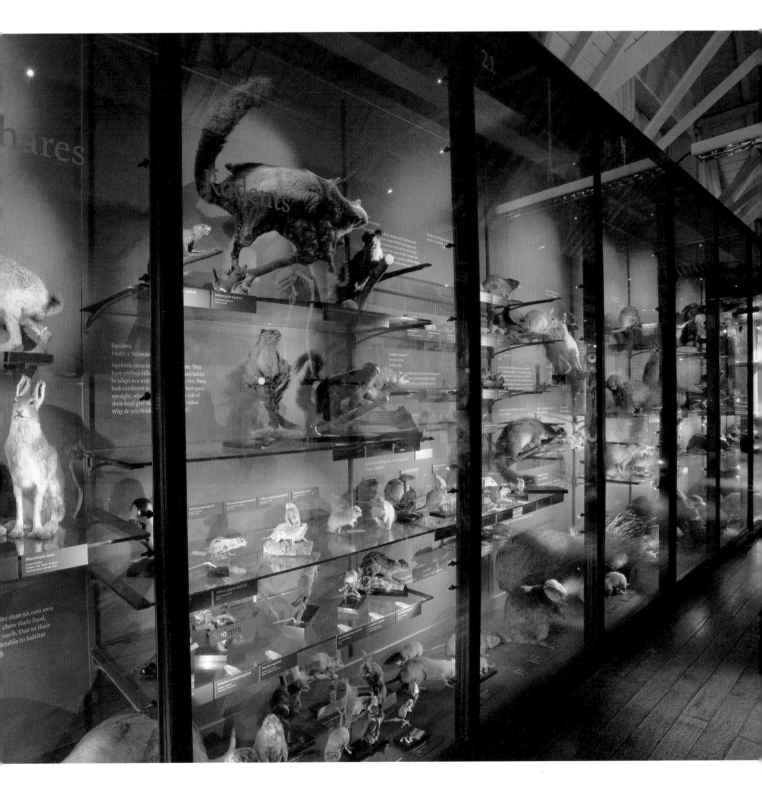

Seal with a trunk

Catching an elephant seal was no mean feat. The Tring specimen is more than five metres long. When alive it weighed over four tonnes – as much as a real elephant. Seals and sea-lions are pinnipeds, a name that means 'flipper-feet', and are all members of the Carnivora group of mammals. It is often said that tigers, or perhaps bears like the polar or grizzly, are the largest in this group. But they are land carnivores. An elephant seal can be almost five times the weight of the biggest bears, and so is by far the champion Carnivora heavyweight. Only the male elephant seals, or bulls, grow as huge as Tring's specimen. And only they have the long, floppy nose that led to the common name, the snout being viewed as a counterpart to the elephant's trunk. The female seals, known as cows, reach less than three metres in length and approaching one tonne in weight. This marked size difference within a species between females and males is a well-recognized biological phenomenon called sexual dimorphism. It occurs in creatures as varied as gorillas, ducks, sharks and spiders.

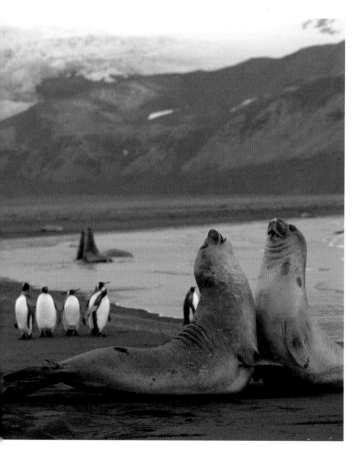

A massive task

Apart from breeding time, elephant seals spend their lives in the open ocean. They hunt fish, squid and similar prey, and have very impressive diving powers. Their average dive depth is down to 500 metres and they usually stay submerged for 20–30 minutes. Such a large, powerful beast must have presented a great challenge to animal collectors as they hunted for specimens. The Tring elephant seal's skin and skeleton were sent back to England packed in large crates, the skin having been rubbed with alum and saltpetre to preserve it. When it arrived, it presented a massive test of the taxidermists' skills. The information on its long-lost card has been copied and added to the main specimen data, but the card itself is now back where it has nestled for 80-plus years. If in doubt, keep the specimen and its label together; how this can go so badly wrong is demonstrated later (see pages 83–86).

Products of their time

Atmospheric displays of real animals like those in the Natural History Museum at Tring are not common today. Many of the species they represent are now very rare. Some, like the zebra variety known as the quagga and the thylacine or Tasmanian tiger (Tasmanian wolf), have disappeared into extinction. Why did people bother to go out and collect so many specimens, transport them back, and then skin, preserve and mount them, and pack them together in neatly ordered glass display cases? Our modern age is teeming with books, magazines, television programmes, videos and movies showing breathtaking scenes from nature, ranging from incredible wide-view aerial spectacles to the most microscopic details. And if we have the means, we can travel almost anywhere in the world and see wonderful wildlife with our own eyes. But when Rothschild was establishing his Tring collections, there was no television and no video. Colour photography was in its infancy. Black and white photography was also relatively primitive, with heavy equipment, long exposure times and blurry results. Long-distance travel to exotic locations was the privilege of a tiny minority. In those days, too, zoos and wildlife parks were less numerous and more limited than today, and often in private hands. For example, London Zoo at Regent's Park was at first intended just for scientific research. It only opened its gates to the public in 1847.

Even so, the Victorians were generally keen on education and widening the experiences of common folk. The main way that the vast majority of people could appreciate the wonders of wildlife, exotic animals from faraway places, and of course the bizarre, peculiar and occasionally ghoulish products of nature, was in museums. Any such establishment worth its salt needed its arrays of rocks and crystals, pressed flowers, pinned insects and stuffed animals. Crucially, these preserved specimens represented a storehouse of knowledge and a scientific resource still expanding today.

Countless creatures

The Natural History Museum in South Kensington itself grew out of this movement, which could only happen through the efforts of collectors and the taxidermist's work. Natural history artists, with their drawings and paintings, were another vital source of visual information, long before the advent of inexpensive colour mass printing and the latest on-screen technologies. Most people today have grown up in a conservation-minded era. We understand the damage done to the natural world, and we are aware of which animals and plants are common, or rare, or on the brink of extinction. or gone for good. True, conservation has been practised for centuries in some regions, especially of valuable forests. But as a general movement among the mass public, it only came to the fore in the 1950s and 1960s, along with related environmental matters such as the damage caused by pollution and the risks from radioactivity and nuclear technologies.

In great contrast, back in the early days when the Natural History Museum was first being populated with preserved wildlife, and collectors were roaming the world, the majority of people had little idea about the need for conservation. They were simply unaware that some species were disappearing. To Europeans especially, far-off places such as Africa, Asia, South America and

OPPOSITE: Watched nonchalantly by unimpressed penguins, two young bull Southern elephant seals square up on the beach at Heard Island, Kerguelen Ridge, Antarctica. These titanic tussles are among the most violent of all mammal intraspecific (within-one-species) conflicts.

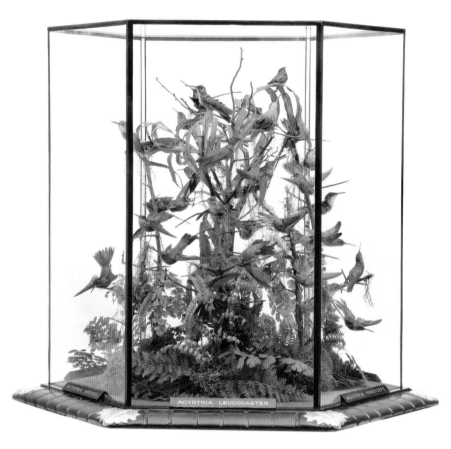

Australia were dark, mysterious and endless. Nature in general was considered inexhaustible. How could taking a few thousand specimens for taxidermy do any harm? That said, Walter Rothschild himself was aware of the need for conservation and in fact leased the whole island of Aldabra in the Indian Ocean for ten years just to prevent the island's giant tortoise population being wiped out.

Art, craft and science

Taxidermy is preserving and mounting animals to make them appear lifelike and last a long time. It is combined art, craft and science that stops the specimen from decomposing and hopefully shows how it looked when alive. A century or two ago, this was the only chance for ordinary citizens to see such creatures up close, and get an idea of their size and shape, their body features, coloration and texture. The most expert conservators and taxidermists were in great demand.

Today the only specimens prepared in-house are for the research collections, so when a display or handling specimen is needed, an expert taxidermist is brought in. When choosing a specimen for this purpose, there is an early question: can it be preserved for display or is it already too damaged or decomposed?

Skinning and mounting

If a specimen is in good enough condition for display, the carcass is skinned. Anyone who has tried this when preparing animals for eating knows that with practice the skin tends to come away in a relatively predictable fashion from the underlying layer, and hopefully in one piece. At this stage it may well be possible to manipulate the skinned body into a lifelike pose and photograph it, or shape it as a plaster or clay version, or even take a direct mould of it. Using an intermediate cast or mould as necessary, this will produce a model of the body, a mannequin, in a substance such as foamed plastic, ready to accept the skin on top. Alternatively, a mannequin is built up separately from reference sources including photographs, films and artworks.

Meanwhile, the skin itself, with its scales, feathers, fur or other appendages, is thoroughly cleaned and treated with preserving chemicals and then dried, ready to mount. Along the way there are anatomical details such as eyes, claws, teeth and horns. Some of these can be detached from the original carcass, treated with chemicals and dried, and made ready for reattachment. A creature's eyes draw our eyes and so are especially important. Glass and plastic versions can be bought ready-made, or hand-shaped from raw material, polished and coloured.

Back to life

Every taxidermy specimen is unique, and the methods are constantly improving with new types of preservative chemicals, mounting materials and laser 3-D scanners to get the best pose. In one sense, stopping decay is a prelude to the main aim of taxidermy: to 'bring the animal to life', in a pose that reflects its behaviour and habits. For this purpose the skilled taxidermist researches the creature in great detail and tries to get into its world of actions and intentions. Should it be in a restful pose taking time out, or looking aggressively for prey, or fearful of approaching danger?

RIGHT: In this 1932 photograph, Museum guide lecturer Mona Edwards (unfortunately positioned in front of a horned antelope) describes specimens in the India-Malaya section, including a Bengal tiger. It was a time before television and long-haul holidays; even cinema wildlife documentaries were in their infancy.

OPPOSITE: Richard Henry Meinertzhagen, here photographed in his mid-40s, cultivated the air of a dashing, successful army officer and intrepid, devil-may-care naturalist and collector. His bird frauds have left Museum specialists with enormous amounts of work to right the wrongs.

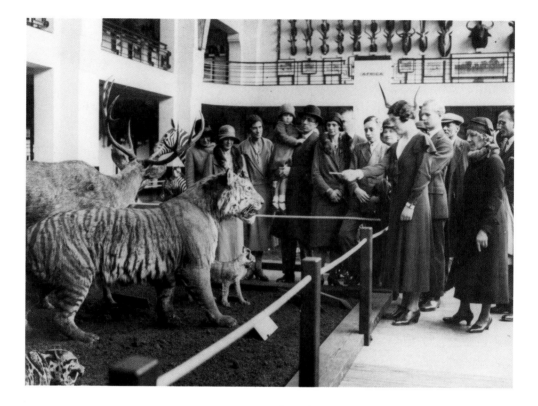

Displaying the result in a lifelike mini-scene involves a vast array of techniques such as moulding, casting, painting, modelling, sculpting and airbrushing, and expertise with a range of materials, from real wood and leaves to papier mâché, plaster, plastics, resins, rubbers, latex and the latest hi-tech composites. The passion of a new generation of conservators and taxidermists, armed with the latest equipment and methods, is helping to preserve and add to the display and handling collections right across the Natural History Museum.

In the modern museum this method of preparation is now only used for gallery displays. Material destined for the scientific collections is prepared in many different ways to ensure the key diagnostic features of the animal are preserved for researchers to study. For such specimens the whole body may be preserved in alcohol or the bones of the skeleton kept or a study skin prepared. Some animals may be too damaged and decomposed to use the skin for either taxidermy or as a flat skin. But it could be possible to extract and preserve the skeleton or other internal hard parts. First, a rough dissection gets most of the flesh off the bones. Then the skeleton can be cleaned in several ways. One is by immersing it in baths of various corrosive chemicals that eat away soft tissue but leave the bones intact. Another method is to leave the specimen in a tank of *Dermestes* flesh-eating beetles. The larvae's tiny mouthparts pick and nibble the soft parts in a most delicate and thorough manner (*see* pages 127–128). The bones can then be arranged on a wire or plastic frame, identified and labelled, and take their place in the collection.

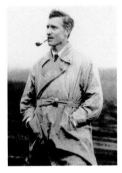

Colonel Fraud

Tring's founder Walter Rothschild would surely have reacted in horror if this next event had occurred in the research collections of his museum. This was a prolonged and serious series of bird frauds perpetrated by 'respected ornithologist' Colonel Richard Meinertzhagen during the early to mid-twentieth century. Like Rothschild, Meinertzhagen (1878–1967) was born into a well-to-do family, then developed a childhood interest in wildlife, principally birds, but was encouraged to join the family bank, where he soon decided that finance was not for him. Young Richard joined the British Army and served in India, East Africa, the Middle East and France. During this time he developed his talents at shooting, trapping, collecting and preparing animal specimens. He also trained as a fine wildlife artist. He remarked that he was only 'incidentally a soldier'.

Meinertzhagen became a regular visitor to the Natural History Museum, especially after his retirement from the Army in 1925, although he went back for a spell in Military Intelligence during the Second World War. To fill his retirement time he wrote and edited works on birds, accessed and studied specimens at the Natural History Museum, and rose to prominence as one of the nation's most accomplished ornithologists. However, this work aroused suspicions from the start. At the beginning of the 1920s Meinertzhagen was banned for 18 months from the Museum's Bird Room for unauthorized removal of specimens. Museum records over the following 30 years contain many mentions of staff who were suspicious that he was misappropriating specimens and library materials. On two occasions, prosecution was planned but never occurred.

With a typical flourish, Meinertzhagen donated his collection of 20,000 bird skins to the Museum in 1954. At the start of the 1970s these were moved with the rest of the Museum's bird research collections to Tring. Then, from the 1980s, scientific publications drew attention to the flawed nature of the Meinertzhagen material. Detective work since has uncovered a large amount of fraud clearly carried out by Meinertzhagen, which has damaged the integrity of the Tring bird research collections and the understanding of when and where the specimens were collected.

It mainly comes down to labels. A specimen is of scientific value only if labelled with the date and location of its collection, and any relevant notes. If the labels are lost, or even worse, faked, then chaos ensues and the specimens lose much of their scientific value.

Senior Museum ornithologists have been investigating the Meinertzhagen matter for several years. For example, the redpoll is a common smallish bird in Europe. There are several specimens at Tring supposedly collected in France in the 1950s, allegedly prepared and donated by Meinertzhagen. But close study reveals that they were probably the work of at least two different

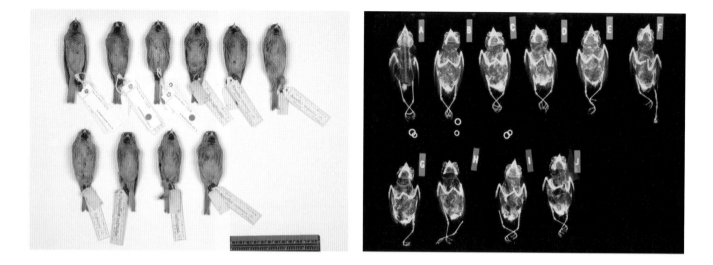

ABOVE: These specimens of the common redpoll, *Carduelis flammea*, look similar to the untutored eye. Meinertzhagen claimed that he collected the three upper left items in 1953. However, under X-ray conditions (above right), the differences between specimen A compared to B and C become more obvious. The first looks quite different to the other two, which date back to 1884.

RIGHT: The falsified label is from a magpie that Meinertzhagen said he collected in 1925 while 'on a yak' along the Sikkim-Tibet border. In fact it dates from the late 1800s.

people. Each individual person skins and prepares in a characteristic way, putting the body into a certain pose and using particular materials for support. These little idiosyncrasies can be recognized by the trained eye, and so it is with the redpolls. Some have the head forwards, while in others it angles back. Some have wooden support sticks, others do not. It becomes obvious that the specimens were not all prepared by one person. Indeed, it turns out that some of the redpolls were the work of Richard Bowdler Sharpe. They were collected in the 1880s, rather than the 1950s, and from Middlesex, west of London, rather than the South of France. How is this known? Because the birds were originally part of the Museum's very own collections.

The fraud exposed

Gradually the extent of Meinertzhagen's fraud has been exposed. He had claimed thousands of specimens as his own, when they were not. He had removed the real labels and added new ones with fictional dates, places and other information, and then included them as part of his generous presentation to the Natural History Museum. And with the greatest irony, he had stolen many of the specimens from the Museum itself. Tracking back through the Museum's records and catalogues showed where the birds originally came from. It seems that the early suspicions, aroused during Meinertzhagen's visits, about taking items without permission, had been the tip of a huge iceberg.

A few examples show the nature of the fraud. A false label by Meinertzhagen identifies a Grey's grasshopper warbler, *Locustella fasciolata*, as one of only three ever recorded in Western Europe. In fact the bird was from its native East Asia, more than 12,000 kilometres away. Meinertzhagen also claimed to have taken rare Blyth's kingfishers, *Alcedo hercules*, in Burma, far from Hainan, South China, where they had actually been collected. The research documenting his frauds has had some surprising spin-offs. Otherwise not seen since the 1880s, Meinertzhagen had a specimen of an exceptionally rare forest owlet that he claimed to have collected in a certain area of India in 1915. Following the discovery that he had stolen and falsely relabelled it, further surveys in the part of India where the owlet had really been found revealed that the species was not extinct after all. In this way the frauds and their ramifications multiply.

Various X-ray and scanning methods, and the latest forensic techniques, add to the evidence that the labels on Meinertzhagen's bird skins are often not telling the whole truth, or even part of the truth. Tests showed that the cotton in the wing seam of the forest owlet, where it has been sewn up, matched the cotton used by another collector – yet Meinertzhagen presented the bird as his. He even concocted notes about how he had shot or trapped the birds. On a magpie he took from the Museum, he wrote on the new label about its capture: 'On a yak, one of a pair'.

Museum specialists estimate that perhaps up to one-third of Meinertzhagen's donated species are fraudulent. However, with two-thirds genuine, this leads to another great difficulty. If all of his birds were falsely acquired and wrongly labelled, it might be easier than having to sort out which are authentic and which are not. There is a truly immense amount of detective work involved in identifying the forged labels, reinstating the correct information, erasing Meinertzhagen's input, and replacing the specimens in their rightful places.

BELOW: This is the forest owlet, *Athene blewitti*, 'collected' by Meinertzhagen and donated to the Museum in 1954. In fact he had taken it from the Museum's own collections, altered its skull and legs, given it a wash, and presented it as his own, with the label carrying false information.

The importance of eggs

Tring's massive collection of bird eggshells might seem an unlikely participant in the story that started modern conservation. Today, people are heartily discouraged from gathering and blowing eggs from nesting birds, simply to possess them. In fact, in countries such as the UK it is illegal. But the Museum's existing eggshell collections are there, available for use, and became vitally important in a way no one could really predict.

In the 1940s and 1950s the World Health Organization began a programme to reduce and even eradicate the tropical scourge of malaria (*see* pages 31–32). Its prime weapon was the insecticide known as DDT, from the chemical name dichloro-diphenyl-trichloroethane. Initially the

85

RIGHT: These British and European eggs of the peregrine falcon, *Falco peregrinus*, are from the Edgar Chance collection at the Natural History Museum at Tring. Examining these and hundreds of other eggs collected over 50 years revealed the sudden decrease in shell thickness, attributed to pesticides such as DDT.

OPPOSITE: The beluga sturgeon, *Huso huso*, is the largest European freshwater fish. It can weigh up to two tonnes and live for more than 100 years. It is the subject of a continuing battle between conservationists and poachers.

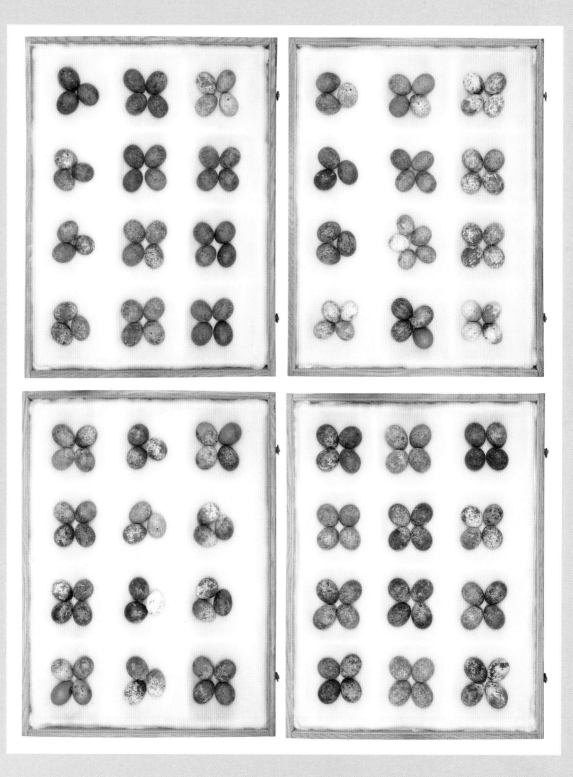

attempts were successful. But naturalists and others soon began to notice that areas sprayed with DDT were suffering damage to their wildlife. In particular, birds were breeding less successfully. Suspicions grew as more information came in.

In 1962, the book *Silent Spring* by US biologist and author, Rachel Carson, drew together many strands of evidence, to show that DDT was poisoning the environment, killing off animals and plants, and even damaging human health. Its title refers to a spring without birdsong and the buzz of bees and other insects. Following further research by Derek Ratcliffe, particularly using peregrine falcon eggs from the Chance collection, it became clear that accumulating DDT affected the breeding biology of many bird species. In particular, it caused them to lay eggs with thinner shells, which were more fragile and cracked before the baby chicks had developed enough to survive. Much data was needed to compare eggshell thicknesses over time, including those from the pre-DDT era, and Tring was one of the sources of this data. This is an example of the way the Museum's collections are used to spot trends that could, eventually, impact on us all.

Stanley takes the limelight

Something of a fishy story, and one that might be quoted in years to come as shedding light on a trend in nature, stars 'Stanley'. At more than three metres long, and weighing in at around 130 kilograms, equivalent to two adult humans, Stanley is the type of fish called a sturgeon. It was thought to have been caught off the coast of Wales in 2004. Since the 1300s sturgeons have been regarded in UK law as royal fish that must be offered to the reigning monarch. Stanley was not the target of the fishing expedition, being part of the bycatch – animals trapped incidentally or accidentally when fishing for other, commercially targeted species such as mackerel, herring or cod. Apparently, Stanley was netted and reported to the local coastguard, who then contacted Buckingham Palace with the news. The Palace replied that Stanley, in effect, was not required to present itself to royalty and could be disposed of by its captors 'as they saw fit'.

Sturgeons are most unusual and primitive fish in the sense that they evolved many millions of years ago and they have changed so little since. In this biological context, 'primitive' is not the same as 'bad' or 'outdated' or 'unsuccessful'. It is more akin to 'early' or 'long ago'.

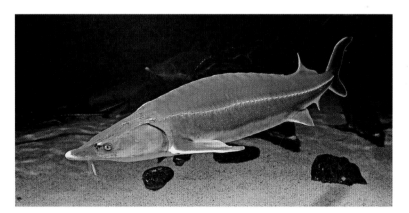

Creatures with primitive features can survive extremely successfully in the modern world, or at least, they would if humans let them. Sharks, for example, are primitive in the sense that the first of their kind appeared more than 400 million years ago. Other groups of fish have evolved since, and some have become very common and widespread. Yet today's sharks, which have retained many of their original features and characteristics, still dominate certain marine habitats. Their group provides the world's largest fish, the whale shark, and the biggest predatory fish, the great white.

The family of Stanley

The sturgeon family Acipenseridae includes about 25 species spread across all northern hemisphere waters. They lack the lightweight, streamlined scales of more modern fish. Instead they have bony plates called scutes over parts of the body, and this is one of their primitive features. Another is a skeleton composed mainly of cartilage or gristle, as in the sharks, rather than being fully ossified or turned into bone. All sturgeons are predators, feeding usually on or near the bottom on fish, shellfish and similar prey. Some species are exclusively freshwater. Others are mainly marine but migrate into fresh water to breed (like salmon), a lifestyle termed anadromous. They are rare out in the open ocean; even the most marine sturgeons rarely stray from coastal waters.

Most sturgeon species are medium to large, with the biggest specimens exceeding five metres in length, 1,200 kilograms in weight and 100 years in age. Such giants are usually from the species *Huso huso*, known by various local names such as great giant sturgeon and beluga. These enormous sturgeons are exceptionally rare today, if any at all survive. They have been overfished for their caviar, the roe or unfertilized eggs of the female, and isinglass from fish swim bladders, which was used to clarify beers and wines.

Disappearing act

Because of fishing pressure, many species of sturgeons have become rare – extremely rare in Britain – or even disappeared from parts of their natural range. So various wildlife laws were introduced to help them recover their populations. Stanley was a fine specimen, big and in good condition. but it was still a protected species in Britain. Was an offence committed by its catch, or especially by its sale? Apparently Stanley was due to be auctioned to the highest-bidding restaurant when the local police heard of its existence. The fish then mysteriously disappeared, as it were, going 'on the run'.

Stanley next turned up at Plymouth Fish Market, but renewed police interest meant it was held back from sale. In fact Stanley became a local star of radio, television and press, with the BBC and the *Daily Mail* reporting on its predicament. There was much speculation about where it had come from, where it was going, whether it was legal or not, and even its age. This was at first estimated as up to 200 years, but later study showed that 40-ish was more accurate.

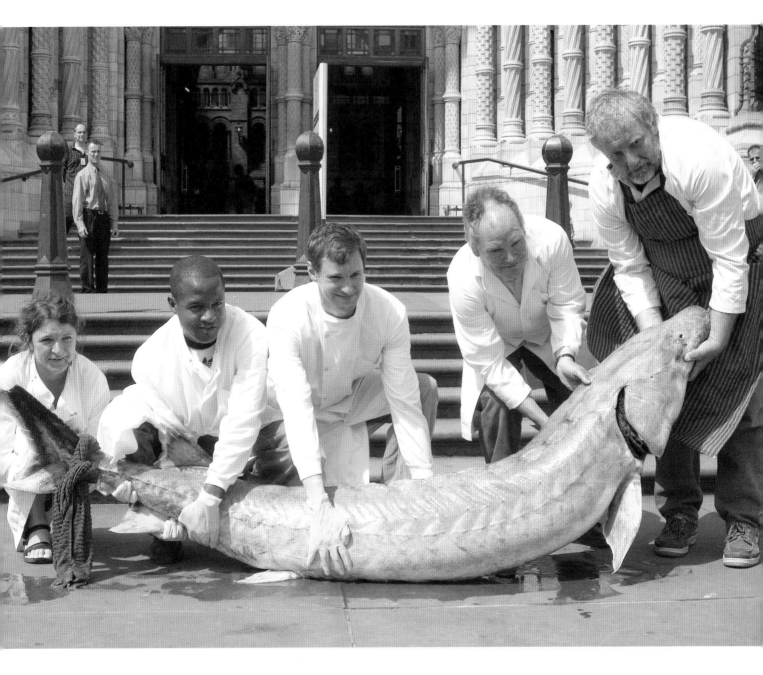

OPPOSITE: The giant ground sloth was the largest of the ground sloths, growing to a length of six metres. It may have used its huge claws to uproot tubers and other underground plant parts, as well as to hook high twigs towards its mouth.

As the Plymouth fish merchants were wary of trying to sell Stanley, protected as it was by the CITES agreement, the Convention on International Trade in Endangered Species, they decided to offer it to the Museum. In early June 2004, amid more media attention, Stanley arrived at the Museum and was installed in one of the freezers.

Several studies on Stanley have produced more puzzles. The sturgeon to be expected off the Welsh coast is the European sea sturgeon or Baltic sturgeon, *Acipenser sturio*. However, Stanley was not typical of this species. It had several unusual features, even accepting that sturgeons are difficult to separate into distinct species. Some kinds interbreed, and also genetic changes or mutations throw up the occasional mal-developed individual. Stanley had a too-blunt snout for a European sea sturgeon, and its barbels, the whisker-like projections from the lower snout, were not in the usual place. Also it's tricky to tell the sex of Stanley. If female, roe would be expected, and if male, testes. But the sex organs seem atypical. In addition, the gut contents consist of just a few stones, rather than part-digested prey food, and there are no gut parasites, which is extremely unusual for such a large, mature, long-lived fish. These loose ends could suggest that Stanley did not come from Welsh waters at all. Was it a different species that had found its way into Britain by some other route, or an altogether previously undescribed species, or some kind of hybrid?

In the end Museum scientists got the answer to Stanley's identity through studying its DNA. This proved that it was *Acipenser oxyrinchus*, the Altlantic sturgeon known only from North America. The adults of this species are very hard to tell apart from *A. sturio*. The question now is has the North American species been here all along, unnoticed amongst the *A. sturio*? We need to check the DNA of more Museum specimens to find out. As for the legality of attempting to sell Stanley, *A. oxyrinchus* is not protected in Britain so there was no case to pursue.

Giant of its time

Like Stanley, any massive specimen arouses great interest both in the scientific community and among the public. One of the Natural History Museum's most misunderstood big skeletons is *Megatherium americanum*, meaning big beast from America. It is more commonly known as the giant sloth. Weighing up to five tonnes, which is as much as a large African elephant, it lived in Central and South America from perhaps five million years ago to about 10,000 years ago. Many visitors mistake the giant sloth, a mammal, for a dinosaur which is a reptile.

The fossils of *Megatherium* have long been known and described by natural historians. More than two centuries ago it was reconstructed in an all-fours or quadrupedal pose, somewhat resembling a massive coffee table. Later scientists decided that perhaps the creature could sit upright in a kangaroo-type pose. Some even suggested that it could stand up on two legs and run quite fast.

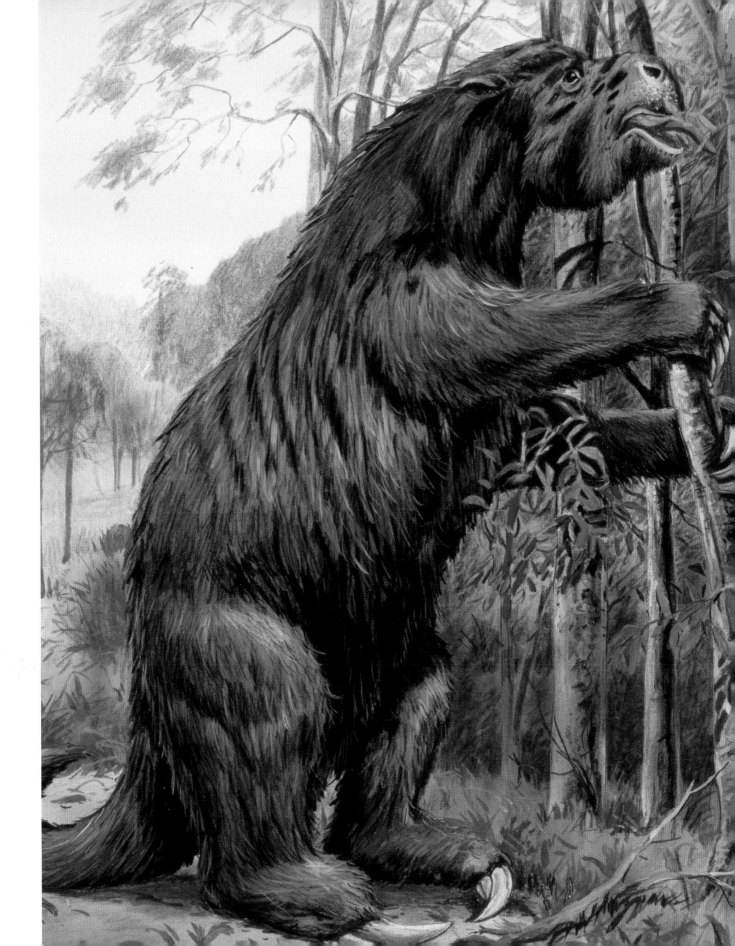

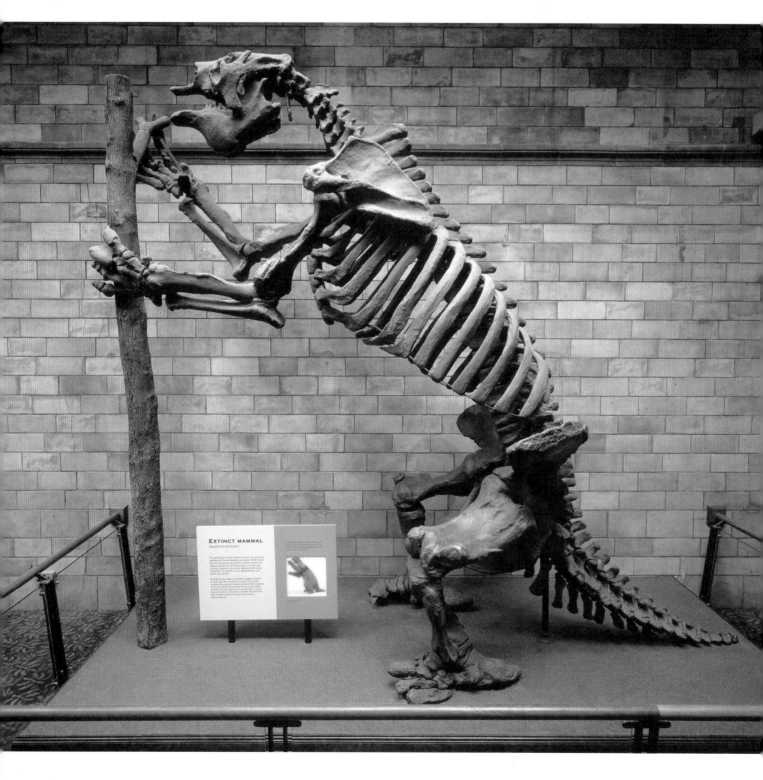

EXTINCT MAMMAL
Megatherium americanum

The Museum's specimen of *Megatherium* is a plaster cast made from a fossil skeleton from Argentina obtained in the 1840s. At the time the huge herbivore's remains were in great demand from several museums in Europe. In life it was a peaceful plant-eater, munching leaves and other plant material. Recent work on what scientists call its locomotion, how it moved about, showed that it could amble on all fours and also stand up on its hind legs, as evidenced by fossil footprints, to reach up to six metres inheight. Its feet are distinctive because it walked on the sides of them, since its large claws prevented a flat-footed gait. In such an upright posture, using its strong tail as a rear support, *Megatherium* could stretch up to reach and pull in foliage with its huge foreclaws, and strip leaves using its long, muscular tongue.

Another idea, working from the details of tooth structure, is that *Megatherium* might have been a scavenger. It could have employed its mammoth size, great strength and long claws to repel hunters like sabre-tooth cats from their kill, and then feasted on the remains.

The giant sloth's disappearance coincided with the extinction of many other large animals, especially to the north, such as mammoths, giant deer and others. The causes of its demise possibly included climate change, and also the spread of humans.

Another giant arrives

Stanley and the giant sloth are big enough to present problems in how they are displayed. Another, more recent arrival at the Museum is even bigger, a giant squid. Measuring 8.6 metres long, it was caught in 2004 in the South Atlantic Ocean near the Falkland Islands. Known scientifically as *Architeuthis dux*, it has naturally been nicknamed 'Archie'.

Despite several catches of enormous squid, both intentional and accidental, these deep-sea inhabitants are still something of a mystery and not until 2004 was a giant squid such as Archie finally photographed in the wild. Sightings of individuals allegedly stretching to more than 18 metres are widely reported but no animals that large have ever been recorded scientifically. Such sizes are almost certainly a case of over-exaggeration or tissue lengthening after death. Recent studies suggest one species of squid may be even bigger. Given the common name of colossal squid, this is *Mesonychoteuthis hamiltoni*, which may not be quite as long as the slender giant squid, but has a bulkier, more heavyweight body.

Monsters of the deep

Such enormous invertebrates, largest of all creatures without backbones, have eyes the size of soccer balls, eight arms lined with toothed or hooked suckers, and two extra-long tentacles to catch prey. They hunt a variety of food, including fish and other squid, grabbing them with the powerful tentacles and pulling them into the fearsome parrot-like beak situated in the middle of

OPPOSITE: The Natural History Museum's giant sloth skeleton was reconstructed in a possible browsing posture. It stands almost upright on its hind feet, front limbs leaning against a tree trunk and tail providing rear support.

93

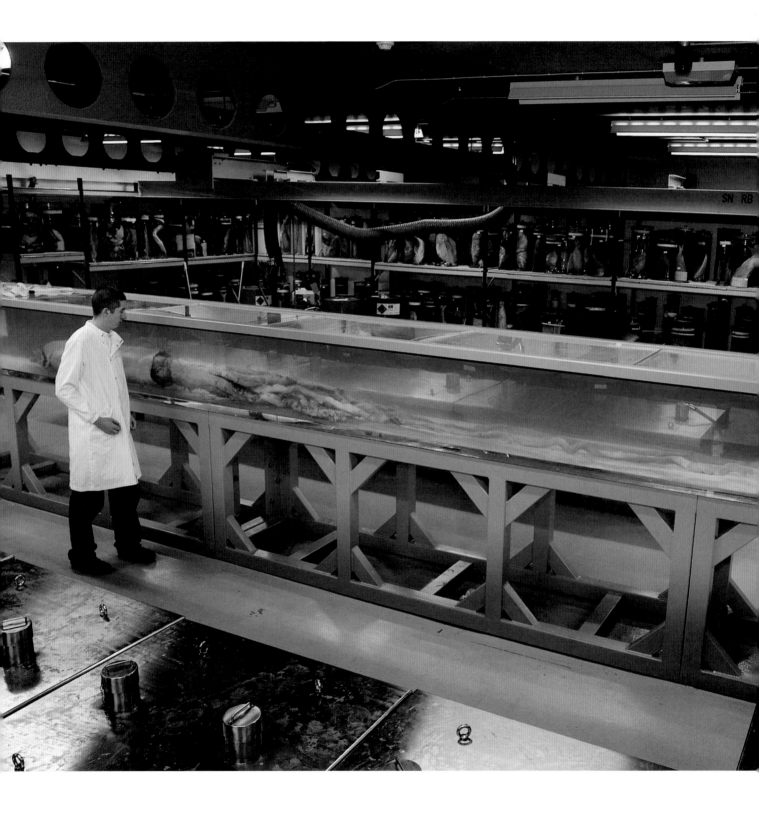

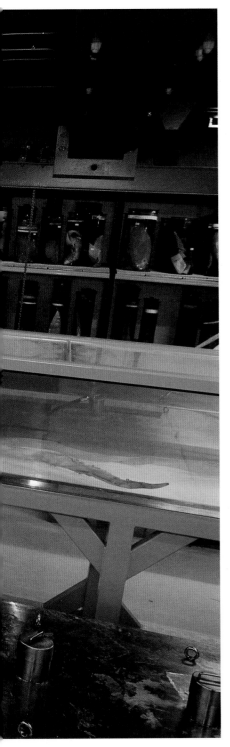

the tentacle ring. These monsters are themselves combatants in the most titanic wildlife battles on the planet, as they struggle to escape the attentions of one of the world's largest predators, the sperm whale.

Archie was caught alive and in good condition. She was frozen soon after capture and then donated to the Museum by the Falkland Islands government. The specimen was then carefully defrosted over a period of three days and transferred to a temporary rubber-lined container holding a bath of salty water and the fixative formalin. After further preservatives, given by injection, Archie was finally moved to her own specially constructed tank, nine metres long and made from see-through acrylic. Now visitors can look Archie in the eye from almost any angle, imagine her exploits in the blackness of the cold South Atlantic Ocean, and wonder how many other giants are waiting to be discovered in the deep.

Biggest of all

Mammoths, giant sloths and giant squid are impressive enough. But the Natural History Museum's most awesome animal exhibit depicts the biggest creature ever known to have lived on Earth, the blue whale, *Balaenoptera musculus*. Old-time whaling records show individuals exceeding 30 metres in length and 150 tonnes in weight. No dinosaur, pliosaur or other prehistoric creature yet discovered can compare. Visitors who enter the Whale Hall, specially built to house it, stare in jaw-dropping astonishment. For a time, many are speechless as they try to take in how enormous it really is.

The Museum's blue whale was conceived in 1936 as an exhibit both to astound and to educate. It was a mammoth task that demanded a huge commitment of manpower and resources. After much research from photographs, artworks and scientific reports, the model-making team began construction using a 2.29-metre-long scale model as reference. The whale was built in place over 20 months, hanging from the ceiling of its newly

LEFT: Archie the giant squid now lies peacefully stretched out in its tailor-made tank. It was caught live and almost complete, making it a very important specimen for research – such squid are not an everyday catch.

OVERLEAF: The blue whale has been wowing visitors since 1938. There was a trapdoor in the underside through to the hollow interior, but this has been sealed. In real life the throat grooves or ventral pleats allow the skin to balloon when feeding.

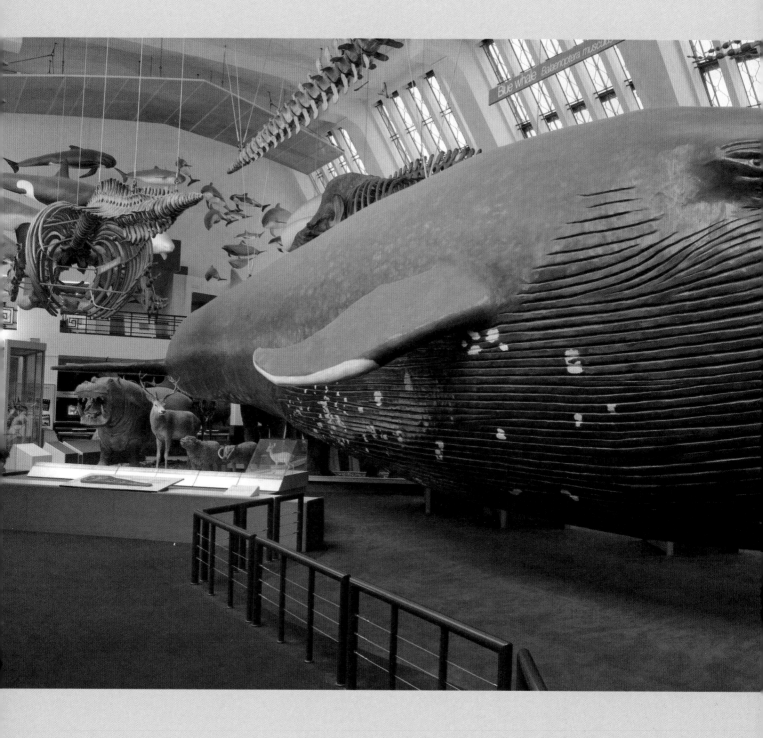

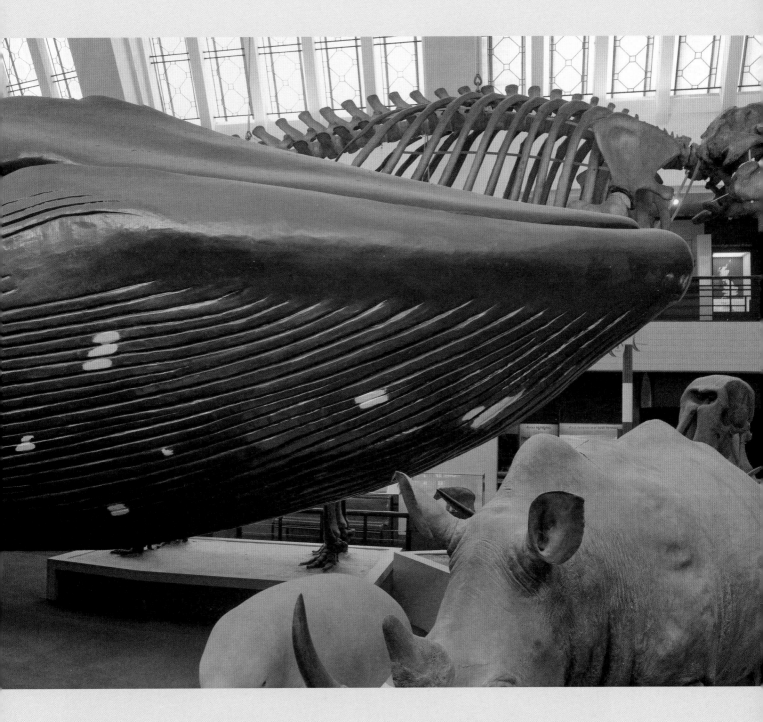

BELOW: The blue whale model takes shape as a row of giant wooden hoops or formers, like all-encircling ribs for its forthcoming skeleton. The construction team pose in front of the whale, which has been clad in lengthways timbers called stringers. Then the painters get to work, brushing onto the whale's white plaster skin. Blue whales are more blue-grey than bright blue, and lighter or even yellowish on the underside due to growths of tiny plant-like diatoms.

finished hall. First a wooden frame was fashioned, which was then coated in wire mesh. The final layer was plaster of Paris, expertly sculpted in every small detail.

With a length of 28.3 metres, the model weighs approximately 10 tonnes, about 90 tonnes lighter than the real thing. As the makers worked on their suspended model, occasionally it swayed. It had to be stabilized with blocks so the team did not feel too seasick. The blue whale was unveiled to the public in December 1938. The initial reaction then, as now, was awe mixed with a degree of shock.

Up to the surface

Impressive though the blue whale is, it has to take its place among the millions of other animal specimens and models at the Natural History Museum. Among these are some of the most common and little-noticed of all creatures, earthworms. These burrowers are vital to the health of our soil, creating tiny tunnels that allow air to penetrate and water to trickle and drain. Surveying the worms, and collecting and identifying the species, is important in finding out how modern problems such

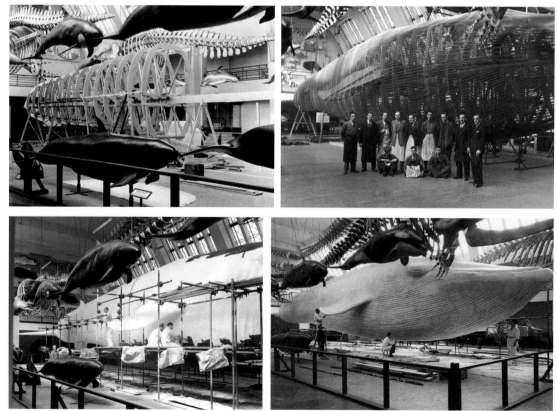

A QUESTION OF SHAPE

IN RECENT YEARS, it has been possible to compare the Museum's blue whale with living whales swimming in the ocean. This has come about through the development of both aerial and underwater photography, which captures stunning sequences of the leviathans swimming, feeding, migrating and even courting. One question now crops up often. Is the Museum model rather too tubby around the chin and belly, compared to the slim, streamlined blues out there in the sea? The answer is the Museum's whale has been portrayed in feeding posture, throat bulging with a vast quantity of water it has taken in, before the water is expelled to leave behind small food items such as shrimp-like krill. This is reasonable enough. The blue whale's feeding mechanism is two rows, left and right, of about 300 brush-edged baleen (whalebone) plates hanging down from its upper jaw. After water is taken in, the mouth almost closes and the baleen acts as a strainer or sieve to filter the food, retaining it as the water leaves the mouth.

In fact the blue whale's normal slender shape, when not feeding, was unclear at the time the model was built. Most visual references came from photographs of individuals hauled onto whaling ships or lying stranded on beaches. In these situations the body tends to sag and flatten, making the throat and belly bulge. But the feeding explanation for the Museum model's shape is usually adequate.

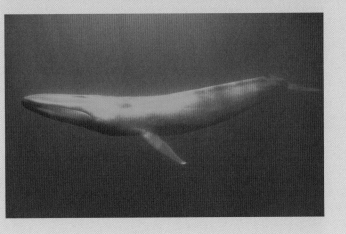

as pollution, acid rain, compaction by heavy vehicles and intensive farming affect the soils in Britain and around the world.

What better way, therefore, to find out which worms are beneath your feet, than by doing some worm-charming? To this end Museum scientists have organized this strange-looking event to launch the Earthworm Society of Britain. All kinds of weird and wonderful charming methods are known, for example, by anglers keen to gather some bait.

Survey results

The worm-charming event held in Hyde Park compared the different methods of charming, and which worm species they yielded, in a scientific way. The rules: each pair of charmers has ten square metres of soil in which to charm. There are also control squares where no charmers work, to see if worms are coming up anyway. Over a set time of 20 minutes, different pairs use one of several techniques. They might simply tap on the ground, or stamp slow or fast; they might jab a fork partway in and then twang it by rocking it to and fro, stick a stake in the ground and rub another implement over the top (called grunting) or even try banging some musical instruments or sprinkling

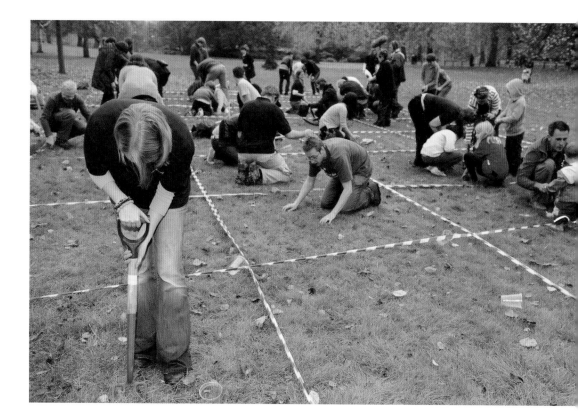

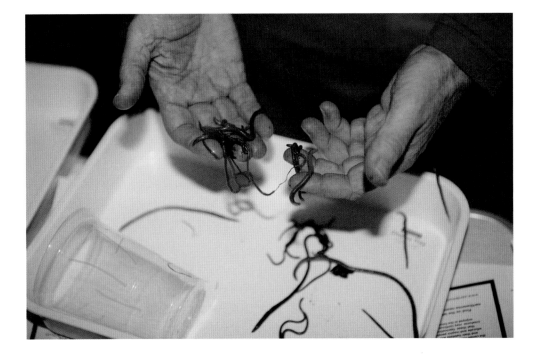

OPPOSITE: The Natural History Museum's 2009 worm-charming event in Hyde Park also marked the launch of the Earthworm Society of Britain.

LEFT: The Earthworm Society of Britain, funded by OPAL, the Open Air Laboratories Project, gives people the opportunity to learn more about earthworms and participate in research. The UK has more than 25 species of these essential nature's gardeners.

a watering can. These various methods are said to mimic rain falling, a mole approaching, and other worm-stimulating situations. From the numbers and types of worms that emerge, Museum scientists can then put together guidelines for charmers taking part in the national survey, to ensure consistency and repeatability. And, of course, the worms are always put back.

Worm-charmers are a dedicated bunch who engage in intense competition. Apart from the fun, their results are scientifically valuable, helping towards data for an earthworm survey that should eventually cover the whole of Britain. Of course digging holes remains the best method for sampling earthworms as the charming methods used seem to have an inherent bias in the types of worms extracted.

Bilharzia

A very different worm-like creature being investigated by Museum staff is the blood fluke parasite *Schistosoma*. Infection with this worm causes the terrible long-term tropical disease known as schistosomiasis or bilharzia. Whilst the mortality rate associated with this disease may be low, it does, however, wreak havoc by damaging internal organs. Unlike the massive amount of attention given to malaria and AIDS, schistosomiasis has become something of a forgotten disease, even though it affects more than 200 million people worldwide, in particular children in sub-Saharan Africa, and treatment of the disease is simply securing better access to medications.

RIGHT: Bilharzia affects children in sub-Saharan Africa in particular. It can cause tremendous damage to the internal organs and yet, if the right medicines are available, treatment is relatively straightforward.

OPPOSITE: This picture of bilharzia's *Schistosoma* blood fluke, a type of flatworm, was made using scanning electron microscopy (*see* page 117). The opening at the front end is the oral sucker, where food is taken in, and behind it is a second, pediculated sucker.

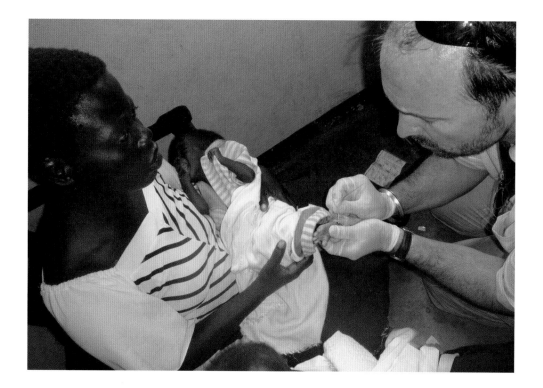

The lifecycle of the worm is complicated and a marvel of evolution bringing together people, parasites and snails. The immature *Schistosoma* flukes, which can be either male or female, enter the human body through the skin, travel to the lungs, and then to the liver, where they further mature and start to breed. Depending on the species of *Schistosoma*, the parasites' eggs pass out in the urine or faeces. In water these eggs hatch into tiny early stages, or larvae, that enter the second host in their complex life cycle – several species of freshwater snails. Here the larvae go through the first set of changes, then break free from the snail, and swim in search of humans to infect as people daily make use of water. So both snails and people are hosts in a single life cycle of the parasite.

In Uganda, Museum scientists are working with the Ministry of Health and undertaking an exciting long-term project to find out more about *Schistosoma* and how people pick up the parasite. In particular, the scientists are exploring how very young children become infected and are determining whether giving medications to such children has a beneficial impact upon their health and control of the disease. Museum staff have now shown how these youngsters are infected by the actions of their mothers who bathe them in water freshly collected from lakes and rivers. This is one of many Natural History Museum projects aiming to change people's lives for the better and bring a happier future to those communities living in poverty.

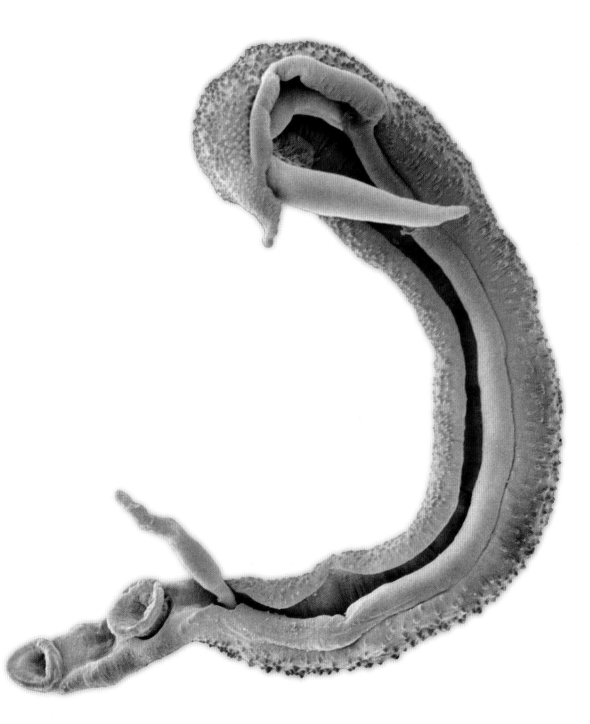

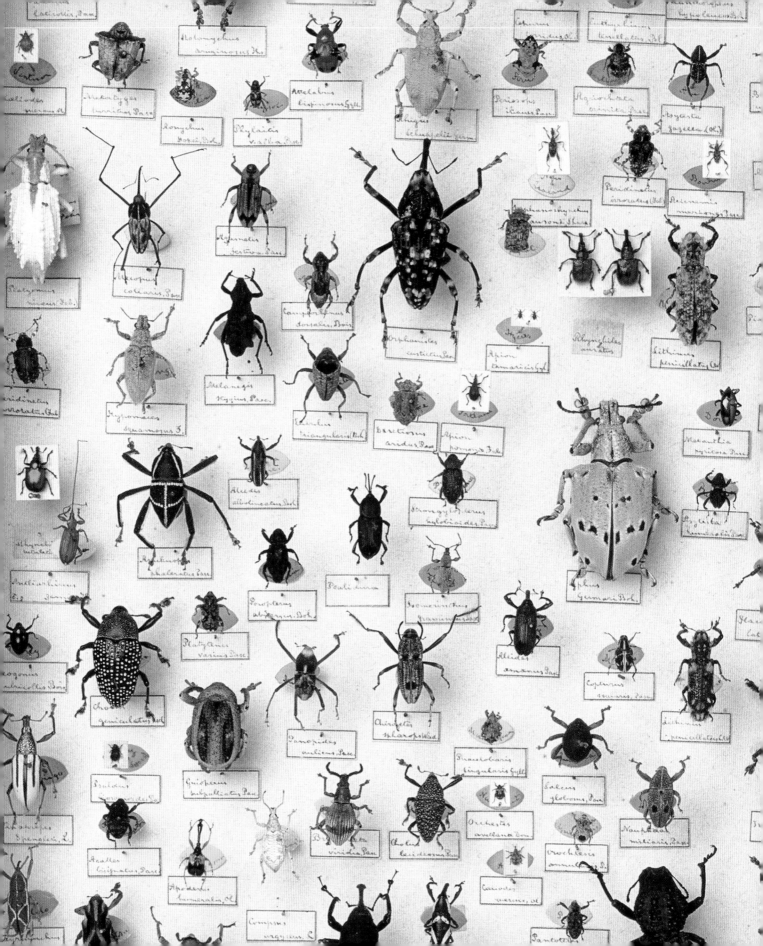

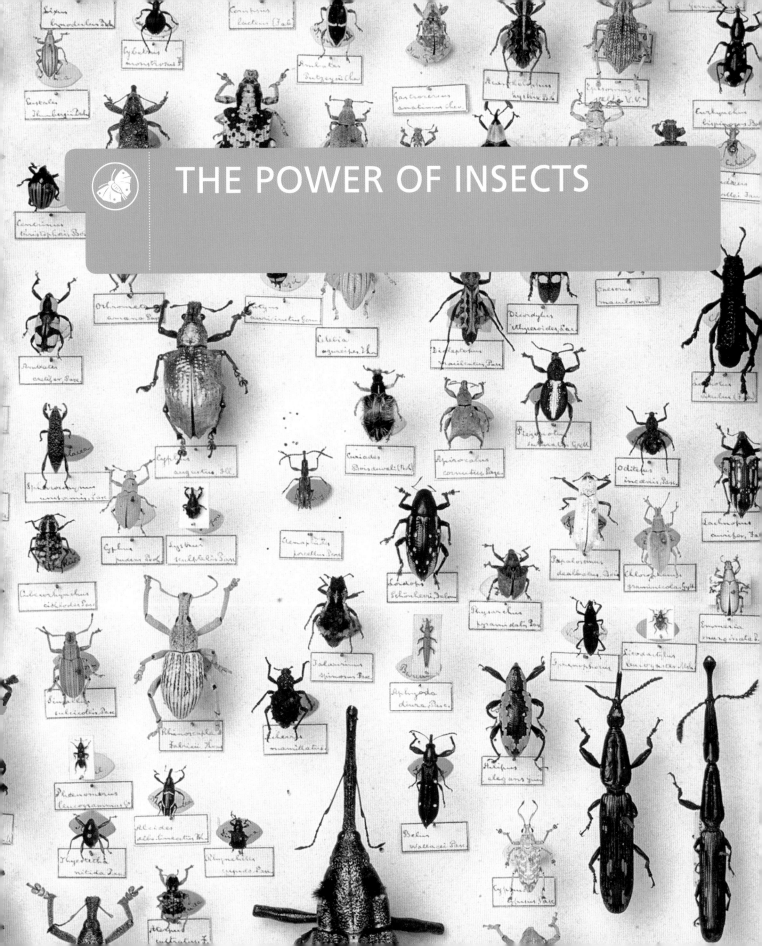

THE POWER OF INSECTS

THE POWER OF INSECTS

We share our world with more than 10 million million million insects. They are nature's great success story. No land habitat is without them. They spread some of the world's worst diseases in people, animals and plants, and they damage up to one-quarter of all our crops. No wonder the Natural History Museum has so many of them, and that the insect specialists, entomologists, are so busy.

ENTOM IS THE SMALLEST AND BIGGEST FIELD in the animal world. Insects are some of the tiniest of all creatures, yet their numbers are mind-boggling. However you calculate it, insects rule. Very roughly, there are between one and a half and two million animal species formally identified, named and described in the scientific literature. More than three-quarters are insects. Their numbers rise daily as more specimens come in for study, curation and preservation. These are not only from remote rainforests, or from strange habitats such as under mountain glaciers, but from familiar places like temperate woods, grasslands, gutters and sewage pipes, where the rarer kinds have simply never been noticed. In hundreds of years, if and when the insect inventory is ever completed, it may extend to 10 million species or more.

The Natural History Museum has more than 25 million preserved insect specimens. If you want to look at each one for just a minute, you will need more than 50 years to spare. It's the biggest and most comprehensive collection in the world. It's also the leading repository for insect knowledge, not just in the form of the physical specimens, but in publications, illustrations, photographs, and in less tangible ways, like the DNA databases of genetic material and records of which species live where.

What are insects?

This seems an easy question. But many people are unclear about how an insect is defined, and how it differs from any old bug or creepy-crawly. The basic description of an insect is a smallish invertebrate (creature without a backbone) that has a hard outer body casing termed the exoskeleton, made

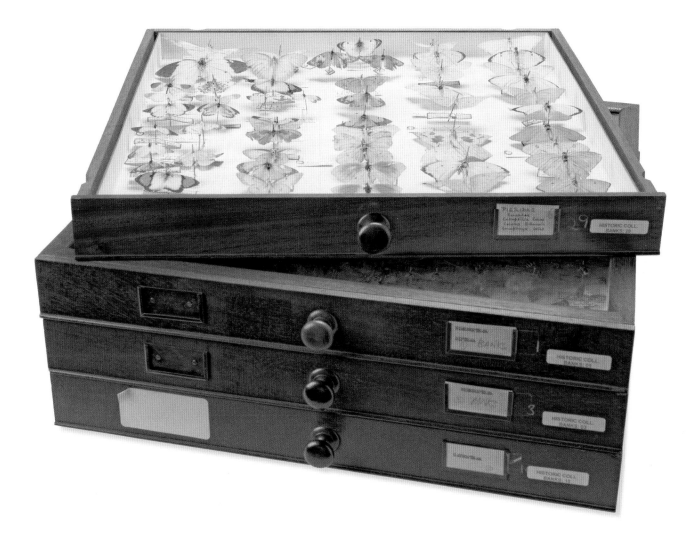

chiefly of the substance chitin; a body composed of three parts, being the head (with a pair of eyes and a pair of antennae or feelers), the thorax in the middle (bearing the legs and perhaps wings), and the abdomen (containing guts and reproductive organs); and three pairs of jointed legs.

Straight away, we need clarification. Flies are only too well known as insects, and true, they have three pairs of legs. They develop from wriggly maggots, yet maggots have no legs at all. The 'legs' part of the definition applies mainly to adult or fully mature insects, not the earlier stages in the life cycle, known as larvae. However, some adult female flies from the Phoridae group are legless. They lose their legs and their wings so that they mimic ant larvae, since they live among Malaysian driver ants and are parasitic on them. There are many similar twists and tweaks to the main definition. Exceptions to the typical insect are legion, which after all, is only to be expected in such a numerous and varied group.

What are not insects?

Amongst the general public, other invertebrates such as spiders, scorpions, mites and ticks are often called insects. These creatures are not insects, they belong, with others, to the animal group known as Arachnida. They have eight legs, two body parts, a pair of appendages called pedipalps

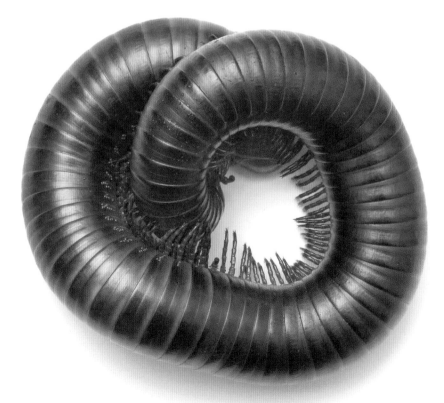

and no wings. Yet again there are exceptions. In some arachnids the first pair of legs are not used for walking. They have evolved as 'feelers', which touch the ground where they walk and feel vibrations and air currents, and detect chemical substances in the environment. These feelers are more like the single pair of antennae or feelers that we see on a typical insect's head, and are called antenniform legs. This is why biologists at the Museum and elsewhere often talk about 'limbs' or 'appendages' rather than 'legs', since the last term implies use in walking and running.

Moving onto more legs, other creepy-crawlies are centipedes and millipedes. And these are not insects. They have a long body with many segments. A millipede has two pairs of legs on each body segment, while a centipede has one pair. Despite the name, many species of centipedes, (meaning 100 feet), have fewer than 50 pairs of legs, although some species have up to 181 pairs. This group is known scientifically as Chilopoda. The Diplopoda are millipedes (meaning 1,000 feet) but many species have less than 100 pairs, although a few species boast more than 375 pairs.

Dedicated work

All of the above groups belong to the animal supergroup known as Arthropoda, meaning jointed legs. The legs bend at specialized joints rather then being generally flexible, like tentacles. Other arthropods include the group that dominates the seas in the way that insects rule the land. This is the Crustacea – crabs, lobsters, shrimps, prawns, crayfish, krill, barnacles, water-fleas and, unusual in that they live on land, woodlice or sowbugs. Detailed descriptions of all these creepy-crawlies fill thousands of books. The knowledge is vital in many fields, for example, in fighting arthropod-borne diseases, in treating their venomous bites and stings, and in consuming them as foods. Such descriptions only exist because of the patient, dedicated study by naturalists and biologists through the ages, including those at the Museum, where new species are added to the specimen collections and catalogues every week.

Naming new species

Each new type of insect or other organism must be studied in great detail, compared to existing similar kinds to see if it might belong to one of them, and then become the subject of a report or paper justifying why it is a species new to science.

There is also, of course, the challenge of giving the new species an official name. It is a process that stimulates much discussion, not all of it serious, among Museum staff. Sometimes the name derives from the place where the creature was found. This could range from a small town to an entire continent, or perhaps a particular type of soil, rock or habitat. For example, one of the earliest insect-like creatures, known from 400 million-year-old fossils, is *Rhyniella*, related to the animals we call springtails. It is named after the village of Rhynie in Aberdeenshire, Scotland, and the Rhynie

OPPOSITE: Often confused with insects are other many-legged creepy-crawlies such as *Archispirostreptus gigas*, the African giant black millipede. Native to subtropical and tropical West Africa, it can grow to a length of 30 centimetres. It is shown here at approximately life size.

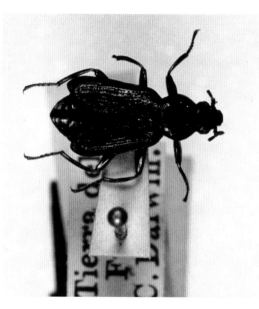

chert, the local type of fossil-rich rock. The insect known as *Belgica antarctica* lives in Antarctica. It is a flightless midge, a type of fly. Although it is small enough to sit on your fingernail, it is that frozen continent's largest terrestrial animal.

Another source of official species names is people. Perhaps the name is from the person who found the specimen. It could be the sponsor of the expedition that discovered it, as described on earlier pages for Walter Rothschild, founder of the Natural History Museum at Tring. It might be a local celebrity or a national figure, especially from the life sciences. The beetle *Parahelops darwinii* was collected by Charles Darwin in Chile, on his voyage in HMS *Beagle*. There are also the Galapagos carpenter bee *Xylocopa darwinii*, Darwin's fungus *Cyttaria darwinii*, Darwin's frog *Rhinoderma darwinii*, the fossil lemur-like primate *Darwinus* or Ida (*see* pages 42-44), and many others named in honour of the great naturalist.

The inspiration for a name could also be a pop star, actor, politician or even a president. Within the vast and varied Insecta, the largest subgroup is the beetles and weevils, known as Coleoptera. There are more than 350,000 kinds, which is almost one-quarter of all described animal species. Recently at the Museum, a group of slime-mould-consuming beetles were identified, completely new to science. There were more than 60 species to name. Time for some creative thinking.

'This is the President'

The entomologists concerned with these beetles, Kelly Miller and Quentin Wheeler, had previously worked at Cornell University in Ithaca, New York State, USA. So maybe an American connection was appropriate. How about *Agathidium bushi, A. rumsfeldi* and *A. cheneyi*? Most readers are probably familiar with the names of the former US President George W Bush, his Vice President Dick Cheney and his Secretary of Defense Donald Rumsfeld. One evening Quentin Wheeler was in his office and the phone rang. A voice at the other end said: 'This is the President of the United States.' Oh dear, what would he think, having a beetle that ate slime mould named after him? The voice continued: 'My colleagues and I are honoured to be immortalized in the names of beetles.' Of course, the entomologists meant no offence. For those keen on *Star Wars,* another species of their beetles was *A. vaderi* after its broad, shiny, helmet-like head.

There is a long way to go in the name game. Scientists believe that there could be another five, seven or even ten million insect types waiting to be described and receive their official designations.

Life on the Commons

Where do all these new species of insects and other organisms come from? Many are collected by intrepid Museum staff and others exploring remote locations for the first time. But others are found much closer to home. Many drawers of British insects in the Natural History Museum have specimen locations labelled 'Bookham Commons, Surrey'. These peaceful mixed-habitat commons just off the M25 London Orbital include pedunculate or English oak and other woods, scrubland, grassy areas, damp meadows, and 12 varied ponds and small lakes, with public access to most areas. The three parts: Great Bookham Common, Little Bookham Common and Banks Common cover 160 hectares and are owned by the National Trust. In 1961, they were declared an SSSI, Site of Special Scientific Interest. Officially sanctioned specimen collecting has been going on there for well over a century. The Museum has many thousands of insects and other items from the locality, making Bookham Commons one of the most intensively surveyed locations, for one of the longest time periods, in the UK.

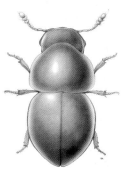

With records going back so far, Bookham Commons are an ideal place to study changes wrought on wildlife by problems such as pollution, local extinctions, and global warming and climate change. The species list here includes more than 2,000 insects, with over 1,000 flies, 1,500-plus beetles and in excess of 300 butterflies and moths. Amazingly, new species are still being discovered – not necessarily new to science, but previously unknown at Bookham. Whether they have always been here and evaded capture until now, or whether they are newly arrived from other sites, perhaps as a result of environmental changes, is another part of the fascinating wildlife jigsaw.

Up in the canopy

Much of Bookham Commons has been minutely surveyed over the decades, probably several times. Enthusiasts from the London Natural History Society have been visiting for more than 50 years, as well as staff from the Natural History Museum and elsewhere. But one area has so far avoided detailed attention. This is the canopy, the woodland's topmost green layer of twigs, flowers, leaves and fruits. Expeditions into the canopies of tropical rainforests show that an enormous amount of biodiversity lives here, yet the canopies of oak forests in southern England are relatively unexplored. At Bookham much of the canopy is just one species, English oak *Quercus robur*. But this famous tree provides

RIGHT: Bookham Commons enjoy the peaceful late summer sunshine, as birds twitter and butterflies flutter. Then the invasion begins ... Museum experts, wearing the latest in protective suit fashions, begin their tree-misting session. Well-aimed spray heads into the canopy ...
The stunned insects and other bugs tumble into the waiting funnels strung in a carefully arranged grid below, and slide into the preserving fluid.

OPPOSITE: The 'insect soup' samples are delicately sorted back at the Museum into their main groups, such as beetles, caterpillars, flies, spiders and others.

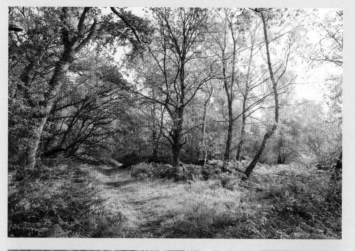

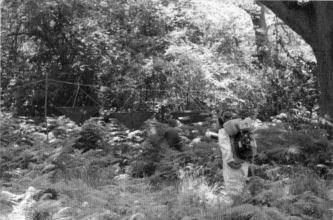

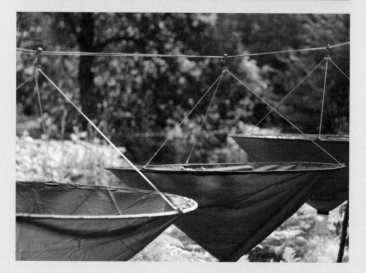

one of the richest and most diverse habitats for many hundreds of animal species that live on it and almost nowhere else, as well as thousands more who climb, feed, burrow, nest and shelter among its leaves, branches, trunk and roots.

Tree misting

Apart from building rope hoists and walkways among the upper branches, another way to gain remote access to the insects living in the canopy has recently been developed. This latest technology is a fine mist of insecticide blown up into the branches and twigs by a mister or fogger machine. The chemical substance is biodegradable and harmless to birds and mammals, but it quickly knocks out insects and similar creatures. They lose their grip and fall down. Hanging low or on the ground is a grid-like system of closely spaced funnels, wide ends facing upwards to catch the specimens, which slide into a container of alcohol. This pickles and preserves the miniature quarry. The fine spray reaches 15 metres up into the branches, and requires an accurate aim and precise timing. The idea is to collect a sample of only canopy insects.

Following the procedure for tree misting, with the correct amount of insecticide, suitable weather conditions, and the recommended numbers and spacing of funnels, is very important. It allows the scientists to repeat the technique on the same tree at different times of the year, and on various tree species at the same time. In this way we gain a picture of how the insect populations change with conditions, year after year.

Insect soup

The alcohol ends up as 'insect soup' that is taken back to the Museum and sorted out, usually under the microscope. Different types of insects are allocated to various tubes or flasks. Then each of these tubes goes to a particular entomologist who is the specialist on that group, such as flies, beetles, moths and so on. The whole sample may need a dozen people to identify everything in it.

A recent tree misting session at Bookham turned up something of a surprise. This was a specimen of tiny beetle just two and a half millimetres long. It is important because it is so scarce in Britain's insect lists. In fact, here is one of less than ten places where it is found. This may be

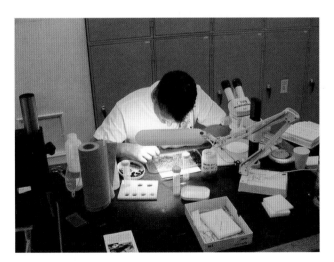

because the beetle is truly rare. Or it could have been in the Bookham canopy before, and the new misting method has at last detected its presence. The overall results of misting reveal that the Bookham oak canopy is alive and well, and that even after a century of intensive study, there are still new discoveries to make.

Big and beautiful

Beetles may be the most numerous insects in terms of species. But most Museum visitors would agree that the most attractive are the butterflies, with perhaps the moths as a close second. These creatures make up the insect group Lepidoptera, meaning scale wing. They are called this because of the hundreds of tiny flake-like scales that coat their four wings and it is these scales that produce the striking colours and patterns. In all there are upwards of 180,000 known lepidopteran species around the world, of which around 20,000 are butterflies and the remainder moths.

The Natural History Museum's butterfly collection is the world's biggest and most comprehensive, with some 90 per cent of all known species represented in the drawers and cabinets. Museum staff and their associates have collected where no one has collected before, deep in forests, high on mountains, in baking deserts and mosquito-infested swamps. Helicopters are hired to reach the most remote locations such as ravines and cliffs. The scientists may be left for a week or more to do their work, with the helicopter their only way out.

On the move

The Museum regularly hosts new butterfly exhibitions detailing the habits and lives of these spectacular creatures. In 2009, *Butterfly Jungle* included a temporary tropical butterfly house and a jungle playground amid the traffic and bustle of South Kensington. Behind the scenes, more specimens are continually coming in for identification, or to add to the vast research and study collections.

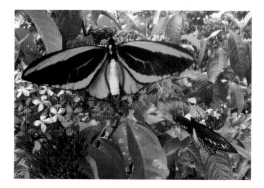

Prize specimens include the Queen Alexandra birdwing, *Ornithoptera alexandrae*, which is the world's largest butterfly. The female has a wingspan of up to 30 centimetres and a finger-sized head-and-body length of eight centimetres. Old-time collectors usually netted or even shot down these magnificent bird-sized insects, and some of the Museum specimens have pellet holes from the gunshot.

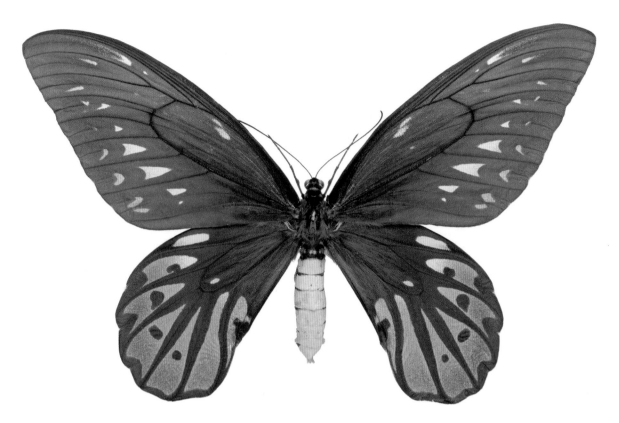

In 2009, more than eight million butterflies and moths were moved from their old homes to the Museum's new Darwin Centre, with its highly controlled environmental conditions and a degree of public access. There are more than 23,000 drawers of Lepidoptera, including 5,578 containing solely British species, as well as 10,000 drawers of another excessively numerous insect group, Hymenoptera – wasps, bees and ants.

Butterflies old and new

The Lepidoptera relocation to the Darwin Centre was done with tremendous care and attention since some of the specimens have become very fragile. This is not surprising given that the oldest date back more than 300 years to 1680. Butterflies and moths are preserved by a process known as setting, which has changed little from that time to the modern era. Each entomologist has personal preferences and techniques for setting, but in general the specimen is gently opened, if possible while still fresh, so that the wings lie flat to the sides rather than being folded together over the back. This can be aided by pressing with a needle or probe against the base of the strengthening tube or vein in the wing, near where it joins the body, rather than pressing the outer part of the wing. Butterflies differ from moths in several ways, although none is foolproof for distinguishing them. One is that the former generally rest with their wings out flat, while the latter hold them together; but there are exceptions. Another, more secure distinction is that butterflies have antennae or feelers with expanded club-like tips, while moth antennae look thready or feathery.

115

BIO-INDICATORS

THE MOST RECENT ADDITIONS TO the Lepidoptera collection include the new species *Idioneurula donegani*, a medium-sized coffee-brown butterfly with eyespots on the hindwings, shown below. It was discovered by Museum workers during the first expedition to the highest peaks of Colombia's Yariguies Mountains, an area that has now become a national park. After comparison with similar specimens in the Museum's collections, and DNA analysis, the new species was confirmed. A few years previously it had been the turn of ornithologists to get excited here, with the discovery of a new variety of bird, the Yariguies brush-finch, *Atlapetes latinuchus yariguierum*, a subspecies of the yellow-breasted brush-finch.

Like many insects and other creatures, butterflies and moths are bio-indicators. Their presence or absence can indicate the health of a habitat or environment and whether or not it is undisturbed by pollution and other damage. Insects go through several life stages during which their body shape changes dramatically, a phenomenon known as metamorphosis. In lepidopterans the stages are egg, larva or caterpillar, pupa or chrysalis, and adult or imago. Each of these stages has differing needs from its environment and so provides a searching examination of the local conditions.

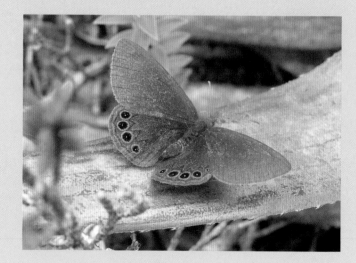

Great care must be taken with the antennae or feelers as the lepidopteran is prepared for setting. If they break, they are extremely difficult to reattach. When the specimen is flat, it is gently placed between sheets of special paper, which are then pinned around the edges, near to the creature but without impaling it, onto a cork board. It is left to dry and harden somewhere dark, since bright light is the enemy of Lepidoptera wings and soon fades their colours.

Gold-plated wasps no more

One of the smallest known butterflies is the dwarf blue from Africa, with a wingspan of just 1.4 centimetres. In general, butterflies and moths are large enough to identify from their wing coloration using the unaided eye or a hand lens magnifying, say, 10 times. But many insects are far tinier, and so much more difficult to study. Some of the parasitic wasps would easily fit into this 'o' including the smallest of all insects, the so-called fairy-flies, a group of parasitic wasps with a head–body length as little as one-fifth of one millimetre. Several of them could populate a pinhead.

Historically, these minute specimens have been examined with a light microscope, but this yields magnifications of just a few hundred times. It's especially important to look at details on the insect body to distinguish closely similar kinds or identify a new species. The Natural History Museum's high-tech armoury has included scanning electron microscopes (SEMs) for over 40 years. An SEM uses a beam of electrons which interacts with the specimen. Electrons given off from the specimen are detected and converted to an image on a screen. Electrons have a much shorter wavelength than visible light and so the SEM can produce very high magnifications. Early SEMs could only work with samples which were conductive, any that were not naturally conductive needed to be coated with carbon or precious metals such as gold. The coating was conductive and helped to produce a stronger signal in the microscope. If a non-conductive specimen was examined, electrons could accumulate on the surface, deflect the beam and the image showed dark streaks and bright areas. Modern SEMs help neutralize this effect, so it is no longer necessary to coat samples. This technique, which has been available at the Museum for more than 30 years, yields images at magnifications comparable to those previously achievable on coated specimens. The result? No more need for gold-plated specimens! The researchers can remove specimens from the collections, examine them, and return them to the collections

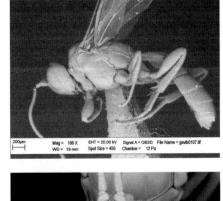

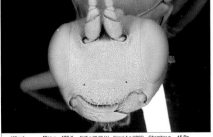

BELOW TOP: Lateral view of the only known specimen of *Perilimicron alticolator*. Scientists hope to find out more about this enigmatic species through detailed SEM study.

BELOW BOTTOM: This is the face of *Lathrolestes* species, a parasitoid of the larvae of sawflies. The classification of *Lathrolestes* wasps is in need of a revisit, which the SEM and other modern techniques should hasten.

BELOW: The nest-in-a-bowler-hat shows how wasps build their dwellings in all kinds of odd places.

OPPOSITE TOP: The Madagascan Darwin's sphinx moth, *Xanthopan morganii praedicta*, has a very long proboscis, which is usually rolled up into a spiral under the head.

OPPOSITE BOTTOM: Made around 1905, these dressed fleas were part of a set given to Charles Rothschild, brother of Walter who established the Tring Museum.

undamaged. The specimen is simply put into the microscope and within a few minutes it shows up on screen in all its miniature glory, perhaps revealing whether it really is a new species.

Insect oddballs

Natural History Museum treasures include some very strange insect-related specimens. One is a wasp's nest constructed in a bowler hat! It was made, not by parasitic wasps, but by the common wasps, *Vespula vulgaris*, which terrorize our summer picnics and barbeques. The nest-in-a-hat came from an outhouse on the estate of Walter Rothschild at Tring which is now part of the Museum. Queen wasps usually select a site such as an animal burrow, natural cave or tree hole to begin their nest construction. This particular queen probably flew into the outhouse in spring and spied the bowler hat as a suitably sheltered, hole-shaped location to set up home. After building a few compartments or cells from chewed wood and her spit, she laid eggs in them. She then fed the hatched offspring on pulped insects through their larval stages until they turned into adult workers. These workers continued to extend the home and cared for the offspring, while the queen spent the rest of the summer laying more eggs.

Another very strange group of Museum exhibits are the tiny dressed fleas or 'pulgas vestidos'. Charles Rothschild, himself an expert on fleas, was expecting a delivery of flea specimens from Mexico and was disappointed to receive two sets of dressed fleas, one a peasant couple and the other two wedding couples together with a full Mexican band. These oddities became popular in Victorian times when fleas of all kinds – human, dog, cat and so on – were much more common and irksome. People made costumes in the shape of miniature human figures from scraps of cloth, and then glued on the flea to represent the head. Most dressed fleas are less than five millimetres tall, about the height of this '1'. Some were mass produced and sold as curios or souvenirs. It's not clear where this trend began. One suggestion is that nuns in convents, known for making miniatures of many kinds, developed the style. Dressed fleas were popular for a time in many lands, from Mexico to Europe, India, China and Japan.

The moth forecast

Among the Museum's more famous Lepidoptera specimens is Morgan's sphinx moth, *Xanthopan morganii*. This is a large hawkmoth from Africa and the nearby island of Madagascar. It is famous because of its link to the two founders of evolutionary theory, Charles Darwin and Alfred Russel Wallace (1823–1913). In 1862, Darwin examined some orchid flowers sent to him by botanist James Bateman. He was struck by the shape of the species *Angraecum sesquipedale*, especially the spur-like part called the nectary which produces sweet, sugary nectar to attract insects for pollination. As the moth sips its sweet bait, pollen attaches to its head, and so the moth spreads the pollen to other flowers. The nectary was narrow and deep, with its base about 30 centimetres from the insect-accessible opening. On first seeing this plant, Darwin exclaimed 'What insect can suck it?'

In his book later that year, *Fertilization of Orchids*, Darwin predicted that the orchid's pollinator could be a moth with hollow, straw-like mouthparts, termed the proboscis, that were long enough to reach the nectar. 'In Madagascar there must be moths with probosces capable of extension to a length of between 10 and 12 inches!'

Wallace took up the idea. He knew of Morgan's sphinx moth on mainland Africa, which almost fitted the bill. He conjectured that a variant with an even longer proboscis would be found on Madagascar. He even made a sketch of this predicted insect in 1867. Both he and Darwin were

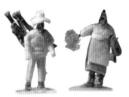

RIGHT: The giant comet orchid, *Angraecum sesquipedale*, puzzled Charles Darwin and other naturalists as to its mode of pollination. It led to one of evolutionary theory's first fulfilled predictions (*see* page 119).

OPPOSITE AND BELOW: Alfred Russel Wallace (opposite) was one of the greatest of all specimen collectors. The 1867 drawing below by him shows how he imagined the Madagascan orchid-pollinating moth might appear, as it sipped nectar with its amazingly extending drinking-straw 'tongue'.

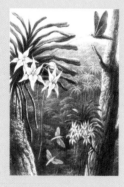

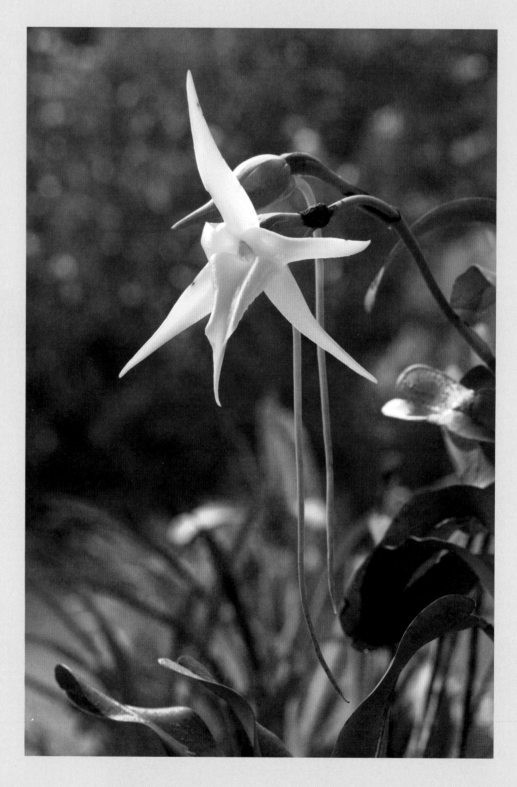

working from the idea that a flower nectary so deep would not be there by accident. It must have evolved for a reason, and what better reason than moths or similar creatures were able to spread the flower's pollen so it could set seed. At the time, just a few years after *On the Origin of Species*, many scientists derided these predictions because they were still sceptical about evolution. In 1903 the moth was finally found and identified as the Madagascan Darwin's sphinx moth.

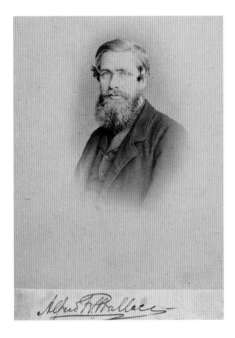

Discovery of natural selection

Alfred Russel Wallace is perhaps best known for developing the theory of evolution by natural selection, independently of Charles Darwin. Wallace sent an essay to Darwin in 1858 sharing his idea, which had come to him while specimen-collecting in Southeast Asia, whilst lying ill with a fever. As he wrote later: 'Why do some die and some live? And the answer was clearly, on the whole the best fitted live.' Darwin was shocked when he received Wallace's letter as he had been working on the same idea for about 20 years. He turned to two friends, Charles Lyell and Joseph Hooker, and they famously managed to arrange for the two men's theories to be published simultaneously. Darwin went on to publish the influential book on the subject *On the Origin of Species,* which came out 15 months after the joint paper was published.

Wallace remained on good terms with Darwin, and wrote many articles explaining, developing and defending his and Darwin's theory during the course of his long life to the age of 90. Prior to all these events, however, he had enjoyed a career as one of the greatest of all travelling naturalists and specimen collectors. His main aim in life was to collect animals, especially insects for his private collection, and he sold duplicates to make his living.

He visited the Amazon region of Brazil for four years and, when sailing back from there in 1852, his ship caught fire. Virtually everything he had collected during the trip – thousands and thousands of specimens and most of his notebooks – were lost. He was luckier in Southeast Asia where he spent a total of eight years. From there he sent back more than 125,000 specimens, including 80,000 beetles. Like Darwin, he is remembered in the common and scientific names of numerous animals. One of the weirdest is Wallace's flying frog, *Rhacophorus nigropalmatus*.

Wallace finally settled in England in 1862 and, amongst other books, authored *The Malay Archipelago,* which is still considered one of the finest books on scientific exploration that has ever been written.

RIGHT: The Wallace Line forms a boundary zone between the wildlife of Asia and Australia. The transition zone, Wallacea, has many endemic species – ones found there and nowhere else.

OPPOSITE LEFT: Many entomological specimens from the Wallace Collection are now held in the Natural History Museum. The Museum has also acquired Wallace's personal papers, documents and library from the Wallace family, numbering more than 5,000 items.

OPPOSITE RIGHT: This Bronze Age piece of bog oak, found by a local farmer, harboured near-perfect 4,500-year-old specimens of the great oak longhorn beetle, *Cerambyx cerdo*. It shows that what are now the Fens were once warmer and covered by forests.

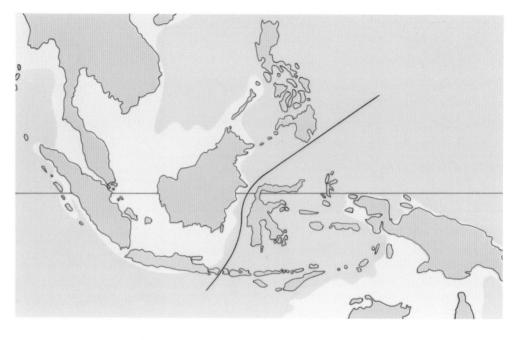

The Wallace line

This great naturalist is also commemorated by the Wallace Line, a zone where animal species undergo a marked change from west to east. The line runs between Indonesian islands, from the Lombok Straits to the east of Bali, northeast to the gap between the large islands of Borneo and Sulawesi. To the west of the Wallace Line, most species are related to those in Asia. To the east, the relationships are more with animals from Australasia. Wallace's studies of the geographical distributions of animals led to the discipline of biogeography, which has since developed into an important branch of the natural sciences. Wallace lived on into the twentieth century, finally dying at the age of 90 in 1913.

Age shall not wither them

Some of the insects in the Natural History Museum's collections are more than 300 years old. But with the best care in the world, nothing lasts for ever. So how long could these specimens persist under optimal conditions before they begin to fall apart and fade into dust? An event from nature itself gives a fascinating clue. It began with an innocent piece of wood dug from the ground by an East Anglian farmer, who took it home to cut up and burn on the fire. During the cutting, he came upon some preserved beetles in the wood. Not recognizing the species, he asked the Natural History Museum to help. Tests showed that the wood had been preserved by falling into a bog. Here conditions were what scientists call anoxic, that is, lacking oxygen. The simple gaseous substance

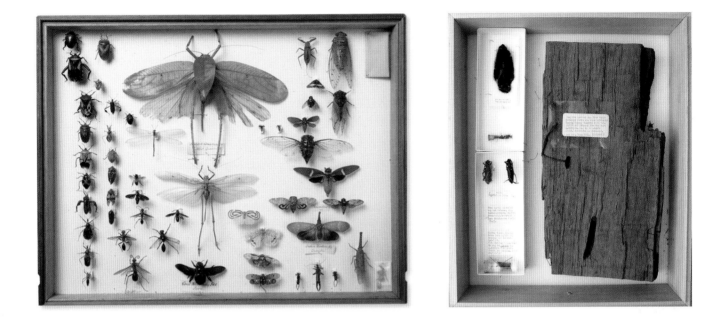

oxygen is the great life-giver on Earth. Almost every type of organism – animal, plant, fungus and microbe – needs oxygen to carry out its life processes. Rotting and decay are mostly the work of worms and other animals, moulds and other fungi, and microbes like bacteria and they all need oxygen. No oxygen no decay. Tests such as radiocarbon dating showed that the preserved wood was around 4,500 years old, which meant the beetles were that old too. So nature can do an excellent job of preserving animals for a time span ten times longer than any Museum specimen, making the staff very envious.

The preserved beetles in question were great oak longhorn beetles or greater capricorn beetles, *Cerambyx cerdo*. They are impressively large, with a thumb-sized body and extremely lengthy antennae, or feelers, providing the longhorn part of the name. Today they are found chiefly on mainland southern Europe and also in North Africa and the Near East, preferring warmer climes. Living beetles are not known from Britain, but fossils and the East Anglian bog-preserved specimens show they once lived here. The deduction is that some 4,500 years ago – at the time of the Bronze Age – the climate of East Anglia was more like today's South of France. This work is part of the science of palaeoclimatology, which is studying weather and climate back through prehistoric times. Preserved and fossil animals and plants, tree rings, ice sheets, rock types and many other clues yield the information. The expertise is invaluable in helping us to predict what the future holds as we enter a new and rapid period of global warming and climate change.

Deep-seated fears

Great longhorn beetles may be large, as beetles go. But for most people they are not particularly scary. Yet a spider one-quarter of their size can make people jump up and run away screaming. The way people react to bugs, slugs and creepy-crawlies in general is a complicated matter. To some, our responses seem entirely justified and have origins deeply rooted in our prehistoric past. For others, being terrified of bugs is a ridiculous phobia and a sign of weakness.

Whether it is the way they look, or how they move, or where they live, or what they do, many of us have a distrust of insects and similar small beasties. Mostly thanks to their arthropod cousins, the spiders, bugs in general are Britain's number one phobia. Up to 10 per cent of men and 50 per cent of women prefer to avoid these creatures. Yet if we take a few moments of rational thought, we know that they are around us almost every day. So why do we not live in a continual heightened state of fear? Would we ever go into a shed, or tramp through undergrowth, or even pull the sofa away from the wall, for fear of revealing some terrifying multi-legged critter? Most likely, it would race away in fear of its own life, desperate to escape from the sudden giant that has disturbed its tiny and limited existence.

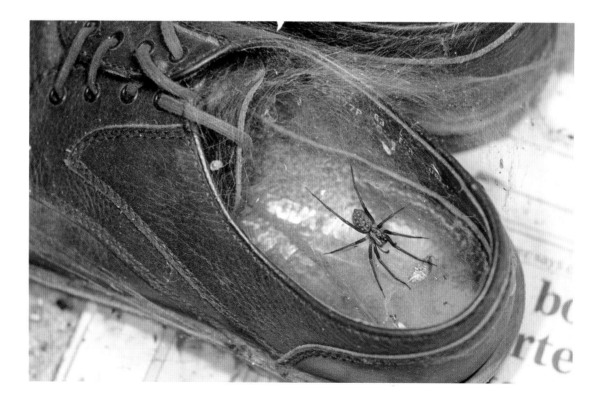

Scientists, psychologists, psychiatrists and others have long debated our worries about insects, spiders and the like. For example, an evolutionary biologist might suggest that yes, there is survival value in being cautious about mini multi-legged creatures coming too near. In tropical areas, especially, they can deliver venomous bites or stings that cause intense pain and even kill. Even if there is no immediately serious harm from the encounter, there could be long-term danger. The mildly irritating and itchy bite of a mosquito or blackfly may deliver a deadly tropical disease, with years of miserable suffering that culminate in a lingering death. It would make sense, therefore, for humans to incorporate some kind of fear, avoidance and self defence into our instinctive, built-in behaviour. Run away, or swipe them and kill them, before they get us – it could be in the genes, as part of our inner nature.

Nature or nurture

Developmental psychiatrists might take a very different view. Such fears are irrational. This is especially true in countries such as the UK where there are no lethal insects, spiders or scorpions, and the only potentially deadly animal is the reclusive snake known as the adder or European viper. Many people encounter spiders and show no special horror or phobia, while others are genuinely terrified. If these fears had survival value in evolutionary terms, surely all of us would show the behaviour, and it would appear in all kinds of situations.

One theory is that irrational phobias are caused by nurture, or the way we are brought up, and not nature, or our genes. This happens mainly during early childhood, to the age of about five years, as part of the period of primary socialization. We learn about dangers such as road traffic and sharp knives from those around us. Often these people transfer their own fears to us, including fears of creepy-crawlies. So if we encounter a spider, or perhaps a mouse or snake, we recall our fear learned from others and have a 'nasty' experience. This then strengthens the fear in our minds.

Probably both of these views, nature and nurture, have some basis. Experiments show that people can develop phobias about almost anything, even flowers or sand. But the experiments revealed that certain objects – snakes, spiders, bugs in general – were much more likely to cause a phobia, and this phobia developed more rapidly than with, say, a flower. So traumatic events during childhood are key in the way we learn our fears from others, but there may also be a genetic predisposition linked to certain objects causing such fears.

Insect cuisine

Tied into learning fear of insects and spiders is another tradition, whether we eat them or not. In some parts of the world, mainly Africa and Asia, fried crickets, boiled wasp grubs or grilled spiders

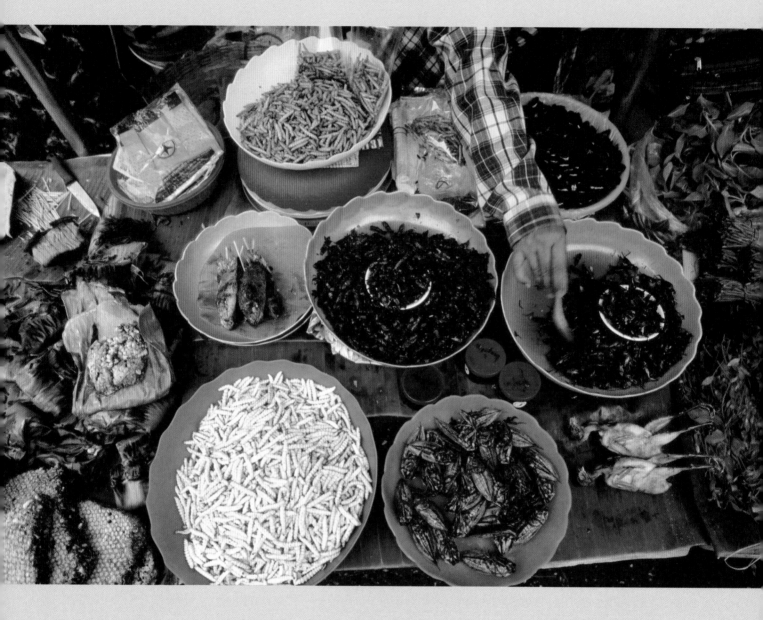

are common foods, displayed invitingly at street stalls and eateries. Honeypot ants and witchetty grubs (beetle or moth larvae) are delicacies in Australia. Fried silk moth pupae are a tasty byproduct of the silk industry. Mosquito pies and termite patties are full of nutrients. Spiders have a nutty taste and roasted, dried locusts, with a sprinkle of salt, are a handy tidbit when peckish. In other regions, especially Europe and North America, people would rather go without and even starve than munch on insect snacks. It is to do with tradition and the types of foods we are exposed to when young. Will this change? Insects are generally numerous and nutritious, with few truly inedible types. As the world's human population rises, food shortages may become more common. When faced with a food crisis, part of the solution could lie in insects. As a nutritional resource, they may become something of a necessity. In the future, Museum staff could be called upon to advise, not just on identification, but about flavours, ingredients and menus.

Stripped to the bone

For anyone studying anatomy, morphology or biology, skeletons are essential. Human skeletons for doctors, pet and farm animal skeletons for vets, and skeletons of all kinds for Museum scientists, are vital tools of the trade. Once cleaned and dried, they contain a mass of information, are easy to handle and store, and last for centuries. Reducing deceased creatures to skeletons has always been an important, if grisly, pastime at the Natural History Museum. It can be done with various dissection techniques and baths of enzymes and other chemicals. But why not let nature lend a hand? It's a task for the smallest workers in the Museum. These are the bone-stripping beetles, official species name *Dermestes maculatus*, also called hide beetles, leather beetles or larder beetles. They are natural scavengers and 'cleansers' that preserve a skeleton by eating all the soft tissues, leaving the bones intact and unchanged. In the past, chemical methods such as hydrogen peroxide and carbon tetrachloride penetrated the bones, making them fragile and destroying the tiny molecular information. The chemicals were also hazardous substances to handle.

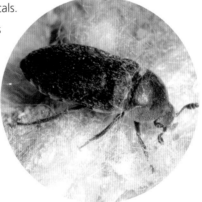

Dermestaria

The most recent batch of beetle staff members arrived at the Museum in 2004, destined to clean up mainly fish and mammal skeletons. The Museum had previous colonies living in containers known as dermestaria (similar to fish in aquaria, without the water), but these had failed for various reasons. Since their arrival the most recent beetles have toiled ceaselessly in their work. About 10 millimetres long, the early life stages or larvae are when they are the hungriest. Of course

RIGHT: A bird specimen is prepared for its visit to the dermestarium by skinning and removing most of the flesh, to speed the beetles' task. Then, the beetle larvae and adults get to work on what's left of the carcass. They carefully consume the soft parts and leave the harder ones – the bones. After a week or two the bones start to show through. The beetles continue their energetic work, secure from escape. The end result is a lightweight, delicate and scrupulously clean bird skeleton, every nook and cranny scoured of flesh, ready for reassembly.

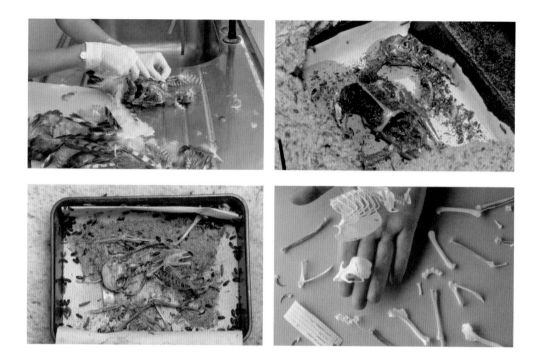

they must be kept under tight security. These beetles are notorious pests in museums and other animal collections, and if they escaped from their containers they could devastate the Museum's collections. In fact, an insect of similar habits, *Anthrenus sarnicus*, is known by the common name of the museum beetle.

Once a dermestid colony is set up and the environmental conditions are right – the beetles heartily dislike light – it is self-sustaining. All that the 1,500 or so Museum workers need are an occasional clean-out and about four kilograms of fleshy food each week. The specimens are usually prepared by skinning and gutting first, and as much of the flesh as possible is removed. From big skulls and limb bones to tiny, delicate mice and shrew skeletons, the beetles use their miniature mouthparts to delicately scrape and nibble every scrap of flesh, 24/7.

Silent witnesses

Earlier pages describe how Museum staff are sometimes called upon as expert witnesses in legal cases, including suspected murder, and the process of estimating the minimum amount of time since death from the fly eggs, maggots and pupae on bodies. The first recorded case in the UK where this type of evidence brought about a successful conviction involved Doctor Buck Ruxton, in 1935. Doctor Ruxton was a general practitioner in Lancaster, in the north of England. He was popular and respected. But privately he became obsessed with the notion that his common-law

FLESHY FOOD

AS WELL AS BEETLES AND THEIR LARVAE, fly larvae, commonly called maggots, are well-known meat-eaters. A few years ago Natural History Museum staff discovered some fly larvae in a small labelled vial in the back of an entomology cupboard. They turned out to be part of the evidence that had been used in a landmark case for forensic entomology in the UK (*see* opposite). Their use showed that insects can provide crucial evidence in murder cases, not just of a specific location, but also of the minimum time since death. Forensic entomology, the use of insect evidence in the legal arena, then became a science in its own right

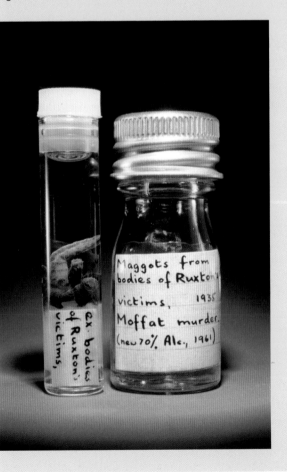

BELOW: This female bluebottle blowfly is feeding with her extended proboscis (mouthparts) on an animal corpse. Around her is a range of developmental stages of the larvae or maggots, hatched from eggs laid earlier.

wife Isabella, a lively lady who socialized widely, was having an affair. Ruxton became increasingly jealous and apparently flew into terrible fits of rage. Finally, he could stand it no longer and he strangled Isabella on 15 September1935. Ruxton killed the maid too, perhaps worried that she might discover the body before he could deal with it or perhaps because she had already discovered it. He cut up the bodies into at least 70 pieces, mutilated them to prevent their identities being discovered, and then dumped them unwisely wrapped in local newspapers almost 100 miles north of Lancaster, in a steep valley near the town of Moffat in Dumfriesshire, Scotland On 29 September the badly decaying body parts in their wrappings were found by passers-by. The case hit the national headlines as the 'Jigsaw Murders'. Ruxton fell under suspicion. The police pieced together various lines of evidence. These included fingerprints, which Ruxton had tried to erase but which were still readable, and forensic anthropology, where a photograph of a person's face can be matched to the contours and features of a skull. Dental records were also requested A fourth line of evidence was forensic entomology. Maggots feeding on body parts were collected and sent to Doctor A G Mearns of Glasgow and Edinburgh Universities. He identified them as bluebottle blowfly, *Calliphora vicina,* and estimated their age at 12 to 14 days. So this was the minimum period between death and discovery, providing vital evidence about the time of death, which had to be about two weeks before the bodies were discovered.

More evidence turned up to implicate Doctor Ruxton. One of the dismembered heads was wrapped in clothing belonging to one of his children. Also, the dismembering had been skilfully

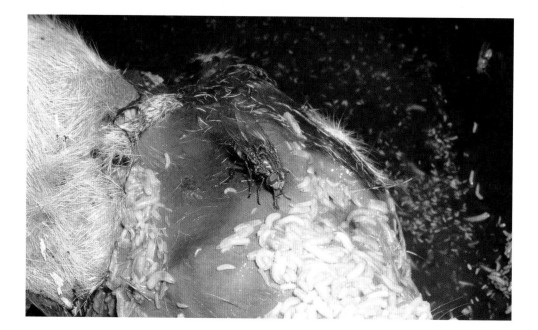

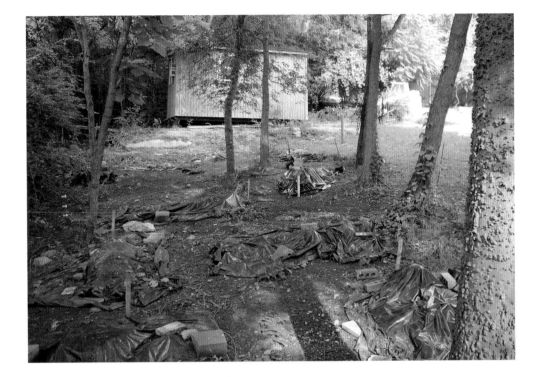

LEFT & BELOW:
At Knoxville's
Anthropological
Research Facility, each
plastic sheet covers a
slowly decomposing
human body, as decreed
by the wishes of its
owner when alive. The
plastic does not keep
insects away, rather
it helps to maintain
high humidity so the
bodies decay more
thoroughly. The original
entrance sign (below)
is now kept within the
site, so it is not quite
so obvious from the
outside what goes on
inside.

carried out, pointing to some knowledge of human anatomy. Combined with the other lines of evidence, legal proceedings ensued. Ruxton's trial began on 2 March 1936, and 11 days later, despite still protesting his innocence, he was found guilty of the murders. The punishment of the time was death by hanging.

Body farms

In 1981, the science of forensic entomology was aided with the opening of the first USA Anthropological Research Facility, the so-called 'body farm' at the University of Tennessee in Knoxville. The bodies, about 120 each year, come from various sources. Some are donated following the wishes of their owners. Others come from mortuaries and medical centres where they have been unclaimed.

Records are kept of the types of flies, beetles and other wildlife that turn up to do their natural tasks of degrading the tissues, eventually recyling them into new life and into the soil. Moulds and other fungi and bacterial microbes are monitored, as are meteorological conditions especially temperature. All of this effort gives forensic

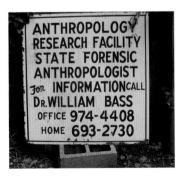

131

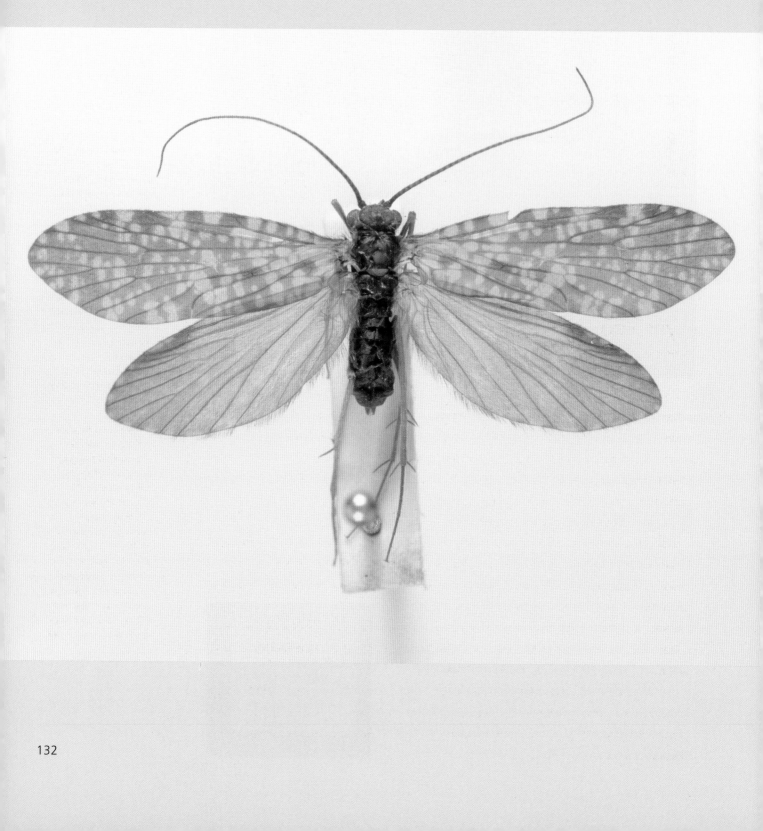

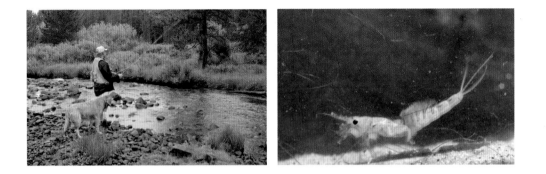

ABOVE RIGHT: Mayfly larva such as this green drake, *Ephemera danica*, live in the water for one or two years, before just a few days or even hours as the winged adult. Each species has its own habitat preferences and is sensitive to tiny disturbances.

ABOVE LEFT: Anglers around the UK are encouraged to take up the Riverfly Partnership's Anglers Monitoring Initiative, AMI, a public participation project in conjunction with the Natural History Museum and Environment Agencies. Thousands of pairs of eyes keep a watching brief on our waterways.

specialists ever more detailed reference information as they carry out their work to ensure justice is done. Forensic entomologists from the Museum have studied insect decomposition of humans at the body farm to relate it to studies on dead pigs, which are the best available proxy for humans in most countries, including the UK.

Fly fishing

A far more palatable way of gathering information is the UK's Anglers Monitoring Initiative, AMI, recently launched by the Museum. Just three minutes doing a kick sample of the river bed, and examining the results on the bank, is enough for anglers to use river fly larvae as a barometer for water quality, and so give our waterways an ongoing health check. A published guide includes notes on the monitoring technique and the insect species to look for. The results are fed to the Environment Agency and the Scottish Environment Protection Agency, making it easier for them to detect and respond quickly to water quality problems such as pesticide spills, pollution leaks, silting up and acidification. The AMI also monitors longer-term changes expected from climate change.

River flies include mayflies, caddisflies and stoneflies. These live in the water during their immature or larval stages, known as nymphs, then emerge as adults to breed. Both below and above the surface they are food for fish, birds and bats, and their variety and numbers are sensitive indicators of environmental conditions. Anglers are keen to help because decline in water quality may well have serious implications for their favoured pastime. They can share their knowledge about rivers with each other and with government scientists and agencies. This is one of several outreach projects being developed by the Museum, to get the public more interested in the environment and wildlife while adding to the body of scientific knowledge.

The AMI's techniques have been developed over more than ten years, involving 500 plus anglers on rivers across the country. The methods are based on the way scientists monitor biological systems and habitats. Healthy river fly populations are a sign of healthy rivers, which means better water quality for everyone.

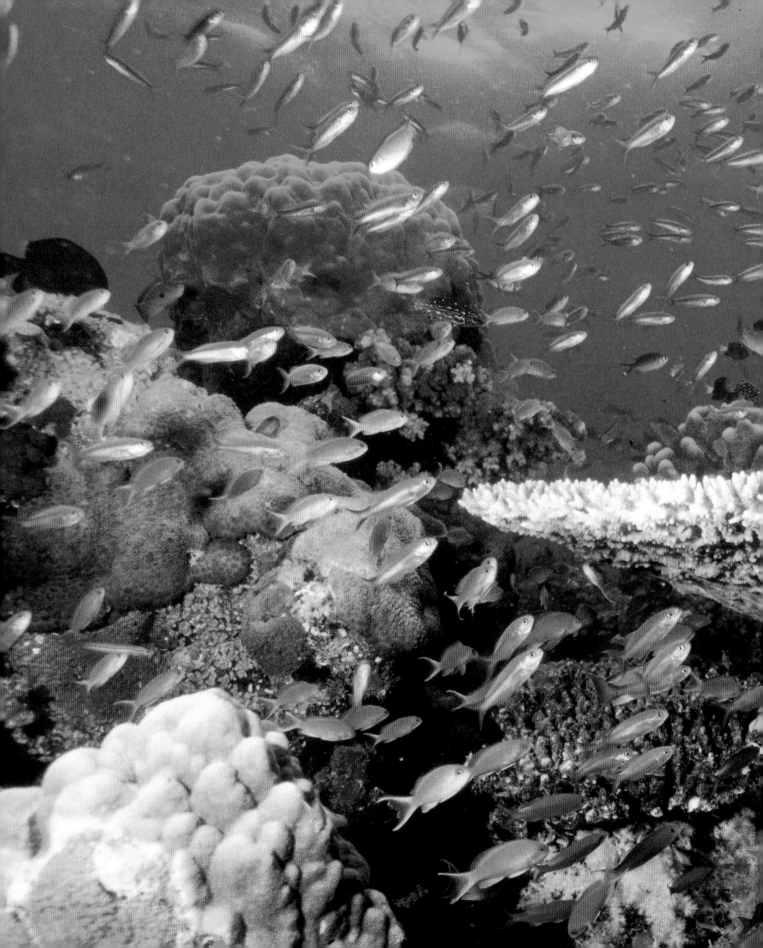

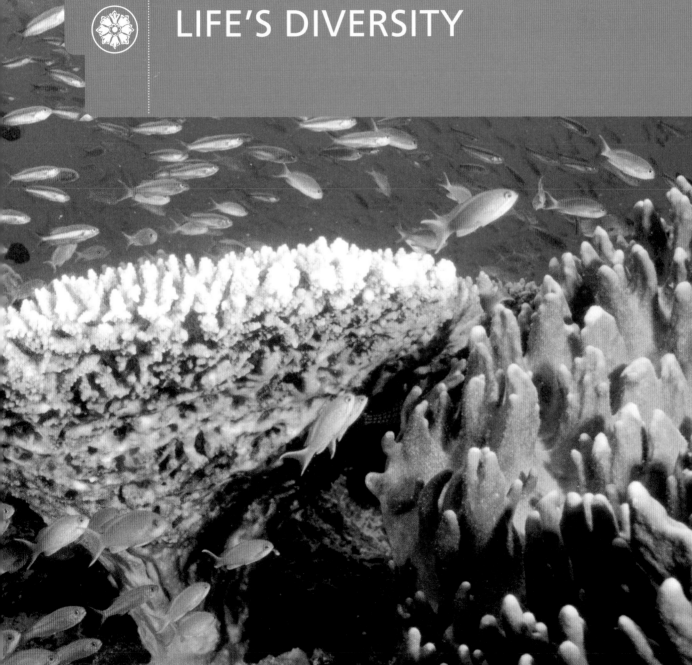

LIFE'S DIVERSITY

LIFE'S DIVERSITY

The term biodiversity is increasingly in the news and on our lips. Simply, it is the diversity or range of life and all its processes in a given place. The United Nations declared 2010 as the Year of Biodiversity in recognition of its economic importance and of how we must renew our efforts to protect biodiversity and halt its accelerating loss.

WE CAN GET A ROUGH IDEA OF LIFE'S DIVERSITY in a habitat or environment by being there and experiencing it for ourselves. A climb into the canopy of a tropical rainforest, or a scuba-dive through a coral reef, reveals the riot of shapes, colours, and teeming activity from thousands of species of creatures, plants and other organisms, living together and interacting in myriad ways. These particular habitats are famous as two of the most biodiverse on Earth. They are warm, wet and sunlit, and these are the three conditions that encourage explosions of life.

Compare tropical rainforests and coral reefs to harsher habitats such as a windy desert, a storm-pounded coastal cliff in winter, or bare -ooking estuarine mudflats. These seem almost empty of life. But not necessarily so. Under the muddy flats of an estuary are probably millions of small snails, shrimps and similar creatures, making a good living in the glutinous mire. They may be from a limited number of species, that is, not very biodiverse, but they thrive in immense numbers, and so they are extremely bioproductive – they produce a large mass of living tissue. In the desert at night, too, various creatures emerge from their burrows to search for food. Then, after a rare shower of rain, seeds nestling in the sand suddenly germinate and flower, covering the surface with a colourful carpet. And if you go back to the rocky cliff in spring, it could be covered with thousands of nesting seabirds, flapping and squawking as they tussle for space and raise their chicks.

The message is that assessing biodiversity depends on careful, detailed, systematic observations and study. The Natural History Museum is at the forefront of such work around the UK and across the world. It is so vital because biodiversity is not just for aesthetic value, as we marvel at

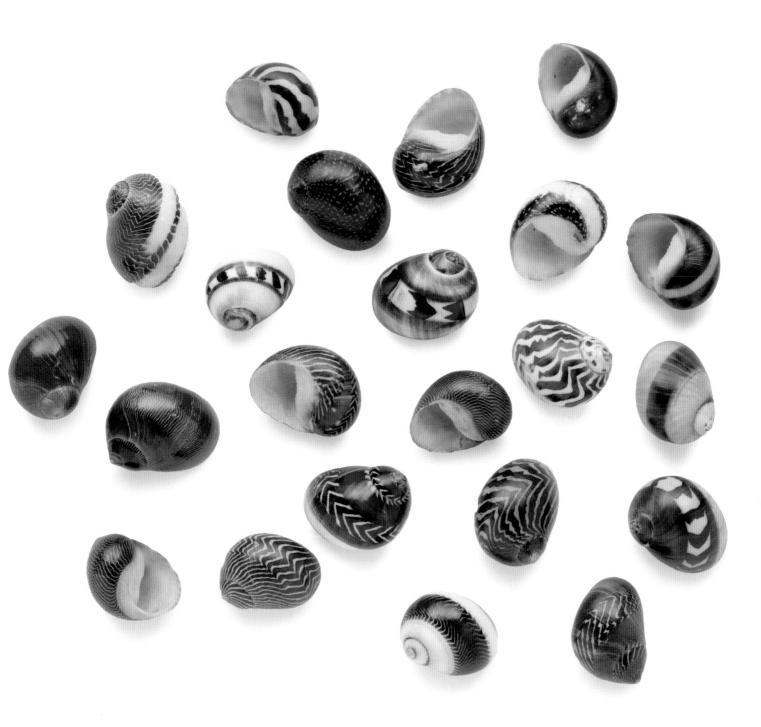

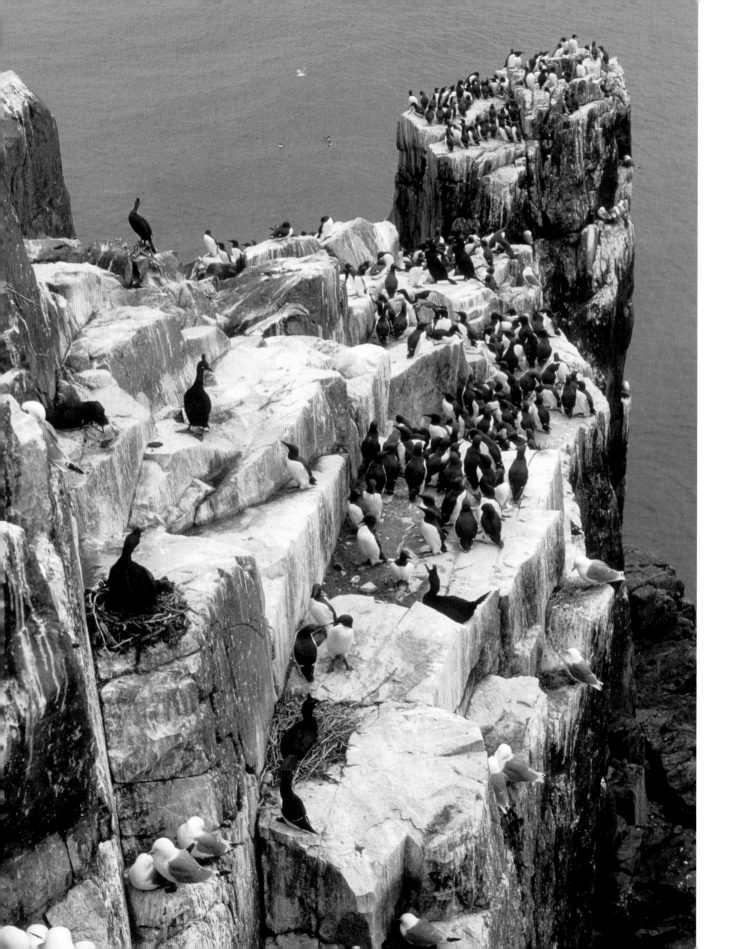

the wonders of nature. It and its basis – genes, many still waiting to be analyzed – have massive and complex implications for our farms and food production, for the raw materials we use in factories, commerce and industries, and for our own human health and the conquering of diseases that afflict so many people.

Undersea work

When we think of biodiversity, probably one of the last images that comes to mind is the carcass of a great whale rotting away silently on the dark, deep sea floor. But recent work involving Natural History Museum staff yields an absorbing insight into what happens to these great mammals when they die. This work has many ramifications, from our understanding of the ocean's biodiversity, to the evolution of life in extreme environments and even how ecosystems respond to pollution events, such as oil spills.

Studies on 'whale falls' in the deep sea began in the 1980s using deep-submergence vehicles first developed by the US Navy. Deep-submergence vehicles or DSVs, also called deep submersibles, are capable of diving much further than the near-surface submersibles which take tourists on trips around coral reefs and marine parks, and deeper even than many military submarines. The most famous is DSV *Alvin*, operated by Woods Hole Oceanographic Institute in Massachusetts, USA. *Alvin*, with its three-person crew, has been diving since 1964. It can descend to 4,500 metres and stay below for almost nine hours.

With its powerful lights and robotic grabber–manipulator arms, *Alvin* has achieved a long line of successes. In 1986, in the northwest Atlantic Ocean it explored the wreck of the great liner RMS *Titanic*, which had sunk 74 years earlier. Before this, in 1977, *Alvin* allowed scientists to study the first 'black smokers' discovered, near the Galapagos Islands in the Pacific Ocean. These are deep-sea hydrothermal vents where superheated water, very rich in minerals, blasts up through cracks in the sea floor. The minerals form solid particles or precipitates as they meet the cold sea-bed water, creating dark rising clouds that look like smoking chimneys. These hydrothermal vents support some of the strangest life forms seen on Earth. They have made scientists revise many of their ideas about how organisms adapt to extreme environments, and even how life is likely to have begun on our planet.

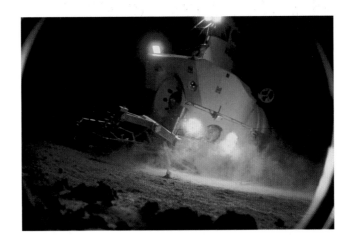

OPPOSITE: Sea cliffs seem either bare, windswept and spray-drenched – or alive with noisy birds such as these common guillemots, shags and fulmars on the Farne Islands, Northumberland, UK. Biodiversity varies greatly with the seasons as well as place.

BELOW: Even after several refits, and an unplanned sinking into 1,500 metres of water, Alvin the deep-sea research vessel continues to make fantastic discoveries. By 2005 all of its parts and components had been replaced, so nothing is left of the original craft except for the name.

BELOW: Crabs are the sea's champion scavengers. Here the species *Paralomis multispina* picks away at the rib bone of a blue or fin whale in the Santa Catalina Basin of the northeast Pacific Ocean.

OPPOSITE: Black smoker hydrothermal vents belch superhot water loaded with precipitating chemicals from the sea bed. The water does not boil due to the immense pressure at depth.

Whale-falls

Today, the majority of dives to the sea floor are made with remotely operated vehicles, or ROVs. These are un-crewed robot submersibles on the end of a long line or tether that carries their electrical power and communications. ROVs are steered by an operator above on the mother ship, who watches the views sent back by its cameras, and manipulates levers to work the propellers, thrusters and rudders. It is rather like flying a helicopter by remote control in the darkness. ROVs can dive even deeper, for longer, than DSVs. They are invaluable in all kinds of deep-sea work, from surveying marine life to looking for mineral resources and checking undersea cables and pipelines.

In 1987, another first for *Alvin*, although this time by chance, was the discovery about 2,000 metres down of a great whale carcass, a blue or fin whale on the sea bed off southern California. Scientists were amazed to see that, even at great depth, it was covered in life. All manner of both familiar and new creatures were active on it, while the surrounding sea floor was relatively bare and quiet. Like a deep-sea hydrothermal vent, the whale-fall was a hotspot of biodiversity and abundance amidst a much less active region. On land, we might imagine the equivalent as an oasis in a desert. Or for land life generally, a comparison could be an island in a vast ocean. Assuming that whales die and sink fairly randomly, and using information about their populations, lifespans and movements, it is estimated that whale-falls are quite common on the sea floor, spaced as little as five to ten kilometres apart along whale migration corridors. Furthermore, these giant carcasses are thought to take over 100 years to disintegrate.

Bone-eaters

Since these early discoveries, several whale-falls have been found by chance. But scientists have also been able to conduct controlled experiments by sinking carcasses or packages of bones.

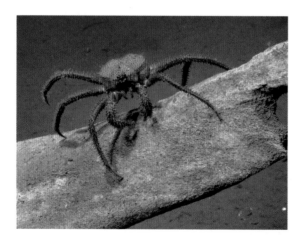

A whale, dolphin or porpoise that has stranded on the shore and died can be towed out to a chosen location and sunk. Scientists can then use DSVs, ROVs and remote cameras to keep an eye on its fate.

The results show that the flesh first is consumed by scavenging crabs, shrimps, worms, hagfish and even deep-water sharks such as the massive six-metre Greenland or sleeper shark. Next a diverse range of creatures move in. Among them are the 'bone-eating worms', species in the

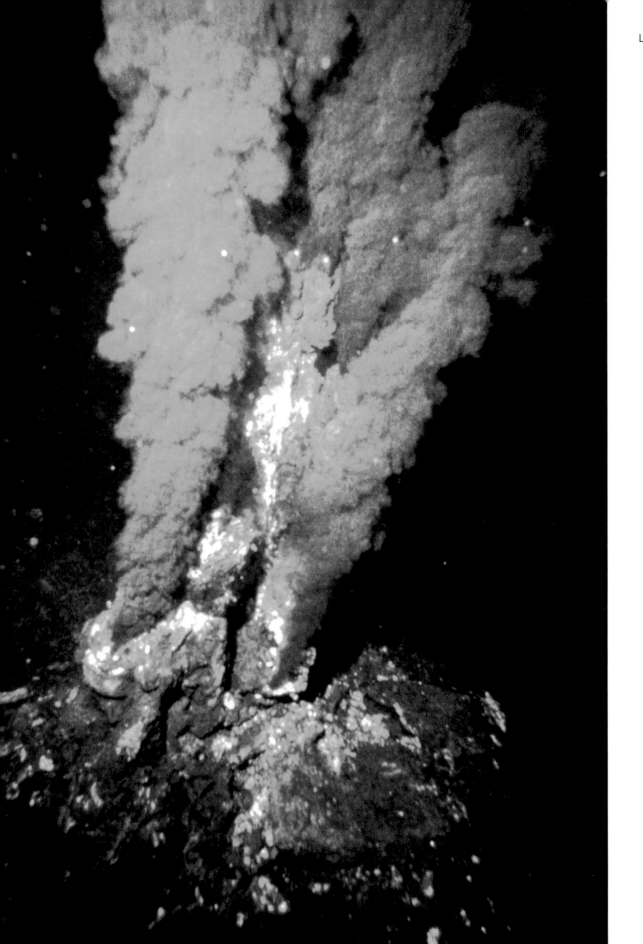

BONE-EATER WORMS

AT FIRST SIGHT A BONE-EATER LOOKS NOTHING LIKE A WORM. The exposed part projecting from the bones is like a red or orange flower housed in a thin mucus tube. This 'flower' grows root-like threads down into the bone to consume the oils and fats (lipids) and bone tissue within them. These substances, in turn, become food for thousands of bacterial microbes living within the worm's tissues. The microbes break down the chemicals in the whale bone to extract energy and provide nutrients. The worm–bacteria relationship is an example of what biologists call symbiosis – two very different life forms that live in close association and benefit each other. The worm gets energy and nutrition from the microbes as its pay-off, while the bacteria have somewhere comfortable and sheltered to live, rather than taking their chances in the open water.

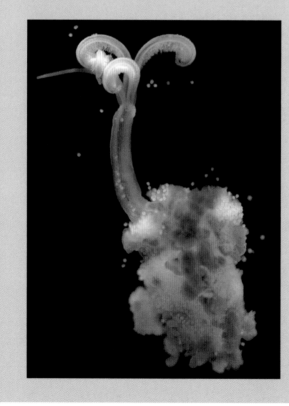

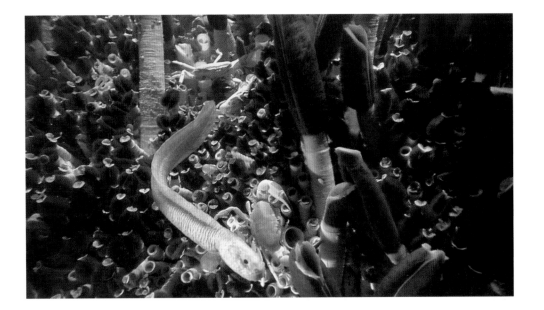

genus *Osedax*. These were first identified in 2002 on bones recovered from a whale-fall almost 3,000 metres down at Monterey Canyon, in Monterey Bay on the coast of California.

Bone-eating worms are relatively new to science and continue to amaze us. At first their bizarre structure puzzled experts until DNA analysis showed that they are true worms, or annelids. This means that they are related to earthworms and, more closely, to the marine worms known as polychaetes, or bristle-worms. Bone-eaters look different to other polychaetes as they have no mouth or gut and they can absorb the nutrients processed by their 'friendly' bacteria. The frilly, flowery and slimy exposed parts are gills to provide oxygen to these bacterial farms in their roots. The worms have evolved a unique reproductive strategy, with tiny 'dwarf' males sitting on the sides of the much larger females, waiting to fertilize eggs as they are released into the water.

In 2005, in the relatively shallow waters of a Swedish fjord, a new type of bone-eater was discovered by Museum staff. It was given the scientific name *Osedax mucofloris*, literally the 'bone-eating snot-flower worm'. This creature opened up a new area of scientific research on whale-falls as it was found in less than 150 metres of water, rather than thousands of metres down like its close relatives. As work continues, scientists are sure that the number of bone-eating worms will increase dramatically.

Island-hopping

Bone-eating worms, sometimes called 'zombie worms', gain their energy from their bacterial partners, who obtain it from the substances in whale bones. This same type of partnership between bacteria and host worm is found in the giant two-metre-long tube worms first discovered on hydrothermal vents in 1977. However, in bone-eating worms the ultimate source of food is the bone and fats – in hydrothermal vent worms it is the chemicals that leach from the volcanic chimneys. Symbiosis between bacteria and hosts is also found in animals that live in cold seeps – areas of the sea floor where oil and other hydrocarbons are seeping from the sediments below.

Whale-falls, hot vents and cold seeps have many parallels. They are high-diversity, food-rich 'islands' surrounded by vast tracts of food-poor ocean floor. It is thought that some species present on vents, seeps and whale-falls may be able to hop between these habitats, using them as stepping stones for dispersal across the huge ocean floor. Abundant whale-falls on the sea floor may aid this dispersal process and answer questions as to how the same type of animals may be found on one side of the Pacific Ocean as the other. As Charles Darwin recognized, island ecosystems are crucial to the evolution of new forms of life.

Wider interest

Natural History Museum scientists and their collaborators have sunk several whale-fall experiments, including a five-tonne minke whale in 120 metres of water in 2003. It is regularly visited to monitor its progress. Recently a stranded porpoise was sent down too, 16 metres under the surface, set up with its own webcam. Waterproof cameras were attached to a tripod near the fall carcass, sending their images via long wires to the nearby shore, where computers and other technology record the pictures and broadcast them on the internet.

More new species of worms discovered at whale-falls are being given fanciful names such as the carpetworm, candyfloss worm and snowboarding worm, all of them apparently specially evolved to live on this unique habitat. And it's not just marine biologists who are interested in these peculiar, new-found goings-on. Palaeontologists like to study how the whale bones go through stages of decay as they are eaten, to make comparisons with the fossil whale remains

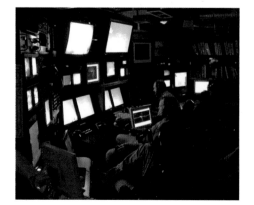

they dig up from millions of years ago. The study of how living things decay and rot, and then perhaps form fossils, is known as taphonomy. It can be described as the passage of plants, animals and other life forms from the biosphere to the lithosphere (the world of rocks). Taphonomy aims to understand how and why only certain organisms become fossilized, how certain kinds of fossil assemblages come about, and therefore why the fossil record is not simply random, but biased or skewed in various ways. By knowing more detail about death, decomposition and

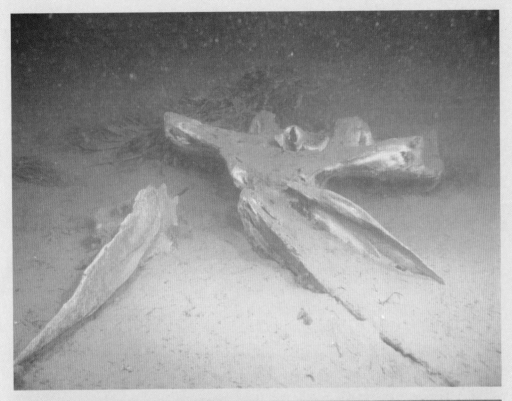

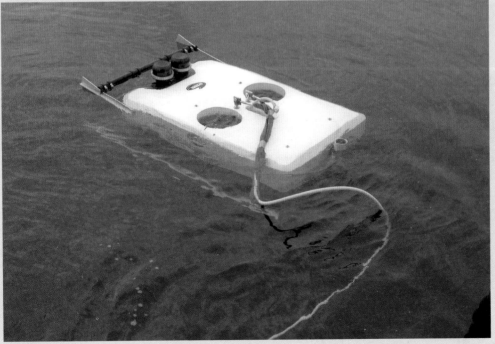

OPPOSITE: In the mother-ship control room for a remote submersible, or ROV, experts watch progress via cameras and monitor the condition of the ROV and its surroundings, from water pressure to emergency battery charge.

LEFT: After five years on the sea bed, at a depth of 120 metres in a Swedish fjord, a minke whale is still being reduced to bones, bits and pieces. On land, an equivalent animal such as a hippo would probably be long gone.

BELOW LEFT: ROVs, Remotely-Operated Vehicles, are the workhorses of deep-sea research. The long cable or tether brings electricity for the propeller motors, cameras, sensors, grabber arms and other equipment.

fossil formation, we can work back to learn more about those long-gone organisms when they were alive.

Studying new strange species from the ocean floor can inform us not just about specific questions such as what happens when a whale dies, but about general problems in all of biology. How does life evolve in extreme environments? Why are there so many kinds of species? What might life look like on other planets? The unusual chemicals that some of these animals produce may even one day have industrial or medical applications. Documenting and understanding biodiversity is key to these discoveries.

Bottlenecks

As more data come in about bone-eating worms and other whale-munching life, there's an intriguing line of background research to follow. The whaling industries of the nineteenth and twentieth centuries devastated whale populations in all oceans. Some great whale species suffered more than a 90 per cent fall in numbers. The International Whaling Commission was established in 1946 to monitor trends in whale fisheries, and in 1986 it announced a worldwide moratorium on mass whaling.

The drastic fall in great whale numbers means that some species are going through what are called population bottlenecks. A risk here is reduced genetic diversity and dangers associated with interbreeding, increased mutations and a smaller gene pool. Intriguingly, the same bottlenecks may also affect species such as the bone-eating worms which feed exclusively on whale carcasses. Museum scientists are studying the DNA sequences in these worms to look for bottleneck effects. The worms themselves may be useful indicators of the degree of whaling in the recent past.

Seaweed survey

It is often said that we know more about the surfaces of the Moon and Mars than we do about the deep seas on our own planet. It's not just the deep, either. There are many discoveries waiting to be made along our own shores and shallows in the UK. A recent initiative from the Natural History Museum is the Big Seaweed Search, where people at the coast help to monitor the effects of climate change and invasive species among Britain's seaweeds.

Seaweeds are relatively simple plant-like organisms from seashores and shallows throughout the world. They have no flowers or seeds, and no proper roots or leaves either. Some anchor themselves by root-like structures known as holdfasts, and others have broad leaf-like parts called laminae. But these do not have the tiny tube-like vessels that carry around water and nutrients, as are found inside more

LEFT & BELOW:
The unusual brown seaweed, *Chorda filum*, reaches eight metres in length. The beautifully branching red seaweed, *Scinaia forcellata*, occurs in the west and south of Britain, and along both sides of the Channel. Green lavers of the genus *Ulva* are edible and also known as sea lettuces or aonori.

147

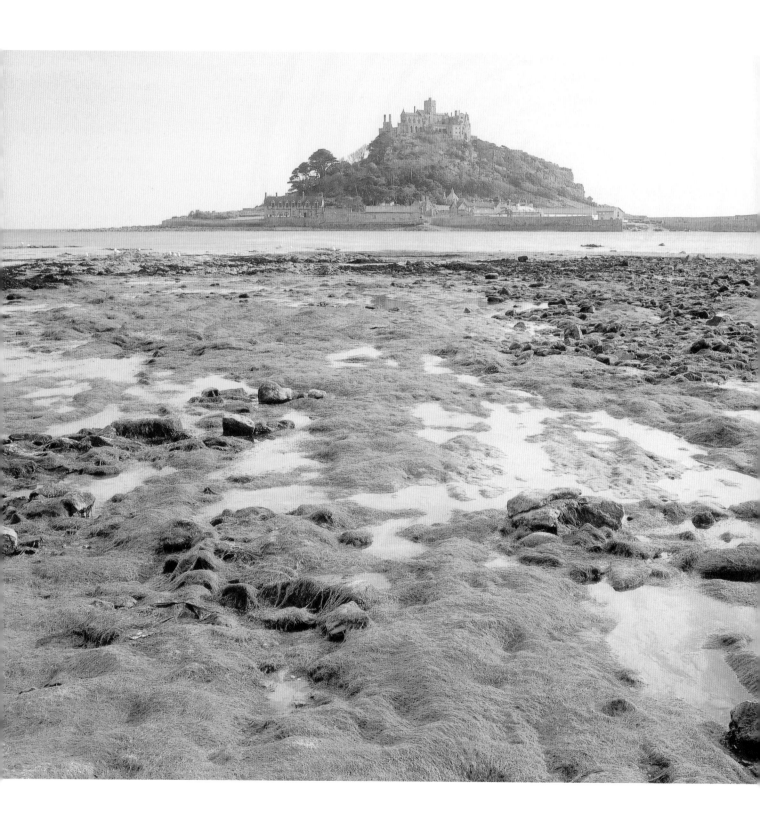

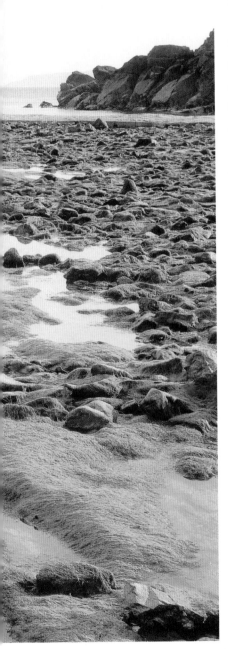

complex plants. The name seaweed is a relatively loose term for several different groups known as algae. Most seaweeds belong to the red, brown or green algae groups. The familiar wracks are green, kelps and oarweeds are brown, and carrageen (Irish moss) is a red type.

There are an amazing 650 seaweed species around the UK. They are the primary food in their habitats, as they are organisms at the base of the food chains. They also offer shelter and safety to many shore creatures, from fish and crabs to sea-snails and shellfish. They help to dampen down wave energy and protect coastlines. They are also collected for many reasons, including foods such as laver bread. In sushi dishes, the wrapping around the rice is called nori and is made from *Porphyra* red seaweeds. Agar and other seaweed extracts are used for an enormous range of processes – making paper, shampoos, toothpastes, cosmetics and medicines, and even as an ingredient in ice-cream.

Under threat

However, the biodiversity of UK seaweeds is under threat in several ways. Polluting chemicals from coastal outfalls and rivers wash into the sea and along the shore. Invasive species from faraway regions have arrived over the years. And climate change is already having an effect. Scientists need more information to work out what is happening and why. The Big Seaweed Search is one of many outreach Museum–public partnerships where people can gather information from nature, and contribute to the scientific databases for future reference.

The aim of the search is to map the distribution of twelve key kinds of seaweeds found around the UK and track how these distributions change through time. For example, climate change has an effect on water conditions and sea levels, which may affect seaweeds as well as other marine life. Non-native species are also causing trouble. For example, wireweed or sargassum weed, *Sargassum muticum*, was first recorded in the UK in the early

LEFT: The UK's rocky shores, especially the south and west with their warmer currents, are some of the world's most diverse for the marine algae we know as seaweeds. Once such place is St Michael's Mount, Cornwall.

149

1970s, along the Isle of Wight and in Southampton Water. Quite how it got there from its native Japan and China is unclear. It could have arrived with other marine life. One possible route is the oysters brought from Japan, or from British Columbia across the Pacific, to France for commercial growing, and then bits of weed drifted across the Channel. Or this seaweed may have travelled as tiny spores or fragments stuck to ship hulls or in their ballast tank water. As a pest, wireweed is now found around much of England and it's still spreading. By 2008, it had reached as far north as the Isle of Skye in Scotland, which is much farther and sooner than previously predicted. Wireweed can grow so thickly that it blocks out light and stops native seaweeds growing, with knock-on effects to other plants and animals. It also clogs water intakes and fish-farming equipment and tangles boat propellers.

Bio-Blitz!

The Big Seaweed Search includes identification guides for the main species found around the UK. With help from the public, Museum specialists can begin to map changes in seaweed biodiversity and work out what is happening around our shores. The search launch, as an ongoing nationwide project, coincided with a rather different type of Natural History Museum anyone-can-help survey. This was the Wembury Bio-Blitz at Wembury Bay in Devon, southwest England. It is part of a series of 24-hour full-on surveys of all the plants and animals in one limited site. There are two aims:

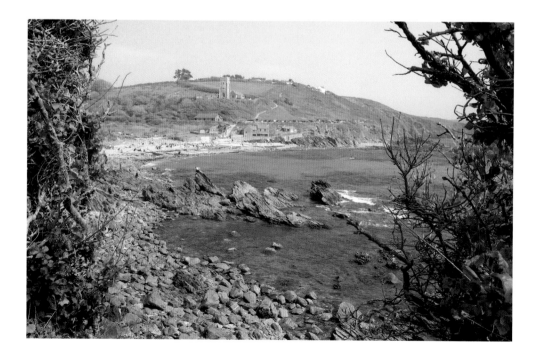

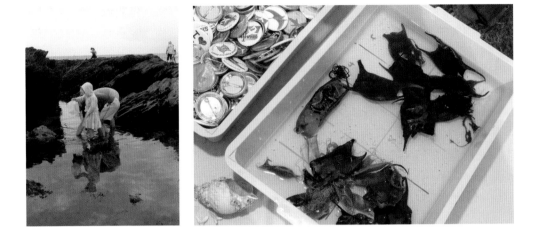

OPPOSITE: Wembury Bay, in Devon, was bio-blitzed in August 2009. For 24 hours non-stop, professional scientists and eager volunteers surveyed and identified almost every living thing.

LEFT: As part of the Wembury Bio-Blitz, volunteers of all ages were encouraged to get active with nature and see what they could find. These empty egg cases of fish such as skates and rays, popularly known as mermaid's purses, are being sorted for counting and closer identification.

to raise public awareness of topics such as biodiversity and environmental care, and to gather data against which future changes can be measured. Wembury is a nationally important nature conservation area with habitats that include sub-tidal waters, rocky shore, beach, coastal cliffs, wet and dry meadows, scrub and a freshwater stream. Apart from the Museum, other organizations were involved, including the Marine Biological Association and the Devon Wildlife Trust.

A Bio-Blitz is basically an intensive search for as many species of plants and animals as can be found in just 24 hours. About 100 scientists and 1,000 volunteers took part in the Wembury event, during the 24 hours from midday on Friday until midday Saturday. More than 900 species were detected, including the beautiful and delicate autumn lady's tresses. This orchid is known from well-drained grasslands but it also appears on cliffs and sand dunes, and is tolerant of some salt spray. Like many other flowers, it has suffered greatly from modern agriculture, such as ploughing grasslands and intensive grazing, as well as our desire to have neatly mowed lawns, rather than leave bits of rough, long grass as havens for wildlife.

The last time anyone looked this closely at the Wembury shores was back in 1957. The idea is to compare Bio-Blitz's intensive biological inventory of all the species here today with those records from 50 years ago. And the same event, at the same time, year after year, should provide linear records that show trends in how our coasts are being altered, gains and losses in biodiversity, invading new species, climate change and many other factors.

Herbaria

Some of the Wembury and Seaweed Search finds will doubtless end up in the Museum's plant collections. The usual way to preserve our green friends is to press them, sandwich the samples between sheets of specialist paper, apply gentle pressure and heat to help them, and wait. If whole

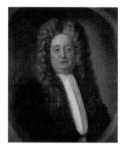

plants are small enough they can be included intact. Bigger species are usually dismembered and then selected representatives of the main parts are placed on the page – stems, leaves, buds, flowers and fruits. Very damp, moisture-filled specimens need changes of paper to soak away the water, so that they dry out nice and flat before moulds and other destroyers gain a hold. The compressed and fairly brittle, fragile, almost two-dimensional results are then placed into more permanent long-term storage, preferably as stacks of sheets in dry, dark drawers. In the past the specimens might be incorporated into massive leather-bound volumes, just like books. Admirers would leaf through the pages and comment on the species therein. But many viewings gradually loosen and crack the specimens, so that fragments of leaves and petals fall out.

The Sloane Herbarium

A herbarium is a collection of preserved plants, or the building where they are kept. It is a staple reference source for botanists or plant biologists involved in their scientific study. A good herbarium is a record of plant diversity from a particular time and place, all specimens labelled with the usual information about where and when collected, notes on weather and conditions, and other relevant details. The herbarium includes not just herbs as we understand them today, used to flavour foods or for medicinal cures. It comprises any species from the Kingdom Plantae, ranging from mosses and ferns to grasses, conifers and the most complex orchids and other flowers.

Sir Hans Sloane's specimens are the oldest in the Natural History Museum's botany collection, comprising both his personal collections and those he purchased from his contemporaries. They are preserved in the traditional large folio-bound volumes. As mentioned on earlier pages, Sloane (1660–1753) was a physician and businessman as well as a most determined collector. His donations formed the basis of the British Museum and worked their way through to the Natural History Museum when it moved to South Kensington in the 1880s. Sloane was exceptionally well connected. Among his acquaintances were Thomas Sydenham, top dog in British medicine at the time and known as the English Hippocrates, and John Ray, dubbed 'father of English natural history' and author of the epic *Historia Plantarum*.

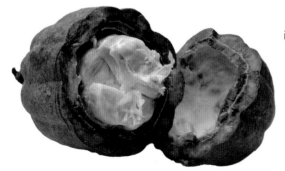

Today, Sloane's collections are important as historical items as well as scientific ones. They provide a snapshot of what existed where several centuries ago, often reflecting habitats and localities that have changed radically. They come from many parts of the world and define a time when natural historians in Britain began to appreciate the enormous biodiversity of plants in faraway places. Sloane's collections include possibly the

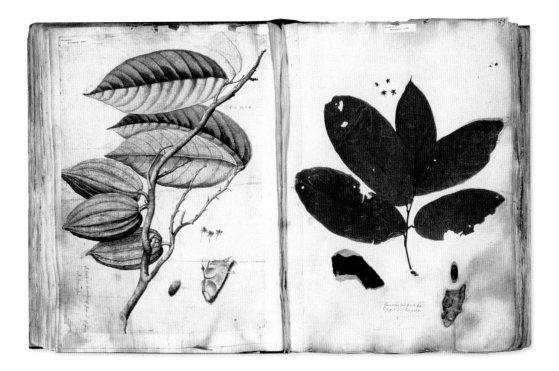

OPPOSITE: Hans Sloane bequeathed his collections and library to the nation in 1753 for the sum of £20,000, which was way below its market value. They formed the basis of the British Museum, part of which later became the Natural History Museum.

OPPOSITE BELOW: Delicious, satisfying and solace-giving, a cacao bean is the source of chocolate (after fermentation), cocoa powder (non-fatty parts) and cocoa butter (the fatty components).

LEFT: Hans Sloane's *Theobroma cacao* specimens from Jamaica are held in the Natural History Museum's Herbarium. Such valuable items are checked regularly and used for study, but with a strictly limited amount of handling.

first example of *Theobroma cacao* to reach Britain. This tropical tree grows seed pods that contain the key ingredient to one of the most tasty and comforting of all foodstuffs, chocolate. Sloane visited Jamaica in 1687 as physician to the Duke of Albermarle and in little more than a year he collected more than 800 species of plants new to science. He tried the local cacao beverage, which was water-based, and considered it 'nauseous and hard of digestion'. However, he devised a way of mixing it with milk and sugar to make what we now call hot chocolate or drinking chocolate. The recipe was marketed by London merchants under the name Sir Hans Sloane's Milk Chocolate and became the fashionable cure, recommended by physicians for any and all kinds of ailments.

Adding to the herbarium

Sloane acquired several sets of herbaria and associated material from other naturalist-collectors and added them to his own. One was amassed by German physician Engelbert Kaempfer during his wanderings across Eastern Europe and as far as Japan. Kaempfer provided Europeans with an early description of the maidenhair or ginkgo tree, *Ginkgo biloba*, which was known in the west only from dinosaur-age fossils and so presumed to be extinct. Another collection was from Englishman James Cunningham, who was the first science-based European plant-hunter to visit China. In 1701, he discovered the Chinese cypress or fir named after him, *Cunninghamia lanceolata*.

Further specimens came from English naturalist Mark Catesby, who produced the first book on the flora and fauna of North America, *The natural history of Carolina, Florida and the Bahama*

RIGHT: At the Natural History Museum, packages of pressed plants flown back from Panama are opened and checked by botanist Alex Munro before they enter the next phase of their preservation and study.

OPPOSITE: Out in the wild, improvization is key. Here in the Costa Rican part of La Amistad International Park, plant specimens are being pressed, as part of their preservation, in a shelter against the wall of an abandoned hut.

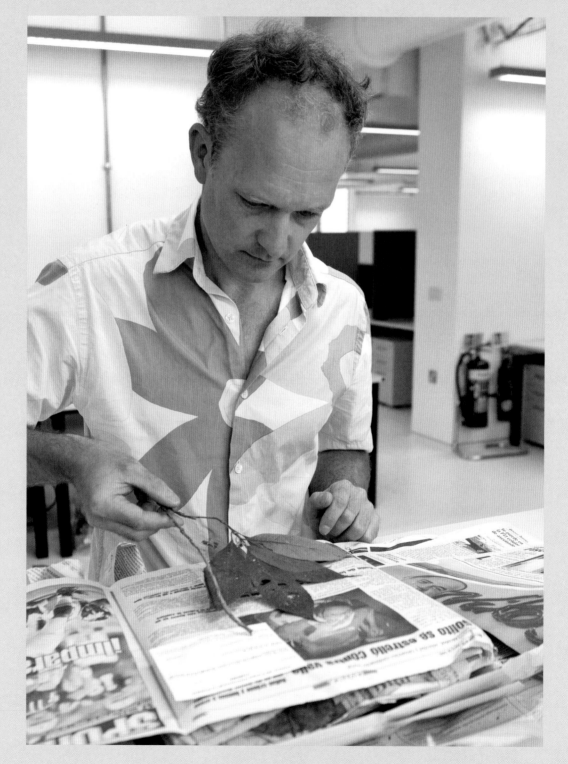

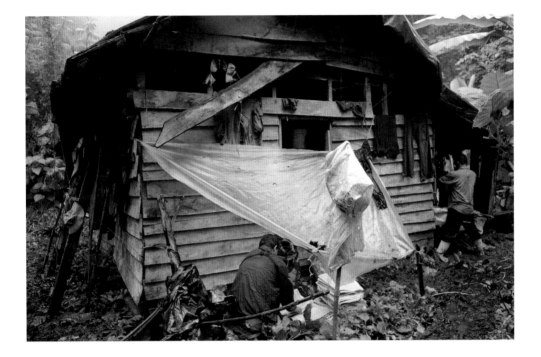

Island (1732–43). Yet more American specimens came into Sloane's collection from Pennsylvanian John Bartram, another father, this time of American botany.

Biodiversity hotspots

The Natural History Museum continues to send exploring and collecting expeditions to the Americas and around the world. One especially magnificent location visited recently is Central America, including Panama. This region, Mesoamerica, is classed as the world's third largest biodiversity hotspot according to Conservation International criteria.

To qualify as a biodiversity hotspot, a region must have a certain number or percentage of the world's plant species, and these should be endemic – occurring uniquely in the region, that is, only there and nowhere else. A wide range of plants, in turn, supports a broad assortment of animals that feed on them or each other. A second hotspot criterion is that the region should have lost a particular percentage, usually at least 70 per cent, of the original habitat that existed before humans started to interfere. The Mesoamerica region has now shrunk from its original area of 1.13 million square kilometres to 225,000 square kilometres, mainly as a result of logging the tropical forests for timber and general land clearance for agriculture. The number of endemic plant species here is more than 2,900. Of the endemic animals, about 30 mammal species are highly threatened, along with 30 birds and more than 230 amphibians, such as tiny rainforest poison dart frogs.

The notion of biodiversity hotspots helps to focus the attention of the public, and scientists, on places where life is incredibly rich in terms of species numbers, and where there has been massive loss of wild habitat that must be curbed and reversed. Globally some 35 hotspots are identified, with more planned to expand the list. Together they make up about one-fiftieth of the world's land surface. Yet they are home to almost one-half of all known plant species and about one-third of land-dwelling vertebrates (mammals, birds, reptiles, amphibians, fish).

Gazing at the ceiling

When the Natural History Museum was being built in the 1870s and 1880s, the term biodiversity hotspot was unknown. But exotic locations were appreciated as places exceedingly rich in wildlife, although perhaps from a different perspective. This is reflected in some of the Museum's exhibits that are rarely studied or even glanced at in passing, yet are enormous in size and always present for everyone to see. These are the paintings and other decorations on the ceilings, especially in the cavernous, cathedral-like Central Hall and the adjacent North Hall.

There are very few records of who painted the original ceiling pictures, or exactly when, or the precise reasons why the particular species were depicted. In recent times much thought has gone into working out the relationships of the groupings, with much more to do. The pictures show plants from around the world, often labelled with their scientific (not common) names in Latinate script. Especially prominent are plants of economic importance.

At the time the Museum's ceilings were decorated, collecting and identifying plant specimens was an important aim. So was investigating each new species for potential use as a food crop, as a producer of something useful to commerce or industry, or for some other practical usage. Newly explored lands, especially those of the British Empire, were seen as providers of materials that would make Britain even greater and increase its power around the world.

Cacao, the chocolate plant, as mentioned above, is

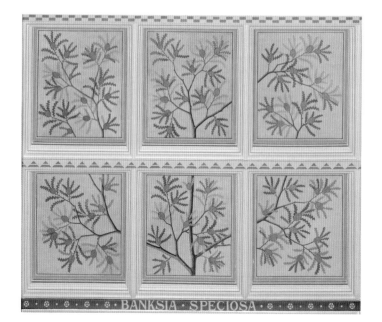

BANKSIA · SPECIOSA

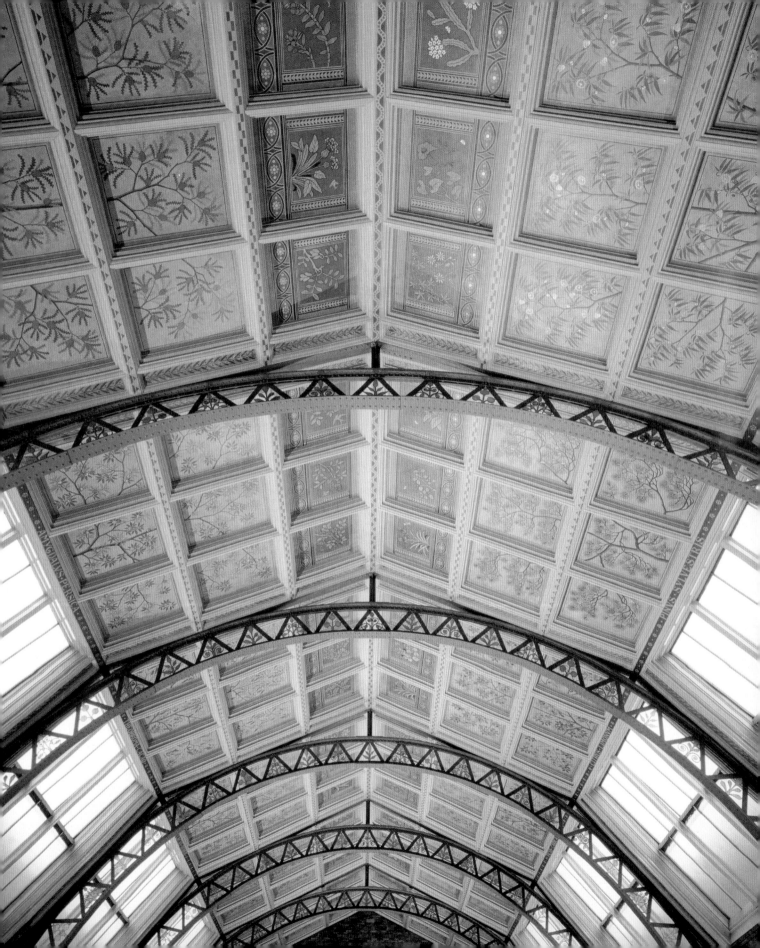

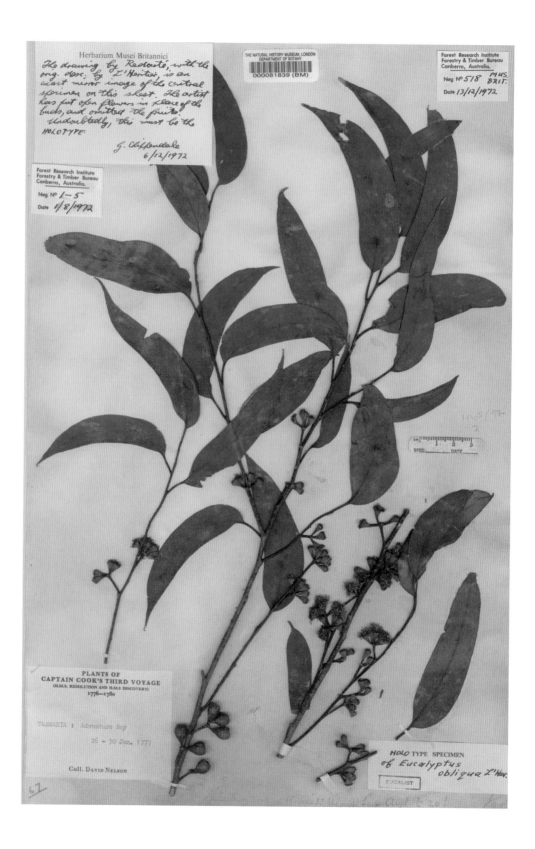

there on the ceiling. So is the species known as showy banksia, *Banksia speciosa*, collected from southern Australia. However, these two seem unusual and out of place, set as they are among much better-known fruits, British trees, and plants familiar to Victorians as mentioned since antiquity. It may be that including these two species was intended to honour two great Museum benefactors, namely Hans Sloane, as mentioned above, and Joseph Banks.

As far as Australia

Sir Joseph Banks (1743–1820) was an independently wealthy naturalist specializing in plants. He was busy, clever and travelled widely, including with James Cook on the latter's first major round-the-world voyage in HMS *Endeavour*, from 1768 to 1771. When the ship anchored in a shallow bay on the east coast of the then-mysterious Terra Australis, Banks had a wonderful time gathering all kinds of marvellous new plants. So Cook decided to name the place we now know as Botany Bay, Australia.

Many kinds of plants are named in honour of Banks, especially the genus *Banksia*. This consists of more than 160 species from Australia, mostly shrubs and trees, some with big, bright blooms. Many have become favourites in parks and gardens. Banks also brought back the first specimens to reach Europe of mimosa, acacia and eucalyptus and was a major figure in establishing the Royal Botanic Gardens, Kew.

As with Sloane, Banks's huge plant collections, including those from the *Endeavour*, were donated to the British Museum and then transferred with the other herbaria to South Kensington. Banks's material also comprises specimens he bought from other collectors, and those gathered by expeditions such as Robert Brown's to Australia and Francis Masson's to South Africa. The Banks herbarium still resides at the Natural History Museum, as a wonderful scientific resource and as a reminder of the stunning biodiversity encountered by early European trips to Australia, South Africa and other far-off lands.

The world's worst journey?

Collectors such as Banks, Brown and Masson endured some harsh conditions on their long voyages, including heatwaves, digestive troubles and plagues of biting insects. However, they mostly visited warm climes, where biodiversity is greatest. At the other end of the temperature scale is Antarctica. Three emperor penguin eggs in the Natural History Museum's collection come from one of the most terrible and tragic of all visits to the great southern continent. This was Captain Robert Falcon Scott's fateful 1910–1913 Antarctic Terra Nova Expedition.

OPPOSITE: This is the Museum's holotype specimen (the originally described one that defines the species) of Australian oak, *Eucalyptus obliqua*. Collected in 1777, it is the first named in the genus *Eucalyptus*.

BELOW: A thin section or slice through the penguin embryo (*see* page 160). It was studied to test the theory that birds evolved from reptiles.

RIGHT: The three eggs collected on 20 July 1911 by Edward Wilson on the Terra Nova expedition are still held in the Natural History Museum's collection. After Wilson died on the tragic Scott South Pole trek, others took up the work and prepared two embryos as slides for microscopic study.

OPPOSITE: This original plate from Audubon's magnificent *The Birds of America* depicts the greater flamingo, *Phoenicopterus ruber*. The great work was engraved, printed and hand-coloured by R Havell (& Son), London.

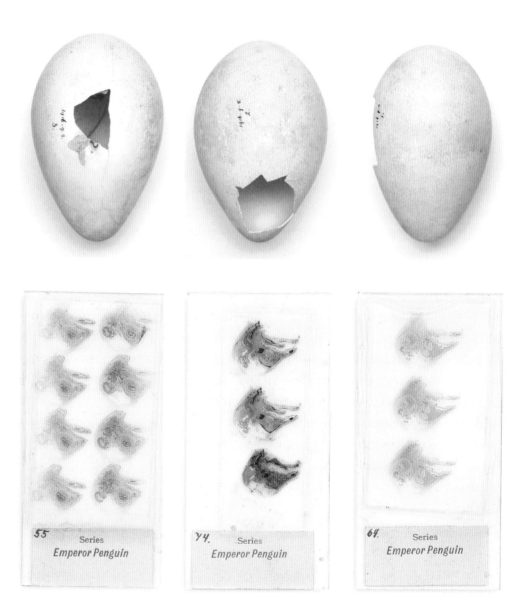

The breeding colonies that these eggs came from were already known from Scott's first voyage to Antarctica on RRS *Discovery* in 1901–04. That expedition's zoologist, physician and natural history artist, Edward Wilson, decided to come back one day to view the breeding colonies and study the birds and their eggs more closely. And he did, on the *Terra Nova*. With two close friends, in mid-winter he left the expedition's main camp to look for the colonies. It was a 225-kilometre return trip in the worst of conditions. The men pulled their own sledges through the pitch dark in flesh-freezing winds, with deep drifts and huge ice ridges blocking their way. After several weeks they arrived at the Cape Crozier emperor breeding area and collected the eggs. The whole journey took five weeks, with average temperatures below minus 40°C.

Finally they arrived back with the precious eggs, but there was no happy ending. Wilson and his friend Henry Robertson Bowers, who had been on the penguin trip, were chosen to go with Scott on his final march. This was the expedition that reached the South Pole just five weeks after Roald Amundsen, and they perished on its return.

Hardship and endurance

Wilson's other egg-collecting colleague, Apsley Cherry-Gerrard, personally delivered the three eggs and their embryos to the Natural History Museum when he finally made it back to England. Two of the three embryos were prepared as hundreds of microscope slides, and one was kept preserved in alcohol. Alas, by the time the final report was published, the theory that suggested the embryos could prove a link between birds and their reptilian ancestors had largely been dismissed. The emperor penguin's own amazing feats have since become famous through television documentaries and films such as *March of the Penguins* (2005). These birds trek more than 100 kilometres from the spreading edge of the Antarctic ice-cap to their age-old breeding grounds. The female produces her egg and returns to the sea. Then the male balances the egg on his feet in temperatures of minus 60°C and 300-kilometre-per-hour winds, for up to two months, before she returns.

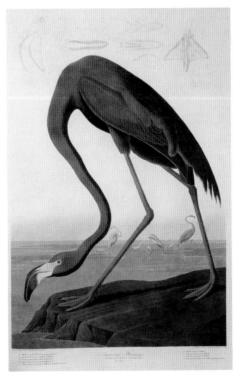

Back in the shelter of the Museum, these three emperor penguin eggs remind us of the hardship and endurance of explorers and scientists who, over the years, have added so many fantastic specimens to museum collections around the world.

The Birds of America

Another bird-related item at the Museum revolutionized the way people watch, study and appreciate our feathered friends. These are the two copies of the book *The Birds of America*, published 1827–38. It was the work of John James Audubon (1785–1851). Born in Haiti and raised in France, he was one of the greatest of all explorer-naturalist-artists. In 1803, John James' father sent him from France to North America so that he would not become a conscript in the Napoleonic Wars. Here the young man fostered his

ICONS OF EXTINCTION

ONE OF THE BIRDS THAT AUDUBON RECORDED was the now-extinct passenger pigeon, *Ectopistes migratorius*. Its story is one of the most extraordinary in the lengthening annals of now-gone species. When Europeans arrived in North America, these pigeons were so numerous that their flocks darkened the skies and took days to fly past. Some estimates of their population go as high as 5,000 million. Yet by the late 1800s they were as rare as hen's teeth. The last survivor of the entire species was poor Martha, named after the wife of first US President George Washington. She (the pigeon) died in Cincinnati Zoo in 1914.

The causes of the passenger pigeon's decline were numerous and intertwined. They included habitat loss and fragmentation, land clearance and exploitation for meat. A similar end for an entire species, although altogether less numerous, involved that most iconic of all creatures – the dodo, *Raphus cucullatus*.

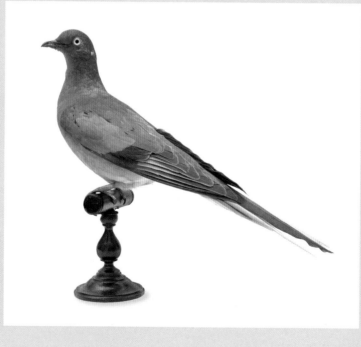

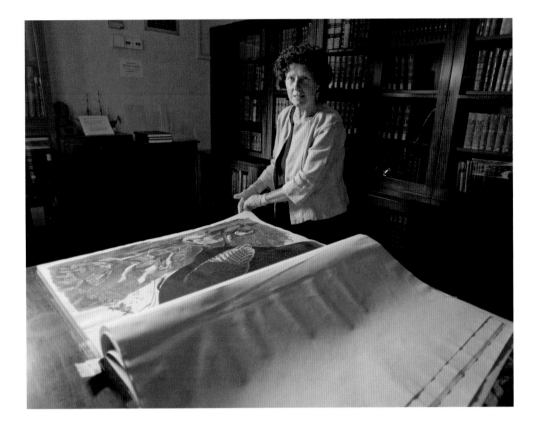

LEFT: Pictured here with Collection Development Manager Judith Magee is one volume of the Museum's *The Birds of America*. Each set has four volumes and the Museum holds two complete sets. There are only 119 complete sets still known to be in existence, each one probably worth over five million pounds.

childhood passions for walking in the country and wondering at all kinds of wildlife, especially birds. He set up his own museum and also had to hunt and fish to feed his family, since business at their general store was often sluggish. He became practised in the ways of the wild and admired native Americans for their expertise. He had ups and downs too. At one time he was rich, with property and booming business interests, then a few years later he was a jailed bankrupt.

By 1820 Audubon decided to follow his first passion. He vowed to record images of every kind of bird in North America. So he roamed the lands for more than 20 years, observing and collecting and painting in every habitat. He explored from the icy north to the Gulf of Mexico, carefully gathering material and making notes.

Audubon's book, with its 435 hand-coloured plates, soon gained its lasting reputation as one of the world's greatest and most beautiful nature works. At the time, many natural history illustrators portrayed birds in stiff, unnatural positions, partly because they worked from skins and unsympathetically mounted specimens. Audubon had his wealth of field observations to call upon. His skills lay in combining scientific accuracy with living vibrancy, capturing his subjects in natural active poses that reflected their habits and behaviour.

RIGHT: This illustration of a group of dodos depicts its ground-nesting habit, with the pale chick slightly to the right of centre being fed by its parent. Ground nesting made the birds 'sitting ducks' for introduced predators on Mauritius.

OPPOSITE: The dodo's traditionally rotund physique has long been the source of amusement. However, new discoveries of preserved remains suggest that, in life, it was somewhat slimmer, even svelte.

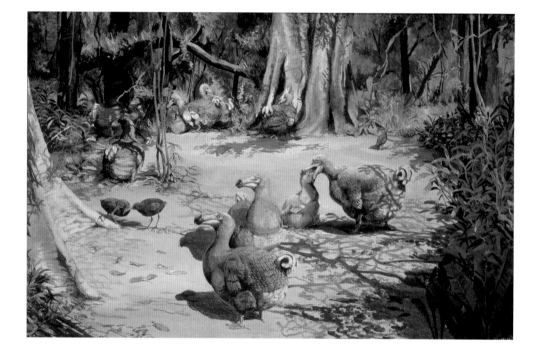

Dead as

A relative of the pigeon, the dodo was once found in plentiful numbers on the island of Mauritius in the Indian Ocean. With no large predators there, and plenty of seeds, fruits and other plant food on the ground, it had gradually lost the ability to fly. But the dodo's quiet world was turned upside down when sailors began to call in at the islands and then settlers arrived. There were introduced species – including monkeys, pigs and rats – which ate the eggs and chicks from their nests on the ground. Early visitors also certainly caught the birds in large numbers as a food source but they were so few in number that their impact was probably negligible. However people certainly altered the island's habitats by felling trees and introducing farm animals, and by 1690 the dodo was no more.

The Natural History Museum displays a skeleton of this species, and a reconstruction using feathers from cygnets and other sources since no complete dodo skin is known to survive. Also staff and researchers from the Museum, working with other scientists, have recently recovered further preserved dodo remains from various sites on Mauritius. Hopefully our knowledge of this celebrated yet doomed creature will continue to expand. Looking back, the dodo's fate, 'dead as', was a tragic early sign of the perils facing species today and the worldwide loss of biodiversity. It is the Museum's aim that, as well as being a repository for the dead from the past, it will help to save the living for the future.

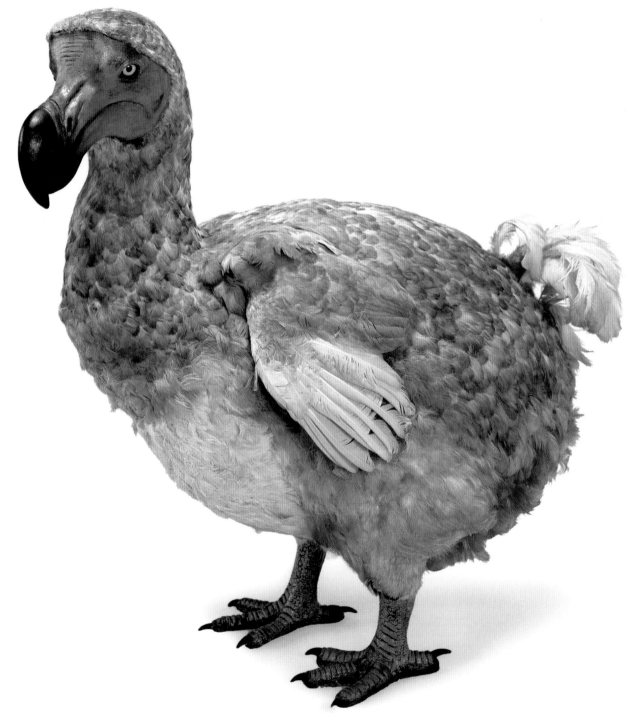

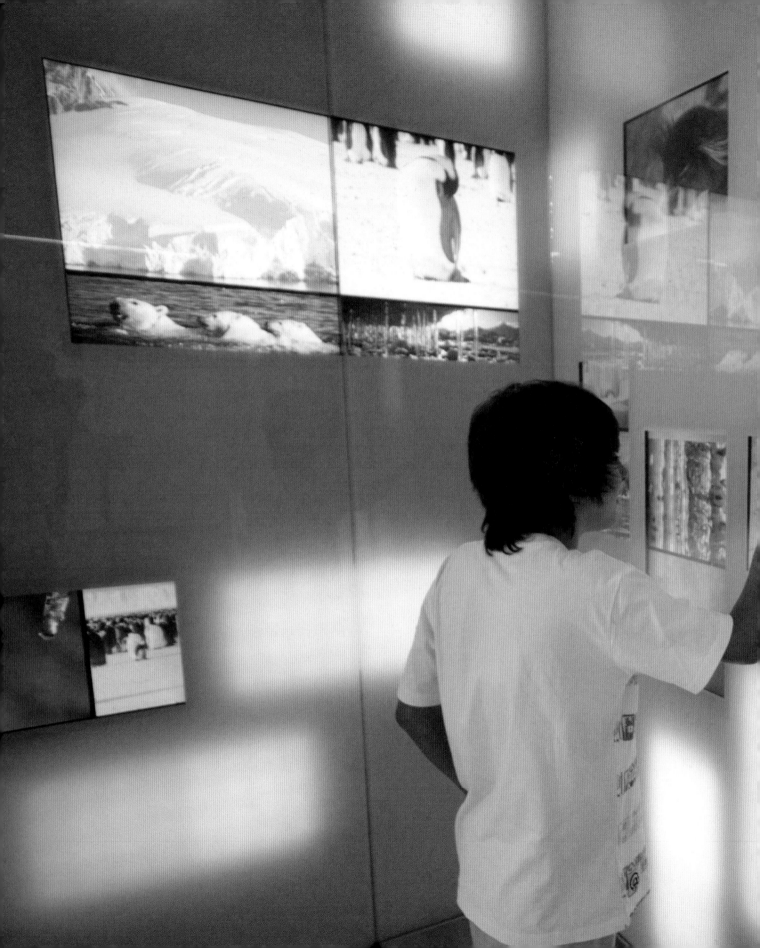

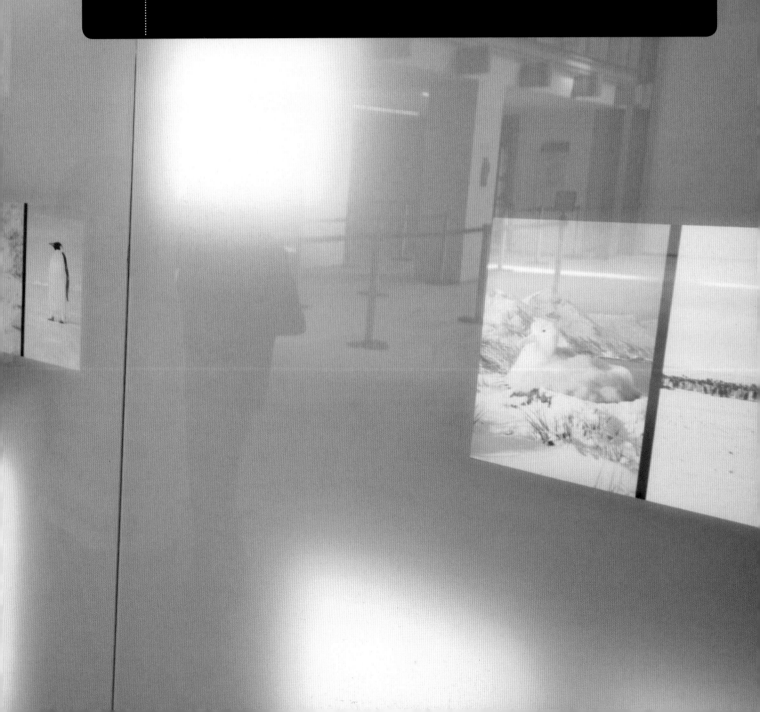

THE LIVING FUTURE

THE LIVING FUTURE

In the future, could museums be a thing of the past? Should they be relegated to a museum? With the world's sum of knowledge at our fingertips on the internet, do we really need them? An immense storehouse of knowledge about all living things, the Natural History Museum is evolving to meet future challenges and to look to the future, you have to start with the past.

The island of Mauritius is noted for its tropical climate, beautiful beaches, tourist facilities, charming local customs – and the disappearance of the dodo. Around the world, species of plants and animals join the lists of threatened species almost daily. The dodo bird has become a symbol of what could happen. The antidote is to get stuck into conservation, save plants and animals, and raise general awareness about rescuing and restoring natural habitats around the world.

Europeans first landed on Mauritius in 1598, with larger-scale settling from the 1630s. Out in the Indian Ocean, 900 kilometres east of Madagascar, the island is about 65 kilometres long by 45 kilometres wide, with an area of just over 2,000 square kilometres. It was once cloaked in forests of ebony trees, with palms and other pristine vegetation. Being of reasonable size but relatively isolated, Mauritius had a large proportion of endemic species – those found only there, and nowhere else. Long, long ago, pioneer creatures and plants had made it to the volcanic island, newly emerged from the sea, and then evolved to fit the island's unique habitats. The same process of island colonization with evolution into unique life forms has been repeated around the world, as Charles Darwin recognized in the Galapagos.

Since human colonization, Mauritius has changed drastically. Much of the original wooded areas have gone, replaced by monocultures of sugar cane and other crops. Introduced species such as rats, mice, dogs, cats, pigs and crab-eating macaque monkeys have also arrived and wrought massive changes on the wildlife. There were no terrestrial mammals before Europeans, only bats in the air, such as the endemic Mauritius flying fox or fruit bat, and various marine mammals such

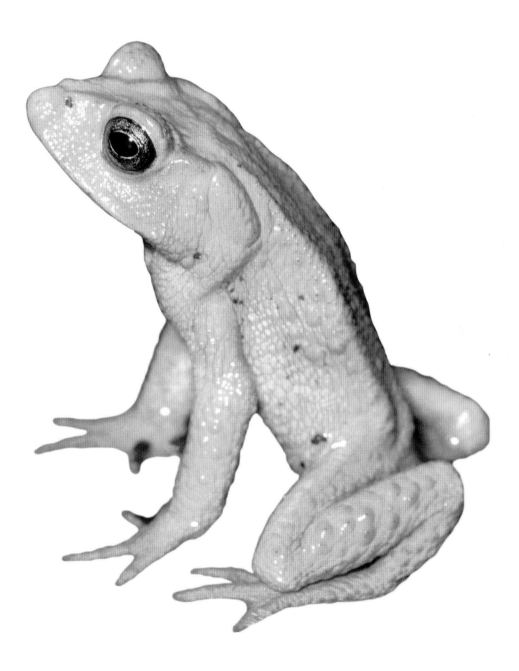

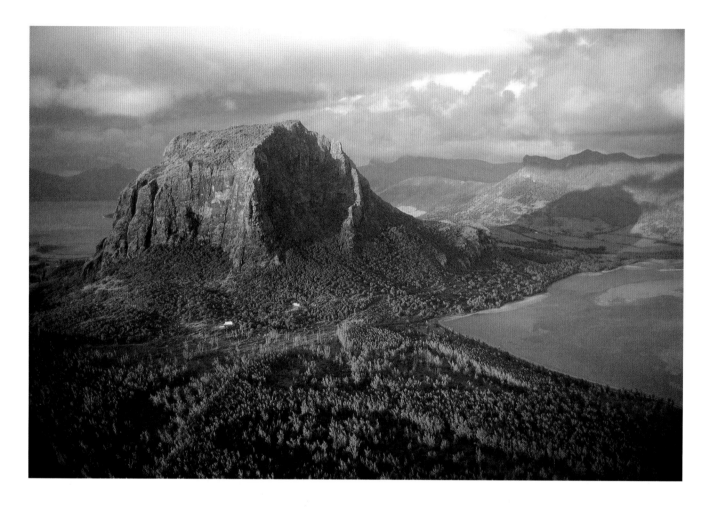

as whales around the coast. The biggest grazers and browsers were one or possibly two species of giant tortoises but they, like the dodo, are long extinct.

Rewilding

Several conservation projects in Mauritius are getting to grips with 'rewilding', restoring the native flora and fauna. Of course the dodo cannot be brought back, at least, not with today's technology. But local tree species have been planted out into protected areas, and the animals encouraged to return and breed.

To rewild, we of course need to know what the original wild was like. Few written records exist of the balance of nature before the European invasion. However, the science of palaeoecology, as described earlier, is helping Natural History Museum experts to find out what lived where on the island. Palaeoecology looks at the range of species long ago and how they interacted with each other and with their environment, each filling a particular role or function in nature known as its ecological niche.

A small marshy area, Mare aux Songes, is playing a leading role in this work. It has been excavated for the preserved remains of animals and plants, from microscopic pollen grains to the bones and shells of giant tortoises. Digging down into the muddy ground reveals cross sections of material including bits of trees and, in particular, bones. Amazing recent finds here have been more than 7,000 bones, including hundreds from the dodo, preserved for more than 4,000 years. These dodo remains represent most parts of the body, from beaks to feet, and from young as well as adult birds. They are helping scientists to revise the physical appearance of this bird away from its traditionally portrayed plump, tubby shape, towards a newer and more accurate svelte, slimline version.

New tortoise for old

Thousands of bones from giant tortoises dominate some parts of the excavated finds. These huge reptiles were obviously central to the original Mauritius ecosystem. By studying giant tortoises elsewhere, including the Galapagos Islands almost half a world away, scientists have worked out the many roles they play. They graze plants, which respond – as gardeners know from pruning roses – by growing more vigorously. The tortoises chomp on fruits, whose seeds pass through their gut and emerge away from the parent plant, thereby spreading the seeds widely. When those

OPPOSITE: Mauritius is an extraordinary island example of evolution going both backwards and forwards. Spectacular Le Morne Brabant is at its southwest tip, a peninsula bearing a giant lump of basalt 555 metres high.

BELOW: Aldabran giant tortoises have been introduced under controlled conditions to Mauritius, to try and fill the ecological niches or roles played by the island's similar species, which both went extinct in the 1700s.

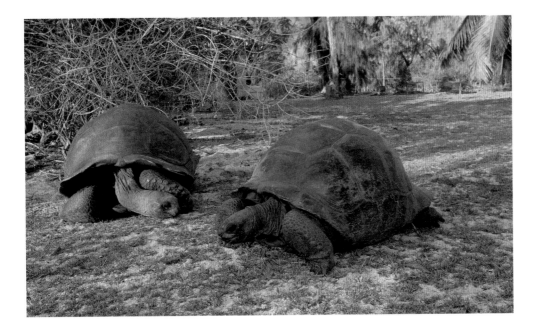

REVIVING THE COMMUNITY

IN 1965 A WILDLIFE PRESERVE WAS SET UP on Ile aux Aigrettes, a small island of some 26 hectares off Mauritius's southeast coast. Introduced species were eradicated and 18 Aldabran giant tortoises were imported in 2000 as an analogue replacement species – one that parallels, as closely as possible, the ecology of the original Mauritius version. After all, the giant tortoise is not just a taxonomic unit, a species to be described and catalogued. It is also an ecological niche-filler and essential part of the balance of nature in its habitat. This part of the rewilding project caused some controversy among conservationists, because the newcomer cannot replicate the original species entirely and could cause problems. In practice, few problems have materialized. In general the tortoises have had a positive effect, showing many interesting interactions with the flora. Their dung spreads ebony and other seeds and enhances their germination. They avoid saplings and young plants and tend to eat the species that are less important. Their grazing opens up new areas along the forest edges. A whole range of plants that rely on these hard-shelled herbivores begins to thrive, rather than continuing to fade away. This helps to recreate, in greenery terms, the lost land of the dodo.

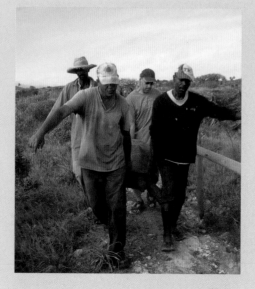

Mauritian giant reptiles disappeared, there must have been a huge impact on the local plant life. Rewilding Mauritius ought to include bringing back the tortoises, since they were such a major component of the ecology. But the Mauritian ones have gone. So an experiment is being carried out using the next best thing, in this case Aldabran giant tortoises, *Dipsochelys dussumieri* (formerly *Geochelone gigantea*). These hail from the islands of that name, which form a coral atoll in the Seychelles group far to the north of Mauritius. Aldabra is a World Heritage Site that retains most of its distinctive and endemic species.

Back from the brink

Apart from tortoises, several birds are the focus of conservation efforts in Mauritius. The Mauritius kestrel, *Falco punctatus*, is found mainly in the island's southwest, and has an amazing survival story to tell. Never especially common, with probably 200–300 breeding pairs in ancient times, in the mid-1970s it had become probably the world's rarest bird, with just four individuals left. The kestrel's population had been devastated by habitat disturbance, introduced species such as macaque monkeys who ate their eggs and chicks, and the spraying of the insecticide DDT (*see also* pages 85-87).

On the nature reserve of Ile aux Aigrettes, eggs were carefully removed from kestrel nests and hatched in incubators. The birds were fed supplements so that they could lay a second

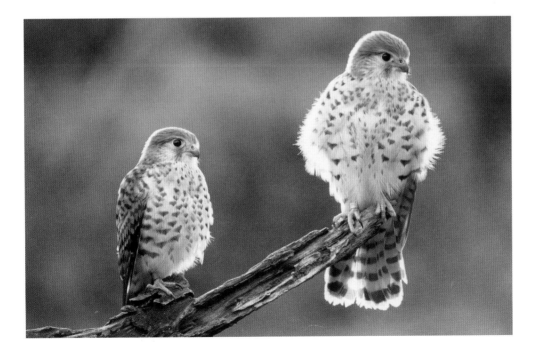

173

replacement clutch without too much strain on their nutrition. Gradually this captive breeding process, along with release and training for life in the wild, became more successful. Ten years later the kestrel numbers reached 50. Today there are more than 800, spread mainly across the surviving forests of the Bambous Mountains on the main island of Mauritius. The population may rise to about 1,000. This is the local area's carrying capacity – the maximum number that the naturally available resources such as food, shelter and space can accommodate.

Pigeons and parakeets

A similar tale of conservation success involves another Mauritian endemic, the pink pigeon, *Nesoenas mayeri*. As with the kestrels, the prime movers in its salvation were the Jersey-based Durrell Wildlife Conservation Trust, established by renowned wildlife author Gerald Durrell, and which has the dodo as its symbol, along with the Mauritian Wildlife Foundation. The pigeon's plight mirrored the kestrel's, but a decade or two later. By the early 1990s only some 10 individual pink pigeons remained. Captive breeding and release were tried, with great success. Some captive individuals were taken to Jersey as a back-up and their offspring then relocated back to Mauritius. There are now more than 300 pigeons living wild in Mauritius.

A third bird with a heartening tale to tell is the echo or Mauritius parakeet, *Psittacula echo*. Like the pigeon, its numbers were reduced to just 10, in this case by the early 1980s. Apart from

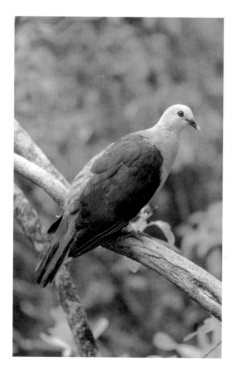

general habitat loss, too few suitable nesting trees, and egg- and chick-stealing by introduced predators, the parakeet also suffered in the face of competition from another newcomer, the rose-ringed parakeet. Once again an intensive conservation effort with captive breeding saw numbers rise, and the current population is around 250–300.

These types of conservation efforts are time-consuming and costly. Provision of nest sites, food supplements and predator-proof fencing, along with constant vigilance for predators and disease, all need money and resources. A scare in the mid-2000s saw the parakeet's numbers fall, probably due to PBFD, Psittacine Beak and Feather Disease, although they have since recovered. Workers must consider factors such as the bird's sex and perhaps releasing mainly young females rather than males, to keep up the breeding success.

Not just birds are exceedingly rare Mauritian endemics. Ile aux Aigrettes protects the ornate day gecko, *Phelsuma*

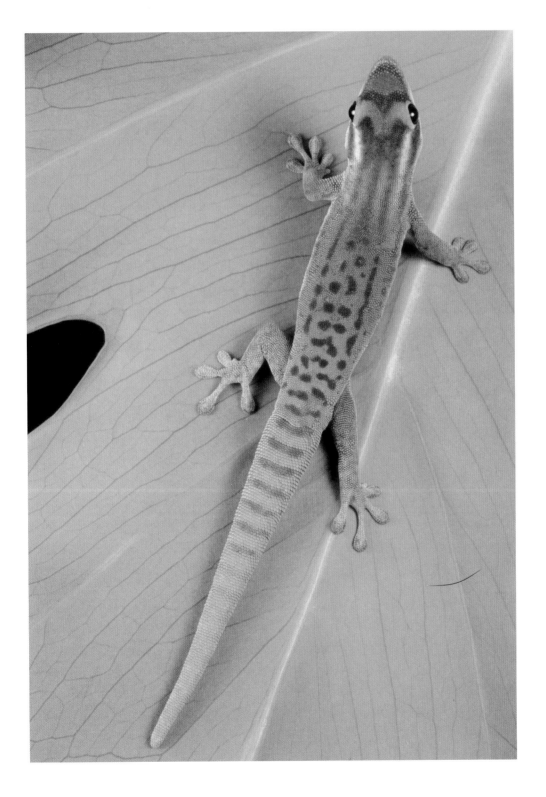

OPPOSITE: The pink pigeon is one of several native Mauritius birds literally saved from the brink of extinction. Gerald Durrell's book *Golden Bats and Pink Pigeons* describes part of the conservation effort.

LEFT: Just 11 centimetres long, the Mauritius ornate day gecko is very variable in colour. It lives in drier parts of the island, adapting to trees or rocky areas, and enjoys a wide diet, from bugs to fruit and nectar.

ornata, a small and speedy omnivorous lizard that has become sought after by reptile-fanciers. The island is also last refuge for the endemic species of ebony, *Diospyros egrettarum*. Formerly logged for timber and firewood, only about 10 trees remain on the main island, and so the patches of ebony on Ile aux Aigrettes are vital for its survival in the wild.

Wartime evacuees

The conservation work pursued so energetically in Mauritius, and hundreds of other places around the world, aims to give all kinds of threatened species a living future – and it relies heavily on a deceased past. The Natural History Museum's immense animal and plant collections and records provide benchmarks against which all kinds of factors can be measured for species, from the physical characteristics to its range, different varieties, preferred habitats and food.

Central to this work is the type specimen or holotype – the individual that defines the species or other taxonomic group. This is usually one of the earliest specimens to be described and identified. An official scientific report points out its unique features and how this specimen – and thus the new species it represents – differs from similar known species. We might imagine that the type specimen should be representative of the whole species, but this is not always the case. Since it is usually an early discovery, biologists do not know whether it is a typical example until more individuals are collected and analyzed.

In the late 1930s, as the Second World War loomed, plans were made to evacuate parts of the Museum collections from London, in case of damage by bombing raids. First on the list were the type specimens which included items in the spirit collections – those preserved in alcohol and other liquids, in glass bottles and jars. Apart from being invaluable in scientific terms, such a vast quantity of flammable liquid as a target for enemy attack was a firestorm waiting to happen. The Museum buildings could be reconstructed, but the type specimens were irreplaceable.

At the quarry

The Natural History Museum at Tring was one of the major storage outposts, but it could not hold everything. Museum investigations turned up a disused quarry near the village of Godstone in Surrey, about 32 kilometres from South Kensington, as a suitable site for the flammable spirit collections. In late 1941 more than 25,000 spirit-bottled type and other important specimens were packed in sawdust in 900 boxes and transported to the quarry's network of tunnels and caverns, which penetrated to 60 metres below the surface.

Even this huge quantity of specimens was only five per cent of the entire spirit collection, but difficult choices had to be made. Other big city museums, such as the neighbouring Science Museum and Victoria and Albert Museum in South Kensington, were also taking away their

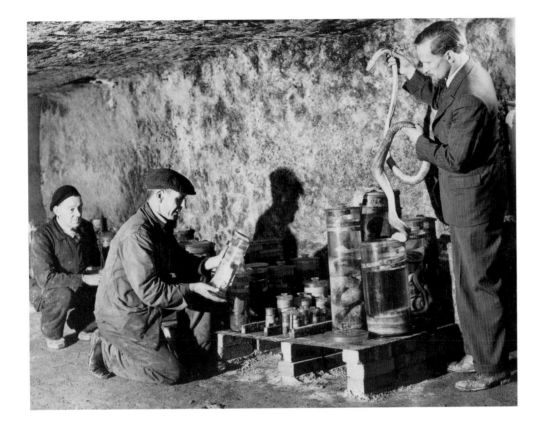

most precious exhibits and items for safe keeping. In the quarry, the boxes of spirit specimens were stacked three high on wood pallets, safe and secure. It was not the best location in the tunnels, because wine merchants had already stacked their bottles in more favoured areas. Now the specimens were safe from one kind of attack. But almost at once, another began. The tunnels were damp and humid, with no ventilation. Various kinds of fungus started to grow on the wood of the boxes and pallets, in the packing sawdust, and even on the specimen labels. As mentioned earlier, a label defines the item it is attached to, and without one, the item is pretty much useless. A team of workers began to paint the wood and labels with preservative varnish. But these men soon started to suffer with their health in the poor conditions, and the fungus continued to run riot. Drastic action was essential.

Saviour of the spirit

The Museum looked for someone to head a task force that could save the day. Alec Fraser Brunner was on the temporary staff as a fish specialist and seemed suited to the job. However, he was called up as part of the war effort in April 1942, just as he was about to put his rescue plan into action.

BELOW: The Museum did not escape the Second World War unscathed. One major hit was in October 1940 when an incendiary bomb seriously damaged the Shell Gallery roof and caused a major fire. Firefighting water then flooded basements below.

OPPOSITE: The Darwin Centre's massive egg-like Cocoon internal structure holds and protects 17 million entomology specimens, three million botany specimens and much more.

A series of high-powered letters between the Museum, its paylords the Treasury, the War Office and the Ministry of National Service managed to keep Fraser Brunner out of military employ until his task was complete.

Fraser Brunner decided that the only way to save the collections was to bring them all out of the tunnels for treatment. He, three labourers and a plucky pit pony carried all 900 boxes out into the fresh air and light.

Each trip took many minutes in dark, damp, cramped conditions. The team threw away the sawdust, which was a major site of fungus activity. They cleaned, dried and treated the boxes and labels, and checked, repaired and renovated the 25,000 glass containers. Some jars and bottles lacked internal labels, preserved within the spirit, so these were supplied. Also all labels were copied as a back-up. Then the whole lot was taken back into the tunnels. This time wooden supports were out of the question since they too harboured the fungus. Fraser Brunner brought in 5,000 bricks and 2,000 pieces of slate to build more than 260 metres of shelving for the specimen jars and boxes. But there were still other troubles to deal with, such as earthworm activity that undermined the tunnel floor and threatened to tip over the shelving.

Back to London

The overhaul of the spirit collection lasted from September 1942 until June 1943. It was largely successful and the work began to tail off. In mid-1944 Fraser Brunner finally went off to join the Army, leaving an assistant to monitor the collections and undertake minor running repairs. Nevertheless,

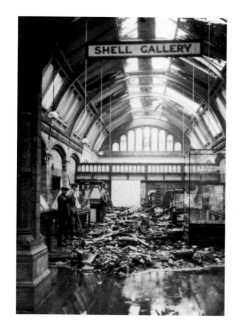

when the war came to an end, the spirit collections could not be moved out of the quarry fast enough. By the end of 1945 they were all back in South Kensington. Ironically the parts of the Museum where they would have been stored were intact, although bombs had damaged other areas.

Fraser Brunner went on to a varied fish-based career running aquaria in Singapore and then Scotland, and founding *The Aquarist* magazine. The quarry is still disused, and its location is kept secret. But a few bits of broken glassware and slate are testament to its vital role in keeping the Museum's most important collections safe.

The Darwin Centre

The spirit collections, along with many other specimens, including insects and spiders, have recently been on the move

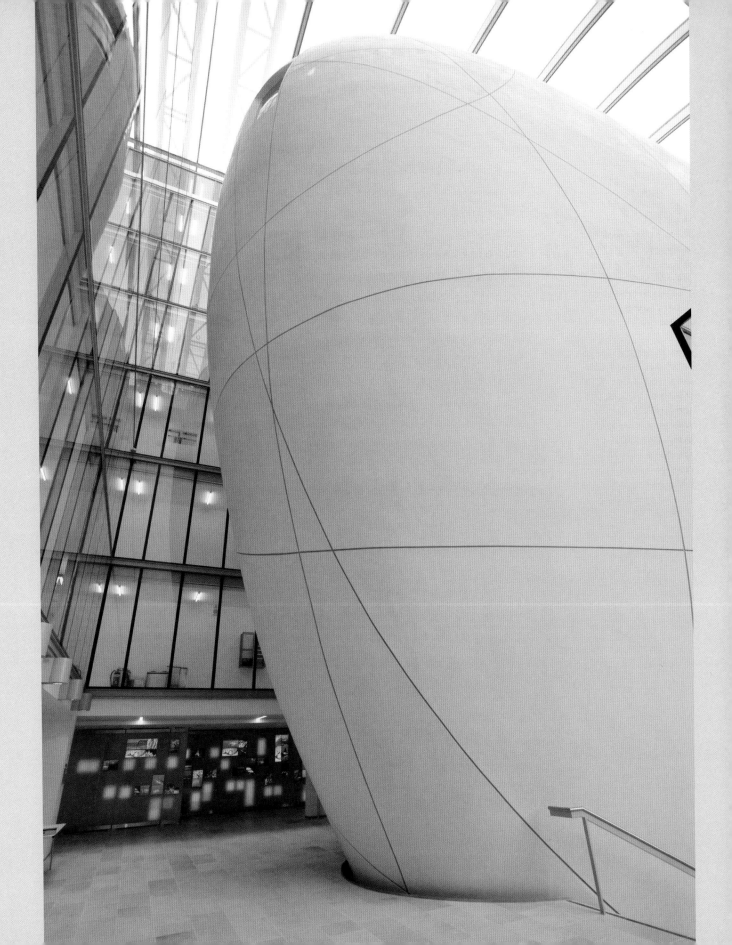

OPPOSITE LEFT: The Angela Marmont Centre for UK Biodiversity occupies the ground floor of the eight-storey Darwin Centre. Workshop space, study equipment, books, online databases and other resources are available to natural history organizations and enthusiasts.

OPPOSITE RIGHT: The red squirrel is now restricted to small pockets in England, although it is less rare in Wales and Scotland. Its demise coincided with the spread of the grey squirrel, but the complex reasons for this are still being untangled.

again. The Museum's newest major building is the 65-metre-long, eight-storey Darwin Centre, named in honour of the great naturalist Charles Darwin. It is at the western end of the main Waterhouse building, overlooking the Museum gardens. From 2009 the public has been able to look around parts of this state-of-the-art facility, with its environmentally controlled conditions, to see some of the research collections and behind-the-scenes activity of scientists going about their daily labours. In the Zoology Spirit wing of the Darwin Centre are 27 kilometres of shelving for the 22 million specimens, some collected by Darwin himself.

The architecturally stunning Darwin Centre is the Museum's most significant expansion since it moved to South Kensington in 1881. As well as harbouring the past, it is definitely looking to the future. There are exciting displays and interactive exhibits, including the high-tech Attenborough Studio. The Angela Marmont Centre for UK Biodiversity is a hub for amateur naturalists, enthusiasts and societies to study all aspects of the natural world in Britain, from animals, insects and plants to fossils and minerals. The Centre also has a dedicated drop-in identification service where experts can give advice to members of the public about strange finds.

The 12-metre Climate Change Wall in the Darwin Centre responds to passing visitors, showing hundreds of images and films about the beauty and diversity of the natural world, with touch-screens giving examples of climate change and how the Museum staff are leading researchers in this field.

Alien invaders

One of the busiest areas for Natural History Museum research is the problem of introduced species. They affect all kinds of habitats in the UK and around the world. Some newcomers slip in quietly, take their place almost unnoticed among the native flora and fauna, and cause little fuss. Others soon become notorious as widespread invaders, like the seaweed known as wireweed, described earlier (*see* page 149). Why are some introductions so aggressive? How do they alter the local ecology, what damage do they cause, and which natives species are threatened? Scientists need to know the answers to all of these questions before making plans to repel the invasion – if that's still possible.

For many invasive species, the more we study them, the more complicated the picture becomes. A familiar example is the story of two squirrels, red versus grey. The grey squirrel, *Sciurus carolinensis*, arrived towards the end of the nineteenth century. Bigger, bolder and more aggressive than the UK's long-time resident, the red squirrel – which is not solely British but has a Eurasian distribution – the grey has spread widely. Since it appeared, the smaller, shyer red, *Sciurus vulgaris*, has suffered a shrinking range. It is now found mainly in Wales and Scotland, with smaller refuge populations elsewhere, such as the Isle of Wight.

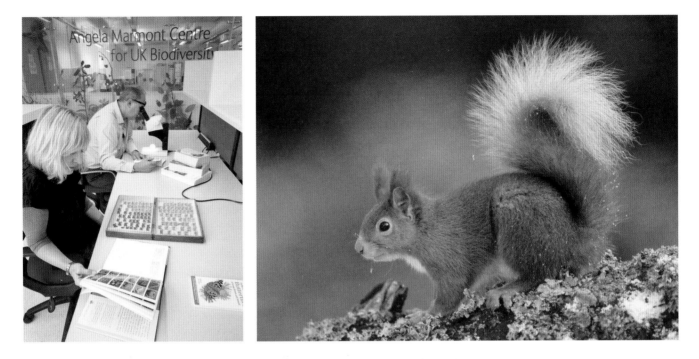

Complicating factors

The image of the big American squirrel scaring away the smaller British one fits many stereotypes. However, it is by no means the whole story. There is almost no direct combat or paw-to-paw fighting between the two. Reasons lie elsewhere. For instance, the grey competes better for limited food sources and survives harsh winters more successfully than the red. In biological language it is fitter, as in 'survival of the fittest'.

Habitats also play a part. Red squirrels once thrived in Britain's ancient woodlands, but these are mostly gone. The remainders are often altered or managed to include non-native trees. The reds are not as happy in these places, but the more adaptable greys are. In addition, the grey squirrels carry germs known as the squirrel parapoxvirus, yet they are little affected by this disease. The reds are, and in some regions more than three-quarters of them die. The greys also fare better than the reds against a range of predators, such as foxes and domestic cats. There are other factors too. Overall, it's a tangled web. Museum experts, working with naturalists' trusts, countryside agencies and many others, are still helping to unravel the situation.

Battle of the bluebells

There are similar new versus native tussles to the squirrels' going on in the UK's plant world. The buddleia, *Buddleja davidii,* is fine at attracting insects such as butterflies, but its speed and vigour

OPPOSITE: English
bluebells form stunning
spring displays in
woodlands. But the
future of this lovely
flower is unclear, with
threats varying from
illegal collecting to
global warming and
competition from
Spanish bluebells.

as a colonizer of disturbed ground means that it crowds out other species. The loquat, *Eriobotrya japonica*, also from China, is raised for its apple-like fruits. But it too can monopolize the local flora, and its fruits alter the balance of herbivores in unusual ways. Japanese knotweed, *Fallopia japonica*, is a notoriously aggressive invader that stifles other plant growth. In Britain, landowners are legally required to deal with it quickly and prevent its spread, and not just by cutting it down and throwing it onto the compost. It is 'controlled waste' and should be incinerated in an approved way or go to landfill. Not just the UK suffers from this plague plant. Japanese knotweed is listed as one of the world's 100 worst weeds.

The 'Battle of the Bluebells' pits the common or English bluebell, *Hyacinthoides non-scripta*, against the so-called Spanish bluebell, *Hyacinthoides hispanica*. The former epitomizes the English wood in spring with its brilliant blue carpet and wonderful scent. The latter is more erect, with larger leaves and more open flowers, although little scent. It tends to tolerate more varied conditions than the English or common bluebell, may outcompete it and is subtly damaging to it in other ways. It seems that the delicate fragrance of our woodlands is in danger of being lost to a brash but odourless Iberian invader. As a consequence the continued survival of our iconic woodland species has become a cause for concern.

Almost two species

Like the squirrels, the bluebells' relationships are not quite so simple. The two kinds can in fact breed together or hybridize. Looking closely, there is now in Britain a whole range or spectrum of physical shapes and types between the two, which is termed a morphological continuum. Both species grow naturally in Spain and where historically they have grown together there are also zones of hybridization, as in the more urban parts of Britain, between the different bluebell varieties. However, the majority of bluebells that grow in Spain do not resemble what we think of as the Spanish bluebell as found in the UK. These rather gross plants are like neither native Spanish or British flowers. We now think they have a horticultural origin but DNA evidence suggests that their parents may have been Portuguese, brought to Britain as a result of the strong trading links between the two nations

The two best recognized types of bluebell, Spanish and English, share a common ancestor. Both are widespread plants that have been in the process of evolving into two or more species but which haven't yet developed barriers to breeding between each other. Only their geographical isolation has kept them apart and pure. This divergence happened over thousands of years as climates and other conditions fluctuated in northwest and west Europe. Then, suddenly, along came people to undo these millennia of natural divergence. We trade the flowers and bulbs, interbreed them in horticulture to create new strains and plant them out into new habitats. In Britain, dumped garden remnants of the Spanish bluebell have their pollen taken by bees and similar insects to fertilize British bluebell strains, muddying the gene pool.

Bluebell research is ongoing and the scenario should become clearer with time. Meanwhile, is there a positive to the story? Partly. Another threat to the English bluebell could be global warming. As the climate hots up, conditions in parts of England may well become too warm for it to survive. But these changed conditions could be suitable for the Spanish bluebell. Are at least some bluebells better than none at all?

Revolutionary thinking

Puzzles like the bluebells greatly tax the Museum's experts in taxonomy – the science of classifying living things into groups. This has been, and remains, one of the Natural History Museum's prime skills. Its specialists, along with their colleagues around the world, can spend years discussing whether a particular worm or moss should be in this group or that, as they propose the merits of different classification schemes. So much detail may seem baffling to many people. But with a love of order and organization, most of us appreciate the result. This is a taxonomic framework of classification units, systematically organized into a hierarchy from the biggest groups to the smallest – phylum or division, class, order, family, genus, species – into which new finds can be slotted.

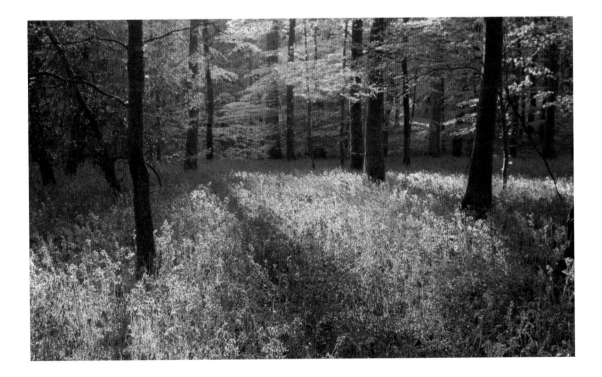

Yet even the seemingly conservative subject of taxonomy has undergone massive changes. In recent decades most biologists have adopted a new way of thinking about the way we classify organisms. This is known as cladistics or phylogenetic systematics. It groups organisms by their possession of what are called shared derived characters. These are traits, features or characteristics of organisms that are presumed to have been inherited from the same common ancestor.

Organisms that share derived characters form what is called a monophyletic group, or clade. A clade is a group in which *all* the included organisms have a common ancestor. That is, they are all presumed to be descendants of the same ancestor (monphyletic means 'one stem or branch'). Any two or more clades may also share a further ancestor, common to them both. Thus, a scheme relating many organisms will have a branching structure, rather like a tree. This is called a cladogram.

As an example, we might note that all known birds have feathers. No other animals have feathers. Therefore feathers are a shared, derived character that distinguishes birds from all other living beings.

Dinosaurs and birds

How does cladistics differ from other methods of classification? First consider the traditional view of birds. Birds were classified in the taxonomic group Aves, which is at the level of class in the classification heirarchy. Reptiles were recognized as another class. Birds and Reptiles are considered to be evolutionarily most closely related. Traditionally Reptiles include crocodiles, tuataras, lizards, snakes, turtles and tortoises. But these animals also share a common ancestor together with birds so the group Reptiles does not include *all* of its descendants. Thus by excluding birds, Reptiles is an artificial group.

The same rationale applies to dinosaurs, different kinds of extinct Reptiles. Dinosaurs include many different kinds of extinct reptiles. It's generally accepted that some of these, probably the smallish meat-eaters known as raptors, are most closely related to birds. Therefore, like the Reptiles above, if birds are excluded from the dinosaur clade, dinosaurs too are an artificial group

Today, most palaeontologists accept that for dinosaurs to be recognized as a clade, they should include birds. Thus, for some, dinosaurs are either still alive and flying around (birds), or are extinct and referred to as non-avian dinosaurs. It is worth remembering that the term 'non-avian dinosaur' indicates an artificial assemblage of organisms. It is this group that most people would consider simply as dinosaurs, because the new way of thinking is taking a long time to seep through into the public domain.

Cladistics has had an enormous effect on the way we classify the natural world. It focuses on the evolutionary relationships of organisms, rather than just their general similarities. It focuses on shared, derived characters rather than simple similarities. More recently, the characteristics of organisms can be organized into computer data matrices and analyzed using computer programs. Scientists are continually examining specimens and discovering new characters to add to existing knowledge and, with more sophisticated programs, offer further insights into their relationships

Natural inspiration

More practical and tangible than computers classifying animals and plants is the growing area of biomimetics. This is mimicking or copying nature – taking natural objects, designs, materials and functions as inspiration for our own artificial versions. It is, in effect, transfer from life to technology. Biomimetics is thriving in engineering, electronics, chemical manufacturing, communications and many other areas of science. And not just in commerce and industry, but in many other parts of life – including the quest for gold medals.

A newsworthy example of biomimetics is the shark swimsuit. Biologists studying how sharks swim have found that their skin has minutely different surface designs over different areas of the body. This is because the water flow varies according to the particular shape of each body part. The shark's snout has to push forwards into new water, the head curves at a decreasing angle to the water flow, the flanks are almost parallel to the main flow, while the fins and tail create eddies or vortexes as water slips off their trailing edges. So the grooves and tiny pointed structures on a shark skin called denticles – in effect, miniature versions of its teeth – vary slightly in their size, shape and spacing, to minimize drag or resistance caused by passing water.

Swimming towards a ban

Swimsuit-makers spent years developing neck-to-ankle shark-mimicking suits. Following the fish's example, the surface textures vary on different areas of the suit, to reduce friction and manage the water flow over that part of the human body. Other swimsuit developments borrowed from nature include new kinds of fabric that offer the human body extra buoyancy. This means the swimmer can put more effort into going forwards (or backwards) rather than expending energy to stay afloat.

BELOW: The shortfin mako, *Isurus oxyrinchus*, is reputed to exceed 70 km/h in short bursts. Under the scanning electron microscope, shark skin shows its tiny, sharply pointed placoid scales, which give it a rough, sandpapery feel and also ease water turbulence over the skin, reducing drag on the fish as it swims. The microscopic structure of the shark's skin has inspired biomimetic specialists to develop a new breed of high-tech, low-drag human swimsuits.

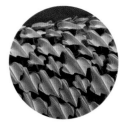

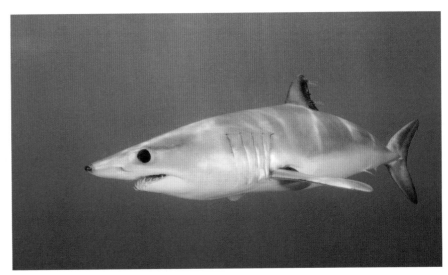

A LACK OF SPARKLE

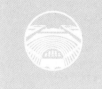

THE LATEST TECHNOLOGY CROPS UP IN all kinds of unusual ways at the Natural History Museum. The Koh-i-noor (Ko-i-nur) Diamond, once the world's largest, has been the subject of a recent study to find out why, once, it did not sparkle as it was expected to. Originally from India, the diamond was put on display with huge fanfare at the 1851 Great Exhibition in Hyde Park, London, in its original mogul cut or shape. However, *The Times* of London reported: 'Either from the imperfect cutting or the difficulty of placing the lights advantageously....few catch any of the brilliant rays it reflects.' The diamond was re-cut the following year, under the orders of Prince Albert. Reduced in weight by two-fifths, the new version had improved brilliance.

Natural History Museum researchers investigated the reasons for this using a unique plaster cast made at the time and kept in the Museum collections. A replica was also built for gallery display, and its shape was programmed into a computer. This shows how the mogul cut, with its wide flat base and 200 facets, instead of the 57 of a modern round brilliant cut, restricted the internal reflections that give diamonds their sparkle. Using the computer-generated model and light sources, scientists were able to recreate the lighting conditions at the Great Exhibition and, with the style of the old cut, re-affirm reports that the stone was best seen to sparkle – and so live up to expectation – for an hour each day, around 2–3pm, when the sun was at a certain angle.

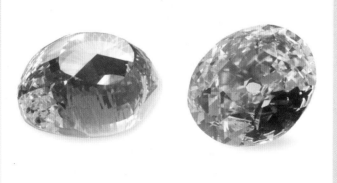

When swimmers wore these new suits, records tumbled but controversy followed. Did the best swimwear technology give those who could afford it an unfair advantage over those who couldn't? Was it turning into a competition for suits rather than for swimmers? In 2009 swimming's world governing body, FINA, Fédération Internationale de Natation, decided to ban high-tech suits from official competitions.

Origins of life

The Museum's mineralogy collections include billions of diamonds. But they are tiny, embedded in some of the oldest objects in existence – meteorites. These rocks from space come from asteroids, the Moon and Mars and, before reaching Earth's surface, their travel through the atmosphere is signalled by a spectacular light display known as a fireball. Meteorites are effectively samples of material from when the Solar System – the Sun, its planets and their moons – came into being. Studying meteorites is sometimes known as astronomy in the laboratory.

BELOW: This 10-centimetre stone is part of the Allende carbonaceous chondrite, one of the best-known meteorites. It is partly covered in jet-black fusion crust caused by high temperature from air friction as it entered the atmosphere.

Dating meteorites using forms (isotopes) of elements produced through radioactive decay, show that many formed almost 4.6 billion years ago, which has become the accepted age of our Solar System.

Chondrites are rocky or stony meteorites, and some of these, known as carbonaceous chondrites, are rich in chemical elements basic to life – carbon, oxygen, hydrogen and nitrogen. In fact some contain chemical molecules called amino acids, which are the building blocks of proteins – vital components in all living tissues. The largest known carbonaceous chondrite was the Allende meteorite which was the size of a car. It fell in 1969 on the Chihuahua region of Mexico and, during its atmospheric flight, broke up into thousands of Allende stones. Long before, this body was born in the disc of gas and dust from which the Sun and planets also came. In fact some parts (components) of the Allende meteorite probably formed even before the Solar System itself. It contains traces of minerals, such as diamonds, which come from distant space, perhaps blown away from an exploding star or supernova.

Lines of research at the Museum look at whether these meteorites could have bombarded early Earth and seeded the planet with life, or at least, ready-made precursors for life. If this happened here, could it have happened on other planets too? In the future, new clues from meteorites may shed light on the origins of life in our Solar System.

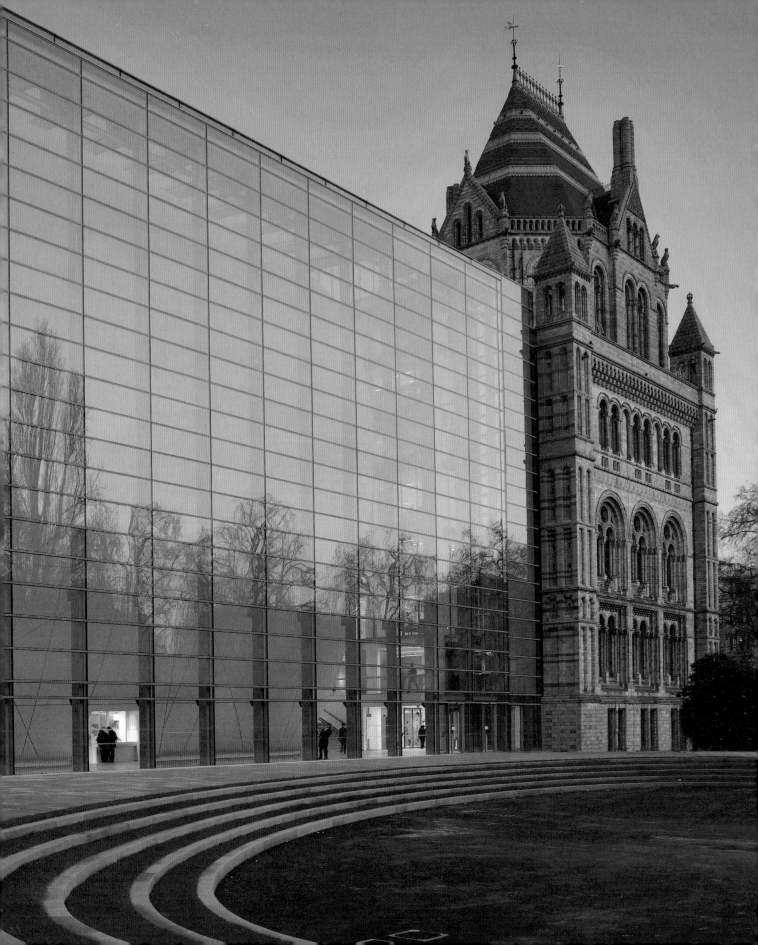

Museums of the future

What does the future hold in store for institutions like the Natural History Museum? The way that information is displayed will doubtless continue to advance. Perhaps nothing will quite match the jaw-dropping awe of seeing real physical exhibits – the blue whale stretching away into the distance, the animatronic *T. rex* baring its teeth in a ferocious roar, breathtakingly beautiful butterflies and flowers, and sinister spiders. But holographic technology, 3D projections, immersive exhibits and more visitor control of what the public see, are all in development. Already there are online virtual tours for many of the Museum's galleries, and these can only expand.

Behind the scenes, progress will undoubtedly accelerate. One hundred years ago scientists knew little of molecular biology and nothing of how DNA works – areas that are absolutely central to today's specialists. Even 50 years ago, DNA's double-helix structure had been worked out, but the genetic code for how its instructions translate into living matter had not. The next 50 or 100 years are bound to open up whole new areas of science that we cannot suspect today. There could be vast new layers of information coded into atoms and molecules. The bizarre phenomenon that physicists called 'entanglement' could lead to matter transfer through space. DNA manipulation might advance to the level where Jurassic Park-style recreated life is possible.

Into the Third Millennium

Can collecting physical specimens continue, with so many species in so much peril? Perhaps this will become virtual, too. Plants and animals could be scanned, and tiny samples of their tissues taken. Then they can remain intact in nature, while also entering the collections, as 3D images showing every tiny detail of anatomy and function, inside and out, and as entries into the DNA and other molecular databases.

As the Third Millennium gets under way, the Natural History Museum – in common with many others – is changing. It aims to be more open and more outward-looking, and less of an aloof academic institution. The latest technology is embraced, from laser vapourizers and X-ray scanners to electron microscopes and DNA sequencers. The Museum is reaching out to people everywhere, to raise awareness and encourage public interaction, online communications, volunteer-driven surveys, the best in conservation projects and much more.

The Natural History Museum works hard to enhance its reputation as a world centre of excellence in the life sciences, and as an innovative and unparalleled exhibition space. The immense collections of animals and plants will become ever more useful, as we look to the past and learn lessons that will help us to cope with the challenges of the future. As well as a museum of the dead, increasingly the Natural History Museum will become the Museum of Life.

OPPOSITE: The Museum's Darwin Centre glows invitingly at the western end of the floodlit main building. Their openings to the public are separated by 128 years. In a similar time span from now, what will the Museum's future hold?

189

INDEX

ACKNOWLEDGEMENTS

The author offers gracious thanks to Natural History Museum staff too numerous to list, who courteously provided detailed information and suggested improvements to the text. The BBC *Museum of Life* television team also gave their time and expertise, in particular series producer Tim Green, directors Sophie Harris and Ian Hunt, and editor Alex Boyle. And thanks are due to the Museum's Publishing staff who monitored the book's evolution and engineered such a wonderfully designed and illustrated product.

PICTURE CREDITS

All images © NHMPL unless listed below.
NHMPL = Natural History Museum Picture Library

p.18 © John Sibbick/NHMPL; p.28 © William Vanderson/Fox Photos/Getty Images; p.32 © Michael Coyne/Lonely Planet Images; p.38 © Lisa Hughes; pp.40-41 © Julius T. Csotonyi/ www.csotonyi.com; p.42 from Franzen JL, Gingerich PD, Habersetzer J, Hurum JH, von Koenigswald W, et al. 2009 Complete Primate Skeleton from the Middle Eocene of Messel in Germany: Morphology and Paleobiology. PLoS ONE 4(5): e5723. doi:10.1371; p.51 © Geological Society/ NHMPL; p.57 © Mauricio Anton/Science Photo Library; p.64 © Peter Snowball/NHMPL; p.67 © John Sibbick/NHMPL; p.78 © Bryan and Cherry Alexander/NHPA; p.87 © Masa Ushioda/Image Quest Marine; p.91 © Michael Long/NHMPL; p.99 © Mike Johnson; pp.100, 101 © OPAL; p.102 © Chris van Tulleken; p.111 Courtesy Quentin D. Wheeler. Artwork: Byron Alexander; p.112 top © Paul Messerschmidt; middle, bottom © BBC; p.113 © Max Barclay; p.114 © Biosphoto/ Gilson François/Still Pictures; p.116 © Blanca Huertas/ Proyecto YARE; p.120 right © Nick Garbutt/NHPA; p.112 Mike Eaton © NHMPL; p.124 © Steve Hopkin/Ardea; p.126 © Kraig Lieb/Lonely Planet Images; pp.130-131 Photo: Martin Hall © NHM; p.133 left © Istockphoto;

pp.134-5 © Mark Conlin/V&W/Image Quest Marine; p.138 © Jouan & Rius/NPL; p.139 © Woods Hole Oceanographic Institution; p.140 © Craig Smith; p.141© P Rona/OAR/ National Undersea Research Program/NOAA /Science Photo Library; p.142 © Adrian Glover; p.143 © Dr Ken MacDonald/ Science Photo Library; p.144 © Adrian Glover; p.145 top © Tomas Lundälv; bottom © Adrian Glover; p.147 right © Maximilian Stock Ltd/Science Photo Library; p.148 © World Pictures/Photoshot; p.150 © David Cranch; p.151 left, right © OPAL; p.152 bottom © Tomasz Zajaczkowski/ Istockphoto; p.155 © Alex Monro; p.164 © Julian Pender Hume/NHMPL; p.169 © Michael & Patricia Fogden/Minden Pictures/FLPA; p.170 © World Pictures/Photoshot; p.171 © Woodfall Wild Images/Photoshot; p.172 © Lorna Steel; p.173 © Nick Garbutt/NPL; p.174 © Julian Hume; p.175 © James Carmichael Jr./NHPA/Photoshot; p.177 © Fox Photos/Getty Images; p.181 © Niall Benvie/NPL; p.183 © Rachel Dewis/Istockphoto; p.185 top © Eye of Science/ Science Photo Library; bottom © Brandon Cole/NPL; back cover top middle © Alex Monro.

Every effort has been made to contact and accurately credit all copyright holders. If we have been unsuccessful, we apologise and welcome correction for future editions and reprints.

First published by the Natural History Museum, Cromwell Road, London SW7 5BD

© Natural History Museum, 2010

BBC and the BBC logo are trademarks of the British Broadcasting Corporation and are used under licence. BBC logo © BBC 1996

A catalogue record for this book is available from the British Library.

Designed by David Mackintosh

ISBN 978 0 565 09260 3

Reproduction and printing by Butler Tanner & Dennis